Charles John Ann Hereford

The History of Spain

From the establishment of the colony of gades by the Phoenicians, to the death of

Ferdinand, surnamed the Sage. Vol. 1

Charles John Ann Hereford

The History of Spain

From the establishment of the colony of gades by the Phoenicians, to the death of Ferdinand, surnamed the Sage. Vol. 1

ISBN/EAN: 9783337246334

Printed in Europe, USA, Canada, Australia, Japan

Cover: Foto ©ninafisch / pixelio.de

More available books at **www.hansebooks.com**

THE HISTORY OF SPAIN,

FROM

THE ESTABLISHMENT OF THE

COLONY OF GADES BY THE PHŒNICIANS,

TO

THE DEATH OF FERDINAND,

SURNAMED THE SAGE.

BY THE AUTHOR OF

THE HISTORY OF FRANCE.

IN THREE VOLS.—VOL. I.

LONDON:

PRINTED FOR C. AND G. KEARSLEY, FLEET-STREET.

1793.

ADVERTISEMENT.

IN submitting the following work to the public, it is incumbent on the author to state the sources of his information:

In the first volume, the history of Spain by MARIANA, has been his principal guide; in the revolutions effected by the arms of the Goths and the Saracens, he has preferred the narrative of Mr. GIBBON; and in distinguishing the ancient and modern names of places, he has had recourse to Monsieur D'ANVILLE.

In the greatest part of the second volume, he has adopted the histories of CHARLES the Fifth, and of America by Doctor ROBERTSON; and the history of PHILIP the Second by Doctor WATSON.

In the third volume, his materials have been more various:
Dr. WATSON's History of PHILIP the Third;
GEDDES's Miscellaneous Tracts;
Anecdotes du Compte Duc d'OLIVARES;
Histoire Generale d'Espagne;
Chronologique de l'Histoire d'Espagne;
Memoires pour servir à l'Histoire d'Espagne sous le
 Regne de PHILIPPE V.;
Mercure Historique & Politique;
Memoires du Marechal Duc de BERWICK;
Memoires pour servir à l'Histoire du 18 Siecle, par
 M. de LAMBERTI;
HUME's History of England;
RUSSELL's History of Modern Europe;
And VOLTAIRE's Ages of LOUIS the Fourteenth and
 Fifteenth.

ADVERTISEMENT.

He must also acknowledge the assistance he has derived from the Travels of Mr. SWINBURNE, and the more recent Journey of Mr. TOWNSEND.

In the perusal of this work, the reader will probably observe, that several circumstances have been slightly passed over which may be thought worthy a more copious detail; the author has only to reply, that he hopes none of the principal events which regard Spain have been omitted; and where the transactions of upwards of two thousand years are to be comprised within three octavo volumes, to be concise, is not a matter of choice, but of obligation.

CONTENTS

CONTENTS

OF THE

FIRST VOLUME.

Chapter the First.

Page

EXTENT and situation of ancient Spain—First discovered by the Phœnicians—Colony of Gades—Invaded by the Carthaginians—Description of the natives—Success of the Carthaginians—The Romans enter Spain—Account of their progress—They divide Spain into two provinces—Wars with the natives—Character of Viriatus—His victories over the Romans—Project of an independent sovereignty in Spain—He concludes a peace with Rome—The treaty is broken by the Romans—Viriatus is assassinated in his tent—The Lusitanians are defeated under Tantalus—They preserve their independence in their mountains—Resistance of Numantia—It is besieged by Scipio, the second Africanus—Despair of the inhabitants—Destruction of Numantia—The Spaniards embrace the party of Sertorius—Death of that chief—Spain subdued by Pompey—Conduct of the Spaniards in the civil wars of the Roman republic—Account of the wealth of Spain—Augustus plans the entire reduction of it—He penetrates into the mountains of Cantabria and Asturia—Submission of the Cantabrians and Asturians—Revolt of the Cantabrians—They are conquered by Agrippa—Division of Spain into the provinces of Tarraconensis, Lusitania, and Bœtica, ————— 1

Chapter the Second.

State of Spain until the reign of Gallienus—Invasion of the Franks—Is usurped by Constantine in, the reign of Honorius—Is betrayed or abandoned to the Suevi, the Vandals, and the Alani—Their devastations—They are attacked by Adolphus—Death of Adolphus—Atchievements of Wallia—Extirpates the Alani—Vanquishes the Vandals and the Suevi—Restores Spain to the Romans—Exploits of the Vandals—They defeat the Romans—They plunder Majorca and Minorca—They depart for Africa—

Devastations

Devastations of the Suevi—Theodoric king of the Goths marches to the relief of Spain—His victory over the Suevi, who retire into Gallicia—Euric the successor of Theodoric completes the reduction of the greatest part of Spain—He is succeeded by Alaric, who is killed in battle by Clovis—Reign of Amalaric—Administration and reign of Theudes—The Visigoths elect Theodigele—He is assassinated—Civil war in Spain—Athanegilde with the assistance of the Romans obtains the crown.--- He is succeeded by Liuva and Leovigild—Leovigild carries on a successful war with the Romans in Spain—His sons Hermenigild and Recared are declared princes of the Goths—Submission of the Cantabrians, &c.—Marriage and conversion of Hermenigild—He rebels against his father—Is vanquished and imprisoned—Escapes from imprisonment—Civil war—Hermenigild is again made captive—He negociates with the Romans—He is put to death—Extinction of the kingdom of the Suevi in Spain—Character and death of Leovigild, —— —— 45

Chapter the Third.

Reign of Recared—The Catholic church is established—His victory over the Franks—Councils of Toledo—His death—Reigns of Liuva, Witeric, and Gondemar—Accession of Sisebut—He persecutes the Jews—He is succeeded by his son Recared the second—Death of Recared, and succession of his brother Suintilla—He expels the Imperialists—He is dethroned by Sisenand—Election of Chintila to the throne—Persecution against the Jews renewed—Reigns of Tulga, Chindesuintho, and Recesuintho—Wamba is chosen king—His exploits—He regulates the national councils—Triumph over the Saracens by sea—Singular manner of his deposition—Usurpation of Erviga—He resigns the sceptre to his son-in-law Egiza—New code of laws promulgated by the Visigoths, —— —— —— 84

Chapter the Fourth.

Conspiracy of the Jews with the Mahometans of Africa—War with the Franks and Gascons—Death of Egiza, and accession of Witiza—The Pope's claim of supremacy is rejected in the council of Toledo—Tyranny of Witiza—Revolt and elevation of Roderic—Treachery of Count Julian—Invasion of the Saracens—Battle of Xeres—Flight and death of Roderic—Exploits of Tarik—Of Musa—Of Abdalaziz—The greatest part of Spain conquered—Recall of Musa—Government of Abdalaziz—His marriage with the widow of Roderic—He is assassinated—Rival factions of the Abbassides and Ommiades—Abdalrahman appears on the coast of Spain—His victory over the Abbassides—He establishes his independent throne at Cordova—The æra of Arabian splendour in Spain—Reign of the third Abdalrahman—His wealth and magnificence—Town and palace of Zehra—His revenue—Trade and natural productions of Spain—Character of Alkalem the second—His justice—He is succceded by his infant son Hassem—Renown of Almanzor, the vizir of Hassem—Overthrow of the house of the Ommiades—Degeneracy and dissensions of the Moors of Spain, 113

Chapter the Fifth.

The Goths maintain their independence in the Asturian mountains—Reign and achievements of Pelagius—Death of his son and successor Favilla—Election of Alfonso, surnamed the Catholic—Reign of Froila—He regulates the Catholic church—His victories over Abdalrahman—His severity—His assassination—Succession of Aurelio, and Silo—Usurpation of Mauregato—Election of Bermudo—He resigns the crown to Alonso, the Chaste—Glorious administration of Alfonso—He is succeeded by his son Ramiro—Reign of Ordogno—Of Alfonso, surnamed the Great—Of Garcias—Of Ordogno the second—Of Froila the second—Of Alfonso the fourth—Of Ramiro—He wrests the city of Toledo from the Moslems—Administration of Abdalrahman the third—Prudence of Ramiro—His victory over the Moors—He is succeeded by his son Ordogno the third—Reign of Sancho—He is deposed—Accession of Ordogno the fourth—Restoration of Sancho—He is poisoned—Election of Ramiro the third—Of Bermudo the second—Of Alfonso the fifth—Of Bermudo the third—His death unites in his brother-in-law Ferdinand the crowns of Leon and Castille, 164

CONTENTS.

Page

Chapter the Sixth.

State of Spain on the union of the crowns of Castille and Leon under Ferdinand the First---War of that monarch with his brothers, the kings of Navarre and Arragon---Account of, and exploits of Don Rodrigo, furnamed the Cid---Death of Ferdinand---Division of his dominions---Sancho the second despoils his brothers of Leon and Gallicia---He is killed in the siege of Zamora---Accession of Alfonso the sixth---Disgrace of the Cid---Establishes himself on the frontiers of Valencia.---Alfonso reduces Toledo---Is defeated by the Moors---His peace and marriage with the daughter of the king of Seville---Invasion of the Almovarides---Defeat of Ucles---Death of Alfonso---His daughter Urraca is acknowledged as his successor---Civil wars with her husband and son ---On her death, Castille and Leon submit to her son Alfonso the seventh---His glorious reign---He receives the title of emperor from the princes of Spain---Divides his dominions between his sons Sancho and Ferdinand---Short but prudent reign of Sancho over Castille---Turbulent minority of his son Alonso the eighth---He assumes the administration ---Is defeated by the Moors near Alercon---He marries his daughter Beregara to his nephew the young king of Leon---Crusade of the Christians against the infidels of Spain---Gallantry of Alfonso in the battle of Toloso---Splendid victory of the Christians---Prudent reign and death of Alfonso---He is succeeded by his son Henry---Disputes for the regency---Death of Henry, and accession of Beregara---She resigns the crown to her son Ferdinand the second, who on the death of his father unites the kingdoms of Castille and Leon, —— 217

Chapter the Seventh.

Final union of Castille and Leon---Rise and progress of chivalry---Orders of St. Jago, Calatrava, and Alcantara---Exploits of Ferdinand, surnamed the Saint---He successively reduces the cities of Cordova and Seville---He meditates the invasion of Africa ---His death---Four hundred years after he is canonized at the request of the king and states of Spain ---Accession of Alfonso, surnamed the Wise.---He aspires to the imperial crown of Germany---Dis-

traction

traction of his reign---Revolt of his fon Sancho---
Death of Alfonfo---He is fucceeded by Sancho the
Brave---Vigorous meafures of that monarch---He
vanquifhes his rebellious fubjects---Dies at Toledo
---The queen dowager is fupplanted in the regency
by Don Henry, uncle of the late king---Stormy
minority and reign of Ferdinand the fourth---Pre-
tenfions of the houfe of de la Cerda---Prudence of
the queen dowager---Perfecution of the Knights
Templars---They are acquitted in Spain.---Hafty
condemnation of two noblemen, by Ferdinand---
Particulars of the death of that monarch---He is
fucceeded by his fon Alfonfo the eleventh---Defeat
of the Chriftians, and deaths of the regents Juan
and Pedro---Alfonfo affumes the reins of govern-
ment---He acts with vigour againft his rebellious
fubjects and foreign enemies---In conjunction with
the king of Portugal, he defeats the Moors at Sal-
fedo---Takes Algezire---Dies of the plague in the
fiege of Gibraltar---Review of his character   262

Chapter the Eighth.

Acceffion of Peter, furnamed the *Cruel*---His perfidy
and barbarity---He is dethroned by his half-brother
Henry, count of Tranftamare---He is reftored by
Edward, the Black Prince---Is a fecond time defeated by Henry, and put to death---Reign of Henry
the fecond---Is fucceeded by his fon John---Pre-
tenfions of John to the crown of Portugal---His defeat at Aljubarrota---Makes peace with Portugal
and England---Felicity of his general adminiftra-
tion---Account of his death---His infant fon Henry
the third, is acknowledged king—Diffenfions of the
nobility—Henry affumes the government at thirteen
—His vigorous conduct—Medidates the expulfion
of the Moors from Spain—His death—Integrity of
his brother Ferdinand—John the fecond is proclaimed—Wife adminiftration of Ferdinand—He is
chofen king of Portugal---Competition of the regency of Caftille---Long and difaftrous reign of
John—Revolt of his fon, the prince of Afturias—
Execution of his favourite, Alvaro de Luna---He
dies, and is fucceeded by his fon Henry the fourth,
furnamed the *Impotent*—His marriage with the
princefs of Portugal—She is delivered of a daugh-
ter---The nobility refufe to acknowledge the child

CONTENTS.

as the king's—Formidable confederacy against Henry
He is solemnly deposed at Avila;—and his brother
Alfonso proclaimed;—Death of Alfonso—Treaty between Henry and his nobles—The king acknowledges
his sister Isabella, his successor, in prejudice to the
princess Joanna—Marriage of Isabella with Ferdinand the king of Sicily, and son of the king of
Arragon—Death of Henry—Ferdinand and Isabella
are proclaimed—The king of Portugal claims the
crown in right of Joanna—He is defeated at Toro
—Death of the king of Arragon—Ferdinand unites
the crowns of Castille and Arragon, — 333

Chapter the Ninth.

State of the neighbouring powers, when Ferdinand
united the crowns of Castille and Arragon—Of
Portugal, Navarre, and Granada—Of France—Italy
Germany—And England—Political state of Spain—
Account of the Justiza in Arragon—Of the Holy
Brotherhood—Address of Ferdinand—He makes
peace with Portugal—Commences the war with
Granada—Various success—Exertions of Ferdinand
and Isabella—Dissensions of the Moors—Ferdinand
successively reduces Ronda, Velez, and Malaga—Domestic history of Abdallah king of Granada—Granada is invested by the Christians—Construction of
the town of Santa Fé—Despair of the Moors—Capitulation of Granada—Triumphal entry of Ferdinand—Description of the Alhambra—Expulsion of
the Jews—Subsequent oppression of the Morescoes—
Progress of navigation—Discovery of the Fortunate
or Canary Islands by the Spaniards—Extensive discoveries of the Portuguese—History and character
of Christopher Columbus;—his idea of new countries in the West—His proposals rejected by Genoa
and Portugal—Are at length accepted by Isabella
—He sails from Palos in Andalusia, — 407

THE HISTORY OF SPAIN.

Chapter the First.

Extent and situation of ancient Spain.—First discovered by the Phœnicians.—Colony of Gades.—Invaded by the Carthaginians.—Description of the natives.—Success of the Carthaginians.—The Romans enter Spain.—Account of their progress.—They divide Spain into two provinces.—Wars with the natives. —Character of Viriatus.—His victories over the Romans.—Project of an independent sovereignty in Spain.—He concludes a peace with Rome.—The treaty is broken by the Romans.—Viriatus is assassinated in his tent.—The Lusitanians are defeated under Tantalus.—They preserve their independence in their mountains.—Resistance of Numantia.— It is besieged by Scipio, the second Africanus.— Despair of the inhabitants.—Destruction of Numantia.—The Spaniards embrace the party of Sertorius.—Death of that chief.—Spain subdued by Pompey.—Conduct of the Spaniards in the civil wars of the Roman republic.—Account of the wealth of Spain.

*Spain.—Augustus plans the entire reduction of it.—
He penetrates into the mountains of Cantabria and
Asturia.—Submission of the Cantabrians and Asturians.—Revolt of the Cantabrians.—They are conquered by Agrippa.—Division of Spain into the provinces of Tarraconensis, Lusitania, and Bœtica.*

O N the western point of Europe, a fertile region extends from the straits of Gibraltar to the
Pyrenean mountains, above five hundred and
ninety miles in length, and, from the Mediterranean Sea to the Atlantic Ocean, five hundred
and eighty miles in breadth. The Phœnicians,
who first discovered this wealthy peninsula, bestowed on it the name of SPAIN; they were attracted to its coasts by the same spirit of nautical
adventure that afterwards impelled the Spaniards
to explore the southern continent of America;
and more than a thousand years before the birth
of Christ, beneath their auspices, the city of
Gades arose on a promontory of the island of
Leon, which was separated by a narrow channel
from the ancient province of Bœtica, and soon
became the emporium of commerce.

A. C. 229. Eight centuries appear to have
elapsed before the establishment of
the colony of Gades seems to have excited the
open jealousy of the natives. At the expiration
of that term, the Phœnicians found themselves
involved

involved in an unsuccesful struggle with the ferocious tribes which inhabited Bœtica; and conscious of their declining strength, they called to their assistance the Carthaginians, who, themselves of Phœnician extraction, embraced with alacrity the kindred cause. The interest of the latter conspired with the resentment of their allies; and a short time after the conclusion of the first Punic war, Amilcar, the father of Hannibal, disembarked the forces of Carthage on the nearest coast of Spain.

He found a warm, but genial climate; the air pure, the soil fruitful, and refreshed by frequent rivers; the mountains abounded with copper, and with the more precious metals. But they were defended by numerous tribes of barbarians, who, although they consented to acknowledge the authority of different princes, were united by similar pursuits, and similar tempers. Bold, subtle, and sanguinary, they disdained the arts of peace, and devoted themselves to the toils of war. Their hours were alternately occupied by the care of their arms and their horses; and deprived of these, the martial Spaniards regarded life with indifference. Their garments were stained with various colours, their bodies painted, and their long hair decked with ornaments of silver and gold. At the distance of above twenty centuries, the same hereditary disposition may be traced:

the haughty spirits of the men scorned, or their indolence rendered them averse to the servile labours of agriculture; and where ever cultivation was necessary, the ungrateful duty was abandoned to a female hand.

The religion of the barbarians of Spain was suited to the rude and ignorant state in which they remained at the invasion of the Carthaginians: they acknowledged and adored one supreme Being, to whom their vows were paid, and their altars erected; deep and venerable groves were considered as the chosen residence of the deity, or the places more peculiarly adapted to his worship; and human sacrifice was deemed the most sacred and acceptable offering.

The jealousy and hatred of Rome, had first prompted Amilcar to aspire to the reduction of Spain. On that theatre he hoped to restore the discipline of the armies, to recruit the exhausted coffers of Carthage, and to enable her to contend with success with the mistress of Italy. Nor was he disappointed in the bold and laborious enterprise. The riches of the country were the recompense of many a bloody and persevering conflict. From the shores of the Mediterranean he slowly advanced towards those of the Atlantic. In nine years of incessant warfare he subdued the province of Bœtica, which corresponds with modern Grenada and Andalusia; and penetrated into the

country

country of the Lufitanians, which is now the kingdom of Portugal. The Lufitanians fupplied their deficiency in arms and difcipline by their native craft and courage. Though they were incapable of preferving their independence, they revenged the lofs of it; and on the banks of the Tagus, Amilcar was encompaffed, oppreffed, and flain.

His brother Afdrubal fucceeded to the command of his army and the execution of his defigns; lefs able in war but more refined in negociation, he conciliated the affections of thofe ftates which Amilcar had endeavoured to fubdue. Lufitania admired his addrefs and acknowledged his influence. The Callaici who ftill perpetuate their origin in Gallicia, the tribes who occupied the modern countries of Leon, the two Caftilles, Murcia, and Valencia, were prevailed upon to fubmit to his authority; even the Celtiberians, the moft powerful of the barbarians, who poffeffed the prefent province of Arragon, and whofe name defcribes their defcent from the Celtæ, and their fituation on the banks of the Iberus, had confented to receive the Carthaginian yoke, when the progrefs of Afdrubal was arrefted by private refentment, and he himfelf fell a victim to the dagger of a fervile affaffin.

The fetters of Spain were riveted by the hand of Hannibal, the glory and the fhame of Carthage;

thage; and who at the early age of twenty-five years surpassed in military skill his father Amilcar, and in political address his uncle Asdrubal. Two years were consumed in securing the conquests of his predecessors, and in the beginning of the third he led his forces to the siege of Saguntum, a city which had been founded by the Greeks on the shores of the Mediterranean, and on the borders of Valencia; the Saguntines confided in the protection of Hercules, and the alliance of Rome. But their hopes of divine assistance, and their expectations of mortal succour, were equally vain; and it was by their native valour, and the strength of their walls, that they were enabled to baffle during eight months the efforts of the besiegers. The fall of a lofty tower at length disclosed to the Carthaginians the secret avenues of the city; but even then their avarice was disappointed by the invincible resolution or frantic despair of the inhabitants; and the Saguntines setting fire to their houses, involved themselves, their families, and their effects, in general destruction.

Beyond the stream of the Iberus, and between that river and the Pyrenean mountains the Vascones and Ilergetes possessed the same districts as compose at present the kingdom of Navarre and the province of Catalonia. They had heard of the fate of Saguntum, and their consternation was

revealed

revealed in their feeble refiftance; they fubmitted to the victor, and Spain tranfiently acknowledged the dominion of Carthage. The terror of arms was probably improved by negociation; the fame qualities which rendered Hannibal the idol of his foldiers, enabled him to reconcile the jarring paffions of hoftile and rival nations; when he prefumed to meafure the ftrength and fortune of the African republic with thofe of Rome, twenty thoufand Spaniards with alacrity marched beneath his ftandard, traverfed with him the Pyrenean mountains, and the Alps; and claimed their fhare in the danger and glory of the bloody fields of Trebia, of Thrafymene, and of Cannæ.

It was not folely on the affections of Spain that Hannibal relied for her obedience during his abfence. Fifteen thoufand Africans were left under the command of his brother Afdrubal, to fecure and protect the country from the mouth of the Bœtis, to the banks of the Iberus; and ten thoufand infantry and one thoufand horfe were entrufted to an officer of the name of Hanno who awed the turbulent hordes between the Iberus and the Pyrenees.

The precaution was the natural refult of the fagacity of the chief who adopted it. Rome fcarce was informed of the defign of Hannibal to penetrate into Italy, before fhe prepared to deprive him of the refources which he might draw from

from Spain, by transporting the war into that country. Cneius Scipio at the head of a formidable army encountered in the country of the Ilergetes the troops of Hanno; the Carthaginians were defeated; and from the Pyrenean mountains to the Iberus, the tribes and cities of Spain submitted to the authority of Rome.

A. C. 204, 196.

The forces of Cneius Scipio were swelled by the junction of the troops of his brother Publius, who with the title of proconsul was appointed to the conduct of the Spanish war. The kindred chiefs extended their enterprises beyond the stream of the Iberus, restored the walls of Saguntum, and during seven years of martial toils maintained the ascendancy of Rome. The Edetani who had seized the moment of their absence to revolt, were severely chastised, and their capital, the modern city of Lerida, was abandoned to the rapacity of the Roman soldiers. Within the hilly district of Lusitania, Asdrubal eluded the pursuit of his enemies; but he was forced to relinquish the open country to their arms; and the Scipios already revolved the total reduction of Spain, when they perished by their own temerity. Elated by a series of victory, they divided their forces to improve their advantages more rapidly. It is probable the natives had always regarded their progress with secret discontent; they embraced the moment

moment when their troops were difunited; to the north of the Iberus, on the frontiers of the Sueffetani, Publius was deferted by his allies, and oppreffed by the forces of Spain, of Carthage, and of Numidia; and as Cneius returned to avert, or avenge the fate of his brother, the levity or treachery of his barbarian followers involved him in the fame deftruction. The Celtiberians retired from his ftandard; and his fcanty band of Romans was encountered and overwhelmed by the hofts of their enemies.

The chaftifement of the Spaniards, A. C. 195, and the expulfion of the Carthaginians, 192. were committed to the kindred hand of Cornelius, the fon of Publius Scipio. That hero, who was afterwards better known by the furname of *Africanus*, was when only twenty-four years old invefted with the proconfular dignity, and appointed to the command which had been held by his father. He found the Romans incamped behind the ftream of the Iberus, and though under the conduct of Lucius Martius they had furprifed the Carthaginian camp, their late fuccefs had not effaced the remembrance of their former difafters. They were taught to contemn the feeble protection of the river by the example of their new general; from its banks to the province of Bœtica their adventurous valour was refpected

by

by the barbarians, and they traversed the extent of Spain without encountering an enemy.

On a peninsula which stretches towards the opposite continent of Africa from the ancient country of the Contestani, and the modern province of Murcia, New Carthage, whose name sufficiently reveals her founders, had under the influence of commerce and civil administration arisen to opulence and grandeur; and had been established by the Carthaginians as the seat of their government, and the repository of their arms and treasures. While Scipio invested the city by land, the Roman fleet under Lælius blocked up the mouth of the harbour; on the side towards the sea the garrison had trusted to that element for their protection, and a low and narrow wall was rather designed to repel the waves than exclude the enemy. The retiring tide left the water fordable at the foot of the rampart; and Scipio was no sooner apprised of the circumstance than he prepared to avail himself of it. Five hundred chosen soldiers were animated by the example of their chief; with venturous steps they explored in silence their course; scaled the wall; and while the attention of the garrison was diverted by a feigned attack from the land, they were astonished by the tremendous sound of the Roman trumpets in the heart of the city. A martial band under the command of Mago in vain endea-

endeavoured to maintain the citadel againſt the ardour of the aſſailants: they were compelled after a ſhort reſiſtance to ſurrender at diſcretion, and the accumulated riches of New Carthage became the prize of the victors.

In the reduction of New Carthage the Spaniards had admired the enterpriſing genius and daring valour of Scipio; in the uſe of victory they were forced to applaud his generoſity and moderation. Among the captives a beautiful virgin who was betrothed to Allucius, a prince of Celtiberia, was preſented by the Roman ſoldiers to their general as the moſt acceptable reward of his martial labours. The gallantry and chaſtity of Scipio might, in a rude and unpoliſhed age, have inſtructed the Romans, and muſt have conciliated the regard of the barbarians. He turned from the alluring charms of the fair, and reſtored her in ſafety to her royal lover, whoſe alliance was the immediate conſequence of his honourable forbearance.

The virtues of an invader are probably the moſt dangerous inſtruments he can employ againſt the people whoſe conqueſt he meditates. The union of the ſtates of Spain might have prolonged at leaſt the term of their independence; but the generoſity of Scipio had been diffuſed through the various tribes of the Celtiberians; the greateſt part of the country from the Iberus to the Sucro, declared in favour of the Romans; and the native

tive bands of Allucius, under the conduct of their prince, marched beneath the banners, and exulted in the dependent title of the auxiliaries of Rome.

Not far from the shores of the Mediterranean where a branch of the Iberus winds towards the Pyrenean mountains, the Lacetani occupied part of the present province of Catalonia. Turbulent in peace, but bold and ardent in war, they were distinguished by the same features as mark the modern Catalans. Jealousy of Rome, or gratitude to Carthage had fixed their prince in the interests of the African republic; and in the destruction of Publius Scipio the name of Indibilis had been transmitted to Italy as the most formidable of the barbarian chieftains of Spain. Steady in his enmity or attachments, he still propped the declining cause of Carthage; and Asdrubal might be urged by his resolution to await the approach of the Roman army. But the contest was fatal to the hopes of the Lacetanian prince, and the Carthaginian chief; the undisciplined valour of the Spaniards, and the rapidity of the Numidian squadrons, were incapable of disconcerting the steady order of the Roman legions; Indibilis and Asdrubal fled; and the recal of the latter to join the forces of his brother Hannibal in Italy, left Scipio to establish his ascendancy in Spain.

The Spaniards in the alliance of Carthage were
a se-

a second time defeated near the Bœtis; and Aurinx, a city of lower Bœtica, was taken and plundered by the victors. But the spirits of the Spaniards were restored by the intelligence that Scipio had passed over into Africa; they had scarce time to resume their arms before they were astonished by the rapid return of the Roman general. The city of Illiturgis, which was situated near the modern town of Andujar, was assaulted and stormed by Scipio; and Astuto, which has dwindled into the insignificant village of Cazlone, was reduced by Lucius Martius.

In the country of the Edetani, and probably not far from the city of Lerida, twenty thousand Spanish infantry and two thousand five-hundred cavalry under the princes Indibilis and Mardonius were assembled to defend their own independence, or to support the fortunes of Carthage. They were attacked, broken, and slaughtered by the Romans; the fate of Indibilis and Mardonius is buried in obscurity, but seventeen thousand of their followers perished on the disastrous field; the open country submitted to the conqueror; and Scipio impatient to expel the Carthaginians from Spain, instantly formed the siege of Gades, within the walls of which the remnant of their armies was united. The fortifications of that city yielded to the machines of the besiegers, and the triumphant eagles of the Romans

were

were displayed from the Pyrenean mountains to the mouth of the Bœtis.

A. C. 155, 192.
When the republic of Carthage sunk beneath the superior virtue or fortune of her rival, the peninsula of Spain was yielded by the vanquished party to the victors; and Rome imposed on that country the name and condition of a dependent province.

It is the observation of Seneca, that wheresoever the Roman conquers, he inhabits; and the maxim was confirmed by the numerous colonies which soon diffused themselves over the face of Spain. The lofty situation of the city of Tarragona protected it from a surprise, and in an age when the art of war was but little known, enabled it to defy the attacks of a numerous army. Its vicinity to the Mediterranean Sea was peculiarly happy for the purposes of commerce in peace; and permitted the Romans, by a short and safe navigation, to pour their forces in war into Spain, without being exposed to a dangerous and tedious march through the hostile and barbarous states of Gaul, and across the rugged and inhospitable heights of the Pyrenees. It soon assumed the splendour of a capital, and became the seat of government for the province of *citerior* Spain, which occupied the northern part of the peninsula from the Pyreneans to the mouth of the Durius or Duero.

The

The province of *ulterior* Spain comprised the rest of the peninsula, which included the modern countries of Portugal, Grenáda, and Andalusia. The first, which had scarcely felt the impression of the Roman arms, was distinguished, as we have already observed, by the name of Lusitania; and the two latter were afterwards confounded in the general appellation of Bœtica.

It is not to be supposed that a people fond of independence, and indifferent to danger, would long endure with patience the yoke of servitude. In hither Spain Sempronius, who, with the rank of prætor, commanded a Roman army, was suddenly attacked and destroyed, with all his forces; and in further Spain the flames of revolt blazed forth with more open violence. But the same spirit of disunion continued to render abortive the struggles of the Spaniards. Marcus Porcius, whose surname of Censor, was the fruit of his austerity in that office, landed with two legions at Rhoda, a port of Catalonia which still subsists under the kindred appellation of Rofes, and in a variety of conflicts restored the ascendancy of the Roman armies. His successor, Fulvius Flaccus, reduced the Vaccæi, whose capital is still recognized on the borders of Asturia by its former name of Palantia. In a bloody battle the Celtiberians paid the penalty of their rashness; and their chastisement seemed for

A. C. 155, 143.

a moa moment to intimidate the haughty spirits of the barbarians.

An hardy band collected in the mountains still preferred the freedom of those barren regions to the subjection of the fertile plains beneath; the oppression of the Romans soon summoned them from their recesses to avenge the injuries, and assert the liberties of their country: Lucullus, who in the quality of proconsul governed *hither* Spain, had been received into the town of Pauca on articles of capitulation; but he basely violated the conditions he had subscribed; and was no sooner admitted within the gates, than he let loose the rage and avarice of his followers; and of twenty thousand citizens, scarce five hundred escaped to accuse his cruel perfidy. In *further* Spain the prætor, Galba, disgraced the Roman name by a repetition of the same sanguinary fraud: a considerable number of the Lusitanians had offered to submit to the authority of Rome; the prætor affected to listen with compassion to their distress, and promised them in a more fertile region those advantages which their own country denied them; but they were scarcely separated before they had reason to repent their fond confidence in the Roman faith; they were attacked, defenceless, and disunited; and the few who escaped served only to inflame their countrymen with an implacable detestation of Rome.

The

The love of freedom, and the thirst A.C. 143, of revenge, had assembled a numerous army of warlike Lusitanians, who retaliated on the Spanish territories of Rome the injuries that had been inflicted on their countrymen; but in their march through Turditania, or modern Andalusia, their impatience betrayed them into the midst of a rugged and mountainous country, the defiles of which had been occupied by the Romans. The difficulties which presented themselves on every side induced them to treat with Vetilius, who had succeeded Galba in command; and the Roman leader readily promised, on condition that they should acknowledge the sovereignty of Rome, to assign them lands that would supply a necessary subsistence to their industry. The recent fate of their countrymen could not but inspire them with some distrust; the moment of hesitation was improved by the remonstrances of Viriatus, who in the obscure station of a private soldier, possessed the talents of a general, and the soul of an hero. "Remember," exclaimed he, "the perfidy of "Lucullus, and of Galba; respect my counsels, "and I will engage to deliver you from the "snare in which you are entangled." The tone of confidence he assumed awaked new hope in the desponding bosoms of the Lusitanians; they committed themselves to his superior genius, and their

their obedience was rewarded by immediate safety. While with a thousand horse he opposed an extended line to the Roman legions, and menaced in appearance a general engagement, he directed the rest in small parties to pursue separate and unfrequented paths, which he himself had explored in search of game, or of spoil; and to rendezvous under the walls of Tribola. His orders were executed with promptitude and success; and no sooner was he assured of the retreat of his infantry, than he followed with his horse their footsteps, with a swiftness and dexterity that eluded all pursuit.

The Roman historians have lavished on Viriatus the opprobrious terms of rebel and robber; they have reluctantly confessed his skill and courage; his temperance and chastity in private, his faith and generosity in public life. His youth had been devoted to the toils of the chace; and in an age and country where the limits of justice and property were slightly traced, he might deem it no ignoble deed to despoil by his single strength the Roman of that wealth which he had extorted from the oppressed natives of Spain. If these practices in a more enlightened and civilized period have reflected some dishonour on his character, they were effaced by the general integrity he observed when possessed of power. The spirit of the hardy hunter, or licentious rover, soon emerged

emerged from obscurity and disgrace; by his late services he was established in the command of the army that he had preserved; his superior fame attracted to his standard a crowd of Lusitanians inured to danger, and enamoured of independence; his authority was founded on the most solid basis, the free suffrages of his countrymen, and Rome must have acknowledged, that he rose to power by the same qualities as Romulus attained it; a more daring valour, and a more sagacious mind.

Those qualities were consecrated to vindicate the independence of Spain, and to check the rapid progress of Roman dominion; his head and hand equally contributed to his glory. He seems to have possessed the peculiar art of directing successfully the impetuous valour of his countrymen against troops not less brave, and better disciplined, than themselves. With him flight was the frequent prelude to victory; and he was never more formidable than when he appeared to dread or to shun his adversary.

The first who felt his arms, and was ensnared by his arts, was Vetilius himself, who, impatient of the triumph that had evaded his grasp in Turditania, pressed forward to seize it under the walls of Tribola; but as he urged his march with inconsiderate ardour through a country embarassed by woods, and broken by mountains, he was suddenly assailed by the fierce and numerous bands of Viriatus. The legions confessed the impressions of surprize and fear, and were confounded by the rapid and desultory attacks of their enemies; they fled; and of ten thousand, near one half perished in the action or pursuit. Vetilius himself fell alive into the hands of the victors; but the barbarians, accustomed only to esteem their captives in proportion to their vigour and activity, regarded with contempt his age and corpulence. Some resentment might be inspired by the remembrance of the perfidy of Lucullus and Galba; and the sword of a Lusitanian deprived Viriatus of the glory of detaining in chains a Roman general.

Viriatus would have ill deserved the reputation of sagacity, had he in the pride of victory neglected the means of improving it. The arms of the legionaries were distributed among the companions of his fortune. The renown of his atchievements allured fresh thousands to his standard; and at the head of a numerous and zealous army he beheld himself capable of undertaking more important enterprises.

Ten thousand foot, and thirteen hundred horse, had landed in Spain from Italy, under the conduct of the prætor Caius Plantius, to support the authority of the republic. They were joined by the troops which had survived the defeat of Vetilius;

lius; and by the Spaniards who still owned the influence, or dreaded the arms of Rome. In their march from Tarragona towards the banks of the Tagus, they were harassed by the attacks of Viriatus; and four thousand who had been detached from the main army were surrounded and cut off by the Lusitanian chief. Encouraged by this second proof of the valour of his followers, Viriatus aspired to a more honourable victory: he met, in an open field of battle, the legions and allies of Rome. The ardour of the latter was probably chilled by the sight of the kindred ensigns of their adversaries; and they might desert without ignominy a field where victory would have only served to have riveted their own shackles. The former were broken, dispersed, or slaughtered; the remnant sought shelter within the walls of the neighbouring cities that were retained in subjection by the strength of their garrisons; but the open country hailed Viriatus as the deliverer of Spain; and his name was the subject of triumph from the Iberus to the Bœtis.

In the hour of calamity and defeat, the fortitude and resources of Rome were most conspicuous: Viriatus had scarcely established his triumph over Plantius before he was informed of the approach of Claudius Unimanus; yet the fate of Unimanus was the same as that of his predecessor

deceſſor; and vanquiſhed in battle, he eſcaped with difficulty from the purſuit of the victors.

The fortune and renown of Viriatus were revealed in the appointment of a chief to oppoſe him, who was deſcended and allied to an illuſtrious race of heroes. Quintus Fabius Æmilianus was the brother of the younger Scipio, and was inveſted with the dignity of conſul when he was named to the conduct of the war in Spain. The virtues of Scipio Africanus were yet freſh in the memories of the barbarians; and the love of freedom might at leaſt be checked by eſteem and gratitude. Several tribes of hither Spain followed willingly a leader whoſe name was ſtill the object of their veneration. Yet Viriatus was neither daunted by the reputation of his adverſary, nor diſmayed by the levity of his countrymen. He frequently defied him to battle; and the conſulate of Æmilianus expired without his being able to obtain any deciſive advantage over his antagoniſt. In the quality of proconſul his military command was prolonged a ſecond year; and although the Roman writers aſſert that he at laſt vanquiſhed in battle the Luſitanian chief, yet the ſtrength of the latter appears to have been unimpaired; and he defeated, the two enſuing years, Quinctius and Servilianus, the ſucceſſors of Æmilianus.

The example and negociations of Viriatus had been

been extended into *hither* Spain; and he had projected an extensive confederacy throughout the tribes of the Spanish peninsula, which probably might have prescribed bounds to the ambition of the Roman republic; but he was sensible that it was alone in the hour of tranquillity that he could firmly establish his authority, and recruit the exhausted strength of his country for the arduous designs he meditated: he seized the moment of prosperity to negociate an advantageous peace. The fears of Servilianus were improved by the address of the Lusitanian; and a treaty was signed by the former, and ratified by the senate of Rome; by which Viriatus was acknowledged as the friend and ally of the Roman people, and the Lusitanians were confirmed in the independent possession of those regions which at that time they had either actually acquired or retained.

It is difficult to discern at this distance, what were the limits of the new dominions of Viriatus; yet we may naturally conjecture that they embraced the greatest part of further Spain. Arsa, which he had fixed on as the future capital of his kingdom, was situated at no great distance from the banks of the Anas, and about half way between the modern cities of Cordova and Alcantara; nor is it probable that the prudence or policy of Viriatus would have suffered him to

have

have established the seat of his government on the utmost verge of his territories.

While Viriatus was intent on the arts of peace, and the embellishments of Arsa, he heard with astonishment the hostile sound of the Roman trumpet. The haughty spirit of Rome had been wounded by the late treaty she had subscribed; and her reputation was mortally injured by the perfidy with which she broke it. The government of whatever remained to the republic in further Spain had been allotted to Quintus Servilius Cœpio, who pressed the senate for permission to renew the war against Viriatus. That assembly was less attentive to the honour than the aggrandisement of the republic; and without any previous intimation of hostilities, Cœpio, at the head of a numerous and well-appointed army, rapidly advanced towards Arsa.

Surprized, and unequal to resistance, Viriatus, on his approach, abandoned with indignation his capital, which he was incapable of defending, and retired within the mountains of the Carpetani, who inhabited the country which is known at present by the name of New Castille. He was pursued and encompassed by Cœpio; but the same arts which had delivered him from the arms of Vetilius, were again practised with success against Cœpio. His followers dispersed themselves by unfrequented paths through the woods and

and mountains; and though the weakness of the barbarians allowed them not to chastise the perfidy, the skill of their commander enabled them to elude the vengeance of Rome.

The assertor of his country's freedom was not indifferent to her happiness; and the lawless rover whose glory had been established in war, sighed for the tranquil blessings of peace. He negociated; but he negociated in arms; and perhaps Viriatus never appeared more truly great, than when with a slender band hastily assembled he observed and harassed the march of the Roman legions, and taught Cœpio to respect his genius in the hour of adversity. In every desultory conflict he maintained his wonted ascendancy; and after every successful action he renewed his proposals for peace. The Roman consul affected to listen with pleasure to the terms that were offered; but beneath the appearance of a treaty, he cherished a dark design as injurious to his own honour as to that of Rome. Open and magnanimous, the mind of Viriatus readily ascribed the same virtues to others as he himself was possessed of. If repeated instances of Roman perfidy might warn him to guard against the artifices of that republic, the consciousness of his own services allowed him not to adopt the slightest precaution against the treachery of his countrymen. But the deputies, whom he
had

had entrusted with the conduct of the negociation, were corrupted by the gold and splendid promises of Cœpio; they agreed to assassinate the defender of their country; and they performed the engagement with infamous fidelity. Viriatus had deserved, and he confided in, the affection and attachment of his followers; the tent of the Lusitanian chief was unprotected by guards or sentinels, and open to access at every hour to the meanest soldier; he was the victim of his honest boldness; and, invincible in arms, he perished by domestic treason. At midnight, as in his armour he snatched a short and necessary repose from the toils and cares of his station, he was assailed by the daggers of the conspirators; their weapons were plunged into his throat, the only part exposed; and he instantly expired, most probably ignorant of the ingratitude and treachery of those whom he had loved and trusted.

In every age and country the same abhorrence of vice has prevailed, though not to the same degree: the treason may be loved, but the traitor must be detested; and when the assassins of Viriatus presented themselves before Cœpio, and demanded the promised reward of their crime, they were admonished by the answer of the consul how little fidelity can exist in the confederacy of guilt: he told them they might retain in safety
what

what they had already received; but infultingly added, it was only from the juftice of the Roman fenate they muft expect any further gratification.

The Lufitanians lamented the lofs, and honoured the memory of their much-loved general. His funeral was folemnized with barbarian magnificence; but their weaknefs allowed them not to fulfil the duty of revenge, which, in their favage ftate, the tribes of Spain would have deemed the moft grateful offering to the fhade of the deceafed hero. Their unanimous fuffrages called to fupply his place Tantalus, who poffibly was recommended by the fame love of independence, but who certainly poffeffed not the fame ability as his predeceffor. He funk beneath the difficulties of his fituation. The very ground which had been the theatre of glory to Viriatus, was the fcene of difgrace and humiliation to his fucceffor: he had rafhly undertaken, and haftily abandoned the fiege of Saguntum; in their retreat the Lufitanian army were entangled within the paffes of the mountains; and the fuperior genius of their former general was acknowledged and regretted in their vain efforts to extricate themfelves; by a difgraceful capitulation they were ftripped of their arms, and were difperfed, by the policy of the victors, to different and diftant colonies; the cities on the banks of the Bœtis returned again to their obedience; the
Roman

Roman eagles were difplayed in triumph through the weftern and northern diftricts of Spain; Junius Brutus paffed the Duero, and penetrated to the coaft of Gallicia; from the utmoft point of Cape Finifterre the Romans caft a look of aftonifhment on the vaft expanfe of the Atlantic Ocean; and on their return, Rome might liften with admiration to the fabulous tales of her enterprifing fons, who boldly affirmed they had beheld in thofe remote regions, the fun yield to the approach of night, and fink into the weftern main, with a mighty and tremendous noife.

The lofty fuperftructure of dominion which had been erected by the ambition or patriotifm of Viriatus, fell with him who had planned it; and from the death of that chief the Lufitanians beheld their fertile fields laid wafte, and their cities reduced to afhes. Yet every want was compenfated, and every calamity atoned, by the enthufiaftic ardour of freedom. In the diftant receffes of their mountains they ftill breathed the pure air of independence; and to the Roman fenate, which endeavoured to impofe on them the ignominious badge of tribute, an high-fpirited people more tenacious of their honour and their liberty than their property, boldly replied, that " their anceftors had left them fteel to defend " their poffeffions, inftead of gold to redeem " them."

While

While the Lusitanians cherished the sacred flame of freedom amidst their barren mountains, its fire had been felt and confessed by the Celtiberians, whose situation exposed them with more facility to the arms of Rome. Near the source of the Duero, and probably on the confines of hither and further Spain, arose the city of Numantia; and the accurate eye of a modern geographer has fixed its situation a little above the present city of Soria. Numantia had listened with attention to the atchievements and remonstrances of Viriatus, and while that chief vindicated the independence of Lusitania, Numantia asserted her native right to the free and equal condition she had known before the intrusion of the Romans; the same cause was embraced by the neighbouring city of Termes, which still preserves her name without her population. Their youth sallied from their gates, repulsed in open fight the disciplined valour of the Romans, and inflamed the spirits of their countrymen by the liberal distribution of the spoil. Intimidated by the approach of Quintus Pompeius at the head of thirty thousand veterans, they condescended to treat of submission; but they rejected with contempt the rigorous and ignominious conditions which would have despoiled them of their fortifications and their arms. " Brave men, exclaimed they, never quit their
" arms

A. C. 142,
128.

"arms but with their lives." Indignation and despair supplied the want of numbers; vanquished in battle, the Roman general was compelled to accept of a treaty by which they delivered up the Roman prisoners and deserters, and engaged for the payment of thirty talents at different periods.

A. C. 142, 128. But when Viriatus was no more, and the imprudence of Tantalus had confined the hopes, or at least the resistance of the Lusitanians within the limits of their mountains, the cities of Numantia and Termes were exposed to the whole weight of Roman ambition and resentment. The senate had sternly refused to ratify the treaty that had been subscribed by Pompey, and without restoring the hostages, or refunding the money, instantly displayed again the signal of hostility. The Numantians beheld from their walls the approach of the Roman army under Popilius Lœnas; and disdaining the advantages of their ramparts and situation, they rushed forth to an open encounter. Their happy temerity was rewarded with success; and the remnant of the Roman army that escaped their fury, preserved during the remainder of the campaign an awful distance.

The succeeding spring the Roman ensigns were again displayed within sight of Numantia, and the inhabitants of that city again sallied forth

forth to engage their adverfaries; twenty thoufand Romans were flaughtered by four thoufand Numantians; and the conful Hoftilius Mancinus, with the wretched fugitives from the difaftrous field, were furrounded by the victors on every fide. They were preferved from famine or the fword by a treaty, which was ratified by the moft folemn oaths of Mancinus and his principal officers. The conditions of it have been buried in ftudied filence by the Roman hiftorians: and the oblivion to which they have configned it, and the fituation of the vanquifhed army, ftrengthen the conjecture, that the independence of Numantia was formally expreffed, and was the ftipulation that ranfomed the lives of Mancinus and his foldiers.

The Numantians were again defrauded of the fruits of victory by the perfidy of their adverfaries, and the treaty concluded by Mancinus was violated by the Roman fenate with the fame facility as that which had been fubfcribed by Pompey. Yet they affected to difguife their breach of faith beneath the appearance of rigid juftice; and by the authority of that affembly, Mancinus was delivered in chains to the refentment of the Numantians. Thefe, with becoming magnanimity, rejected the proffered victim. "It is not," faid they, "the facrifice of a private man that "can atone for a breach of the public faith."

The

The avarice of Emilius Lepidus, who had been appointed succeffor to Mancinus, had prompted him to undertake the fiege of Palantia, the capital of the Vaccæi; and he incurred the double difgrace of abandoning in hafte an enterprife that had been concerted without juftice. His retreat did not efcape the vigilant and active refentment of the befieged; he was purfued, overtaken, and defeated; and fix thoufand legionaries expiated with their lives the guilt of their general.

If the Spaniards were elated by fuccefs, they were foon convinced by mournful experience of the viciffitudes of war. The city of Palantia was befieged, and compelled to furrender by Calphurn Pifo; that of Termes was probably about the fame time obliged to acknowledge the fovereignty of Rome; the Lufitanians were ftill confined within the fortreffes of their mountains; and the Numantians could not hear without fome emotions of fear that a *fecond* Scipio Africanus, who rivalled the martial fame of the *firft*, was appointed to conduct againft them the flower of the Roman legions.

It is not probable that the pride of Rome fuffered her to diminifh the account of the number of her enemies; and by the confeffion of her own hiftorians, the Numantians capable of bearing arms exceeded not ten thoufand. But they

were

were united by the fame hopes, and the fame danger; and had their adverfaries prefumed immediately to oppofe their ardour on the field of battle, the remembrance of former victories might have been the prelude to new ones. But Scipio, though at the head of fixty thoufand foldiers, declined the inaufpicious walls of Numantia; and fuffered an year to elapfe in reftoring and confirming the difcipline of his foldiers before he ventured to approach that city. His march was retarded by the attacks of the Numantians; but their impetuous valour was compelled to yield to the fteady courage of the Romans. When upbraided by their countrymen, that they had fled before thofe whom they had fo frequently vanquifhed;—" The Romans," replied they, " are indeed the fame fheep, but " they have got a different fhepherd." With a figh of defpair and indignation they beheld their fields laid wafte by the invaders; and their laft retreat within the walls of Numantia, was foon followed by the clofe blockade of that devoted city.

The city of Numantia arofe on a lofty hill, and its walls, of three miles in circumference, were manned by four thoufand brave and vigorous citizens, whofe minds were fortified by the love of liberty, and the contempt of death. Could any honourable terms of peace have fatisfied their enemies, they would have willingly fubfcribed them.

Vol. I.   D

them. The intolerant spirit of Rome demanded the surrender of their arms, their city, and their persons, to be disposed of at the discretion of the senate; and the Numantians preferred a glorious death to a life of servitude. They sallied from their walls, and defied the host of their besiegers to battle. But the prudence of Scipio restrained his soldiers within the lines, and the Numantians as they returned revolved in anxious horror a lingering fate by famine. One hope remained, to rouse in their defence the martial tribes of Spain. Five aged warriors, each attended by his son, undertook to penetrate the works of the besiegers; they pierced the Roman lines, hewed down the guard that opposed them, and escaped before the Numidian horse could be assembled for pursuit. But the attempt was more honourable to themselves than serviceable to their countrymen; the emotions of compassion were overwhelmed by those of fear; and of the numerous and powerful states of Spain, one city alone yielded to the noble ardour, and assumed their arms for the relief of Numantia.

The walls of Lutia have been levelled by time or policy; and no monuments remain to mark the spot on which they stood. Yet one generous action has immortalized her fame; and when she embraced the sinking fortunes of the Numantians, she rescued her own name for ever from oblivion.

But

HISTORY OF SPAIN.

But before her youth could buckle on their armour, they were surprised by the appearance of Scipio at their gates. The Roman general had been apprised of their design, and with a select detachment had pressed forward to vengeance. Lutia was incapable of resistance; and four hundred of the noblest youths were the miserable victims to the implacable severity of Scipio. Their right hands were lopped from them; and their mutilated appearance warned the neighbouring nations how dangerous it was to provoke the wrath of Rome.

In the grief of the Numantians for the fate of their generous allies, was mingled some concern for their own safety. Each hour diminished the scanty stock of their provisions, and augmented the number of their enemies. Their councils were influenced by famine and despair; and the deputation which issued from their gates, solicited Scipio to secure their future fidelity by receiving their submission on honourable terms, or to allow them the means of a glorious death in battle. The cold and laconic reply of the proconsul, that they must surrender at discretion, determined the Numantians. Sword in hand they sallied forth on their oppressors, and their bloody despair was gratified by the carnage of their enemies. Their strength was exhausted by the unequal conflict; but their spirits were far from subdued. They that were driven back into the city, set fire to their houses, and with their wives and families rushed on destruction. Fifty alone were with difficulty ravished from the flames to adorn the triumph of the victor; and after defying the power of Rome for fourteen years, Numantia was confounded in an heap of ashes by the indignant rage of her citizens.

A. C. 128, 76. The resistance of Numantia may be considered as the last memorable struggle of Spain for independence; and though the Cantabrians and Asturians, in the mountains of modern Biscay and Asturia, long cherished the sacred flame of freedom, and, confident in their native fastnesses, often invaded the fertility of the plains, and braved in their craggy retreat the resentment of Rome, yet their enterprises were confined to transient and predatory incursions. The greatest part of the peninsula acquiesced under the Roman yoke; and it was only in the civil dissensions of the republic, that her name in the course of an hundred years attracts our curiosity.

A. C. 72, 71. When the party of Marius was overwhelmed in Italy by the superior genius or fortune of Sylla, the remnant found an asylum in Spain. The name of Sertorius is ranked with that of the most celebrated commanders of antiquity; and the mildness of of his civil adminiftration endeared him to the Spaniards, who had long been accuftomed to groan beneath the rapacity of the Roman proconfuls. Yet Sertorius was himfelf diftinguifhed by a quick and lively jealoufy for the dignity of the republic. He was the enemy of the ufurpation of Sylla, but not of Rome. He affumed himfelf the enfigns of a Roman officer; he beftowed on three hundred of his companions the title of Senator; and if he condefcended to treat with the mountaineers of Lufitania and Cantabria as allies, he fcorned to violate the fovereignty of Rome, or to delude the Spaniards with the hopes of independence.

Sertorius was the victim of domeftic treafon; and the tribes of Spain who had embraced his caufe were expofed to the refentment of Pompey, who commanded the army of the republic. In his return to Rome, that general, in his pretenfions to a triumph, reckoned up eight hundred and feventy-one towns which he had reduced; and though many of thefe might be little more than walled villages, yet fome probability muft be allowed to the affertion, fince under the reign of Vefpafian, Pliny exhibited a lift of three hundred and fixty Spanifh cities.

It is probable that Pompey ufed his victory with moderation, fince in the ftruggle for dominion between himfelf and

A. C. 71, 46.

and Cæsar, Spain appears to have supported with ardour the fortune of the former. The banks of the Segra were the theatre of a long and doubtful contest between the lieutenants of Pompey and Cæsar himself. The commanding genius of the latter established his triumph; and Spain professed a reluctant submission to the conqueror.

A. C. 46, 40. When Pompey was no more, his memory was revered, and his sons were protected by the gratitude and affection of the tribes of Spain. The standard of opposition was again erected in that province, and the martial natives joined with alacrity the legions which still adhered to the Pompeian party. Their growing numbers, and rapid progress, demanded the presence of Cæsar. He landed at Saguntum; and in the plains of Munda, which, at some distance from Malaga, still preserve their ancient name, encountered a resistance not unworthy the conqueror of Gaul. The day was, however, unfavourable to the sons of Pompey; the flight of the eldest served only to protract a few weeks a miserable and inglorious existence; he was pursued, taken, and slain by Quintus Didius, the admiral of Cæsar; but the younger gained the shelter of the Celtiberian mountains; and was enabled, by the fidelity of the

the fearless inhabitants, to elude the active enmity of the victor.

Spain was far from acknowledging in the disastrous field of Munda, her own fortune. Quintus Didius, who had disembarked without caution on the coast of Lusitania, was surrounded and killed by the natives; and his death might be considered as an acceptable sacrifice to the shade of the elder Pompey. The city of Munda endured a long and bloody siege; and was at length taken by assault; that of Cordova refused to open her gates but to Cæsar himself. Hispalis, which boasted its foundation from Hispal, one of the ancient princes of Spain, and still subsists under the name of Seville, consented to receive a Roman garrison; but the inhabitants, in the night, admitted a party of Lusitanians; and the Romans were attacked and slaughtered by the citizens, and their new allies. The walls of the guilty city were instantly assailed by Cæsar; the Lusitanians were allured from the safeguard of the ramparts by a fictitious flight of the besiegers; and while they indulged their ardour in the pursuit, they were encompassed, and broken by the Roman cavalry; the citizens, unequal alone to the defence of their fortifications, threw themselves on the clemency of the conqueror. But though Cæsar consented to spare the lives of a prostrate people, he rigidly required and exacted the

the riches they were poffeffed of; and the attachment of Spain to Pompey was atoned by the heavieft contributions.

From the moment that the Roman eagles had been displayed throughout that peninfula, the Spaniards might juftly complain of the infatiate avarice of their new mafters; and their affiduous labour in the mines could fcarcely anfwer the inceffant demands of Rome. The firft Africanus, after the expulfion of the Carthaginians, tranfmitted to the treafury of the republic fourteen thoufand three hundred and forty pounds of filver; Lucius Lentulus collected forty-four thoufand pounds of filver, and two thoufand five hundred of gold; Manlius twelve hundred pounds of filver; Cornelius Lentulius, in two years adminiftration of *hither* Spain, amaffed fifteen hundred pounds of gold, and two thoufand pounds of filver; while the diligence of his colleague extorted from *further* Spain, in the fame fpace of time, fifty thoufand pounds of filver. Within nine years, a fum equal to five hundred thoufand pounds fterling flowed from Spain into the treafury of Rome; and it is probable that the wealth which was diverted from the public channel by the avarice of individuals, was not much lefs. Yet thefe drains were far from exhaufting the country; mention is made by Strabo of a mine near Charthagena which yielded every day twenty-five

five thousand drachms of silver, or about three hundred thousand pounds a year; and according to Pliny, twenty thousand pounds weight of gold was annually received from the provinces of Asturia, Gallicia, and Lusitania.

The total reduction and preservation of so wealthy a country could not but excite the attention of the Romans; and soon after Augustus had extinguished all competition by the battle of Actium, and established himself the undisputed master of the Roman world, he visited Spain in person, and fixed his residence in the city of Tarragona. The predatory incursions of the Cantabrians and Asturians were the pretence for a war, which probably was first suggested by avarice; and the Roman legions were attracted into the mountainous districts of modern Biscay and Asturia by the report of the precious metals with which they abounded. The natives defended their treasures and freedom with a valour worthy of their ancient renown. But the contest was too unequal to last long; twenty-three thousand of the Cantabrians were surrounded by the Romans and compelled to surrender. Ten thousand of the most vigorous were incorporated among the legions, and condemned to employ their strength and courage in the subjection of their countrymen; the rest were sold into servitude; but their despair

A. C. 25, 19.

dis-

disappointed the avarice of their purchasers; and the greatest part embraced with alacrity a voluntary death. The fate of the Asturians was scarce less terrible; two Roman armies entered from opposite sides their country, explored their retreats with persevering caution, and involved them in a general conflagration. The remnant that had escaped from the fire and the sword implored the clemency of the victors. From the northern extremity of the Pyrenees to Cape Ortegal, the fierce tribes of Cantabria and Asturia consented to receive the Roman yoke; a bridge of stone was thrown over the Iberus to preserve the more ready communication between the provinces; and the cities of Cæsar Augusta and Augusta Emerita, which still subsist under the names of Saragossa and Merida, were founded by Augustus on the northern extremity of the country of the Edetani, and on the banks of the river Anas.

The sanguinary chastisement of the Cantabrians had not broken their independent spirits; and five years had scarce elapsed from their late defeat, before they again rose in arms, and attempted to throw off the Roman yoke. Their despair summoned to the encounter Agrippa, the celebrated general, and son-in-law of Augustus; without a hope, or even a desire of pardon, the Cantabrians with tumultuous cries rushed to the charge, and the Roman legions shrunk from the first efforts

efforts of their rage. They were rallied, and conducted to victory by the example of their chief; and after a long and bloody conflict, the barbarians yielded to the superior discipline and arms of their adversaries. Yet Agrippa confessed of the many engagements he had commanded in, this had proved the most severe and obstinate; and his victory was purchased by the lives of his bravest legionaries. Though dear, however, it was complete; and the Cantabrians were never again able to face their enemies in the field. Their strong holds were discovered and forced by the industry of the victors; their castles were levelled; they were compelled to descend from their mountains, and cultivate the plain. They were taught to prefer the flow but certain advantages of agriculture to the precarious success of predatory adventure; and about two hundred years from the first invasion of Spain by the Scipios, the arms of Agrippa extinguished the last sparks of independence throughout that great peninsula, and reduced it to the humble condition of a province of Rome.

In an age that had been distinguished by a rapid succession of the most uncommon revolutions, it is not surprising that the prudence of Augustus should divide the power of his lieutenants, and endeavour to disarm the ambition of an individual from aspiring to empire. It was
this

this jealousy that probably suggested the new arrangement of Spain, which was distributed into three provinces, Tarraconensis, Lusitania, and Bœtica. Tarraconensis corresponded nearly with *hither* Spain, and embraced the modern countries of Gallicia and the Asturias, Biscay, and Navarre, Leon and the two Castilles, Murcia, Valencia, Catalonia, and Arragon; it occupied all the northern part of the peninsula from the foot of the Pyrenees to the mouth of the Duero, where Lusitania commenced; from the Duero the confines of Lusitania were extended beyond those of the kingdom of Portugal, to the mouth of the Anas. From the Anas Bœtica stretched along the western extremity of Spain, included the city of Gades and the rocky height of Calpe, whose ancient name is lost in that of Gibraltar; its boundaries were marked by the mountains of Orospeda, or Sierra Morena, which invelope the source of the Bœtis, and by the city of Urci on the confines of Tarraconensis. Yet even broken and disjointed, the different provinces of Spain were still capable of relieving the poverty or of satisfying the avarice of their respective governors; and the administration of them for near four hundred years was deemed by the Romans the most desirable reward of their services.

Chapter

Chapter the Second.

State of Spain until the reign of Gallienus.—Invasion of the Franks.—Is usurped by Constantine in the reign of Honorius.—Is betrayed or abandoned to the Suevi, the Vandals, and the Alani.—Their devastations.—They are attacked by Adolphus.—Death of Adolphus.—Atchievements of Wallia.—Extirpates the Alani.—Vanquishes the Vandals and the Suevi.—Restores Spain to the Romans.—Exploits of the Vandals.—They defeat the Romans.—They plunder Majorca and Minorca.—They depart for Africa.—Devastations of the Suevi.—Theodoric king of the Goths marches to the relief of Spain.—His victory over the Suevi, who retire into Gallicia.—Euric the successor of Theodoric completes the reduction of the greatest part of Spain.—He is succeeded by Alaric, who is killed in battle by Clovis.—Reign of Amalaric.—Administration and reign of Theudes.—The Visigoths elect Theodigele.—He is assassinated.—Civil war in Spain.—Athanegilde with the assistance of the Romans obtains the crown.—He is succeeded by Liuva and Leovigild.—Leovigild carries on a successful war with the Romans in Spain.—His sons Hermenigild and Recared are declared princes of the Goths.—Submission of the Cantabrians, &c.—Marriage and conversion of Hermenigild.—He rebels against his father.—Is vanquished and imprisoned.—Escapes from imprisonment.—Civil war.—Hermenigild is again made captive.—

captive.—He negociates with the Romans.—He is put to death.—Extinction of the kingdom of the Suevi in Spain.—Character and death of Leovigild.

From the division of Spain by Augustus, to the accession of Gallienus during more than two hundred and seventy years, that country in the humble condition of part of the Roman empire, enjoyed or abused the advantages of wealth and luxury. Twenty-five colonies which had been established by the care or interest of the parent state, soon diffused throughout the most remote districts of the peninsula the blessings of agriculture, and the monuments of public splendour. The rapacity of a needy or avaricious governor might transiently interrupt the general happiness; but the wounds which his administration could inflict were soon healed; the internal resources of the Spaniards restored their wonted prosperity; the grape and the olive were transplanted into Spain, and have flourished on the banks of the Tagus and the Bœtis; and the advanced state of Spanish husbandry under the reign of Tiberius has been elegantly described in the treatise of Columella, who was himself a Spaniard. The aqueduct of Segovia, and the stupendous bridge of Alcantara which was thrown over the Tagus by the contribution of a few Lusitanian communities,

evince

evince the spirit and ability of the provincials to project and execute the most useful and noble undertakings; and the curious eye of the traveller may discover at Tarragona, in the ruins of the palace of Augustus, of the circus, and the amphitheatre, the ancient magnificence of those structures.

Yet it was not only by the works of art and labour that Spain was distinguished above the crowd of Roman provinces; in the elegance and vigour of literary composition, she aspired to rival the parent state. Her pretensions to philosophy were substantiated by the two Senecas, who were born at Cordova; the same city might in the birth of Lucan boast an epic poet, deemed by the too fond partiality of his admirers, not inferior to Virgil; Florus was the offspring, and has been styled the ornament of Spain; and Bilbilis, the native city of Martial, has gradually been corrupted into the name of Banbola; but still serves to mark on the banks of the Xalon, the spot where that writer first indulged the sportive sallies of his pointed wit.

To obtain the palm in science and literature was no ignoble ambition; yet, in every age, the prejudices of mankind have preferred the trophies of the warrior to the silent but more useful labours of the scholar. The toils and dangers of a military life can only be compensated or contemned

temned by the hope of immortal fame. The generous paſſion was felt and diſplayed by Spain. Her ſons urged in arms their pretenſions to, and obtained the honours of the triumph. Their names were inſcribed among the moſt illuſtrious of the conſular ſenators; and Rome ratified with tranſport the adoption of her emperor Nerva, when he choſe from Spain a ſon and ſucceſſor. Trajan was born at Italica, which at preſent ſubſiſts in the name of Old Seville; and his countrymen might exult in a ſovereign whoſe virtues have been deemed not inferior to thoſe of the Scipios. The native place of Hadrian was the ſame as that of Trajan. The younger Antonine was alſo of Spaniſh extraction; and Spain might juſtly claim ſome glory from the luſtre and happineſs which, during their various adminiſtrations, her ſons diffuſed over the wide extent of the Roman world.

A. D. 260.
But when the gathering clouds of the north burſt on the Roman empire, Spain was ſhaken by the violence of the tempeſt, and involved in the general night of darkneſs and calamity. The union and cloſe confederacy of the modern kingdoms of France and Spain a few years ſince were conſidered as dangerous to the independence of Europe; but the name of the ancient Franks was firſt revealed to the Spaniards by their hoſtile and deſtructive invaſion. From the

the banks of the Rhine they penetrated through the rugged paſſes of the Pyrenees; Tarragona, the flouriſhing capital of a peaceful province, was ſacked, and almoſt deſtroyed; during twelve years they extended their devaſtations over the opulent and defencelefs peninſula; nor did they abandon it until it was no longer able to ſupply their prodigal rapacity. The veſſels which commerce had collected in the ports of New Carthage and Cadiz ſerved to tranſport them into Mauritania. But the traces of their blind fury and devouring progreſs were long after their retreat to be difcerned; at the beginning of the fifth century of the Chriſtian æra, Ilerda and Lerida ſtill remained in ruins; a few wretched peaſants, the ſole inhabitants of thoſe once magnificent cities, reared their cottages amongſt the fragments of palaces; and amidſt the broken columns of Roman ſculpture, might juſtly accuſe the wanton rage of the barbarians.

Though bent by the ſtorm, yet the grandeur of Spain was far from extinguiſhed; the cities of Merida, Corduba, Seville, and Tarragona, ſtill maintained their ſtation amongſt the moſt illuſtrious of the Roman world; and though an hundred and fifty years of peace had not totally obliterated the footſteps of the Franks, yet her natural productions had been improved by ingenuity and induſtry; her ports were again filled by by innumerable veffels; her fertility and trade attracted the admiration and envy of the moft diftant nations; that martial fpirit which had enabled her fo long to refift the arms of Rome, feemed tranfiently to revive; and an hardy and faithful militia guarded with native valour and vigilance the important paffes of the Pyrenees; and repelled the frequent attempts of the Germans.

A. D. 409. When the feeble fway of Honorius encouraged the ambition of his generals and lieutenants to ufurp the imperial purple, and their rival claims confumed in civil diffenfions that ftrength which might have been fuccefsfully oppofed to the fierce myriads of the north, Conftantine, who had been acknowldged by the armies of Gaul and Britain, atchieved alfo the conqueft, or received the fubmiffion of Spain. The only refiftance he encountered was from the private zeal of the family of Theodofius. The four brothers, after an unfuccefsful effort to maintain their ground at the head of the ftationary troops of Lufitania, retired to their eftates, where they levied and armed, at their own expence, a confiderable body of flaves and dependants, and occupied the ftrong paffes of the Pyrenean mountains. They were encompaffed and oppreffed by the promifcuous band of Scots, of Moors, and Marcomanni, who had been allured into his

fervice

service by the liberality of Constantine. Yet the reign of the usurper was short; and before his death he was mortified by the revolt of Spain, which, at the influence of his general, Gerontius, invested Maximus with the imperial purple. The same fate involved Constantine, Maximus, and Gerontius; and they were overwhelmed by the superior fortune or genius of Constantius, the general, and afterwards the brother-in-law of Honorius.

The mercenary troops of Constantine who had been intrusted with the defence of the passes of the Pyrenees were, on the death of that usurper, induced, either by the consciousness of their guilt, or by the hopes of rapine, to abandon their station; and about ten months before the sack of Rome by the Goths, the Suevi, the Vandals, and the Alani poured through the straits of the mountains. It is doubtful whether they were invited by treachery, or attracted by negligence; but their irruption was followed by the most dreadful calamities: the barbarians exercised their indiscriminate cruelty on the fortunes of the Romans and the Spaniards; and ravaged with equal fury the cities and the open country. The progress of famine reduced the miserable inhabitants to feed on the flesh of their fellow creatures; and even the wild beasts, who multiplied without controul in the desert, were exasperated

A. D. 413.

rated

rated by the taste of blood, and the impatience of hunger, boldly to attack and devour their human prey. Pestilence soon appeared, the inseparable companion of famine; a large proportion of the people was swept away; and the groans of the dying excited only the envy of their surviving friends. At length the barbarians, satiated with carnage and rapine, and afflicted by the contagious evils which they themselves had introduced, fixed their permanent seats in the depopulated country. The ancient Gallicia, whose limits include the kingdom of Castille, was divided between the Suevi and the Vandals; the Alani were scattered over the provinces of Carthagena and Lusitania, from the Mediterranean to the Atlantic Ocean; and the fruitful territory of Bœtica was allotted to the Silingi, another branch of the Vandalic nation. After regulating this partition, the conquerors contracted with their new subjects some reciprocal engagements of protection and obedience; the lands were again cultivated; and the towns and villages were again occupied by a captive people. The greatest part of the Spaniards were even disposed to prefer their new condition of poverty and barbarism to the severe oppressions of the Roman government. Yet there were many who still asserted their native freedom; and who refused, more especially

in

in the mountains of Gallicia, to submit to the barbarian yoke.

Such, according to an eloquent historian of that country, was the miserable state of Spain, when the same means were employed to restore her to the subjection of Rome, as had been exerted to wrest her from it. Adolphus, the brother-in-law of the renowned Alaric, had been unanimously chosen to succeed to the vacant throne of the Goths. He professed his intention to employ his sword not to subvert, but to re-establish and maintain the prosperity of the Roman empire; and he was confirmed in his attachment to the cause of the republic by the ascendancy which a Roman princess had acquired over his heart and understanding. He admired his captive Placidia, the daughter of the great Theodosius, and the sister of the emperor Honorius. Placidia yielded without reluctance to the desires of a conqueror young and valiant; and her marriage with the Gothic king was celebrated in the presence of Italy. Adolphus marched against the tyrants beyond the Alps; and Honorius accepted from his hand the grateful present of the heads of the brothers Jovinus and Sebastian, who had assumed in Gaul the imperial purple.

It is probable that the Roman emperor regarded with jealousy the military services of his brother-in-law; and the pru- A. D. 414, 415.

dence of his counsellors was displayed in the removal of Adolphus from the peaceful plenty of Italy. The Gothic king was persuaded to turn his victorious arms against the barbarians in Spain; and to undertake the conquest of that peninsula as the ally of Honorius. From Gaul he passed the Pyrenees; and surprised, in the name of the emperor, the city of Barcelona. But he had scarce time to exult in his success, before he fell the victim of domestic treason: he had imprudently received into his service one of the followers of Sarus, a barbarian chief, who had been sacrificed by Adolphus to a long and hereditary enmity; the death of Sarus was avenged by that of Adolphus, who perished in his palace of Barcelona by the hand of the daring assassin; and Singeric, the brother of Sarus, in the moment of consternation usurped the Gothic throne, put to death the children of his predecessor, and compelled Placidia to attend on foot through the streets of Barcelona the triumph of her consort's murderer.

A. D. 415, 418. The cruelty of Singeric probably hastened his destruction; seven days after his usurpation, he also in his turn perished by the resentment of an individual; and the Gothic sceptre was, by the choice of the nation, committed to Wallia. From Barcelona, the new monarch marched in arms through the modern provinces of Valencia,

Valencia, Murcia, and Grenada; and from the rock that is now covered by the fortrefs of Gibraltar, he revolved the invafion of the oppofite coaft of Africa. He was diverted from the enterprife by a violent tempeft, and by the remonftrances of the imperial court; and in a folemn treaty Wallia engaged to imitate the example of Adolphus, and to draw his fword in the fervice of Honorius. The barbarian princes of Spain were animated by the fame paffions, and were excited by the fame pretenfions; the flames of war blazed forth from the foot of the Pyrenees to the mouth of the Bœtis. The contending chiefs are faid to have addreffed their letters, their ambaffadors, and their hoftages, to the throne of the weftern emperor, exhorting him to remain a tranquil fpectator of their conteft, the events of which muft be favourable to the Romans by the flaughter of their common enemies. The fuperior genius and fortune of Wallia eftablifhed his triumph; yet it was not until the valour of his Gothic followers had been approved in three obftinate and bloody campaigns, that his competitors acknowledged his claims to conqueft. The province of Bœtica, which had been the fcene of devaftation to, became the grave of the Silingi. Lufitania was ftrewed with the flaughtered Alani, whofe king perifhed on the fatal field. The remnant of the Scythian wanderers who escaped from the sword of the Goths, ranged themselves under the standard of the Vandals and the Suevi; yet neither the kindred strength of the Vandals, nor the more desperate courage of the Suevi, could avail them against the martial ardour of Wallia. After a variety of unsuccessful engagements, the promiscuous herd of the barbarians were driven into the mountains of Gallicia. A broken and intractable country opposed the pursuit of the victor; and within a narrow compass, it might be reasonably expected that the mutual jealousy of the rival warriors would precipitate their destruction. The most wealthy cities of Spain recompensed the toils of the warlike Goths; and it is probable that Wallia indulged his followers in an ample privilege of rapine, before he fulfilled his engagements and restored his Spanish conquests to the obedience of Rome; even then the natives regretted the fidelity with which he executed conditions he had subscribed; and they asserted that the violence of their barbarian conquerors was to be preferred to the steady and indefatigable extortion of their Roman governors.

A. D. 428, 429. Honorius had in person triumphed for the advantages that had been obtained by the conduct or courage of Wallia; yet but a short time elapsed between his celebration of the conquest and his final loss of the kingdom

of

of Spain. The Vandals, on the retreat of the Goths, had emerged from their faftneffes in the mountains of Gallicia. The Suevi who had prefumed to oppofe, were the early facrifice to their valour and renown; they quitted the ungrateful country between Leon and Oviedo, to revel in the plenty of the plains of Bœtica; the approach of Caftinus with a numerous army of Goths and Romans, excited their ardour, rather than awakened their fears; the degenerated Romans probably fled; and if the Goths afferted their former reputation, their obftinacy only ferved to fwell the flaughter. The prefumptuous Caftinus found fhelter in the walls of Tarragona; and it is moft likely that he foon paffed over into Italy. Seville and Carthagena opened their gates to the victorious Vandals; and the veffels which the northern warriors found collected in the port of the latter, tempted them to undertake a new, and not lefs profitable enterprife.

The name of the Baleares was limited to the two iflands of the Mediterranean oppofite to the fhore of Valencia, which, from their different extent, obtained, and have preferved the expreffive appellation of Majorca and Minorca. They had been early occupied by the Phœnicians; had, from the time of Scipio Africanus, been conquered and poffeffed by the Romans; and

and during the irruption and bloody contest of the barbarians, had become the asylum to the most opulent Spaniards, who had retreated thither, from the tempest of war, with their families and most valuable effects. The thirst of plunder allured the Vandals to surmount their native aversion, and to commit themselves to the perils of the sea. They probably availed themselves of a favourable wind; and, with a steady breeze, they might in twelve hours accomplish a navigation of scarce fourscore miles. The wretched fugitives, who trusted to the protection of the elements instead of arms, were stripped of the remnant of their former opulence; and the Vandal fleet, laden with spoil, steered back its successful course into the ports of Spain. The barbarians renewed their depredations; but their active rapacity had already exhausted the country; and they listened with pleasure to the invitation of the governor of Africa, whose personal resentment solicited them to the invasion of that province. The vessels to transport them across the straits of Gibraltar were furnished by the Spaniards, who anxiously wished for their departure, and by the African general, who impatiently awaited their arrival; yet before he quitted the coast, Genseric, the king of the Vandals, admonished Spain, by one instance of tremendous vengeance, how dangerous it was to

provoke

provoke his resentment. Hermanric, the king of the Suevi, had descended from the mountains of Gallicia, and presumed to ravage the Spanish territories, which the Vandalic monarch was resolved to abandon. Impatient of the insult, Genseric pursued the hasty retreat of the Suevi as far as Merida, precipitated the king and his army into the river Anas, and calmly returned to the sea-shore to embark his victorious troops.

The retreat of the Vandals was far from atchieving the deliverance, or establishing the tranquillity of Spain. A. D. 456. The Suevi deplored their monarch and the bravest of their warriors overwhelmed in the waters of the Anas; but they reviewed with pleasure the numbers which still survived in the mountains of Gallicia. They gradually issued from their dark recesses, and indulged in the plenty of the plains. About thirty years from the departure of Genseric, their increasing strength, under their king Rechiarius, afflicted the provinces of Carthagena and Tarragona, and threatened to extinguish the feeble remains of the Roman dominions in Spain. The emperor of the west was moved by the cries of the oppressed Spaniards; but the effeminate Romans would not have presumed to have met in arms the hardy emigrants from beyond the stream of the Elbe. The chastisement of the latter was intrusted to a kindred hand. The sister of Theodoric

Theodoric the king of the Goths had been married to the king of the Suevi; but the Gothic prince preferred the ties of public, to those of private connexion: as the ally of Avitus he declared, unless his brother-in-law immediately retired from the imperial territories in Spain, he would arm in support of the pretensions of Rome. His menaces were derided by the fierce Rechiarius: "Tell him," replied the haughty king of the Suevi, " that I despise his friendship, and his " arms; and that I shall soon try whether he will " dare to expect my arrival under the walls of " Thoulouse." The martial impatience of Theodoric allowed him not to wait the promised attack of his adversary; and his policy might suggest to him to keep Rechiarius involved in all the disadvantages of a defensive war. But though he undertook the expedition, as the obedient soldier of the emperor of the west, he was not indifferent to the motives of interest or ambition; and he privately stipulated for himself and his successors the absolute possession of his Spanish conquests. At the head of a promiscuous army of Visigoths, Franks, and Burgundians, Theodoric passed the Pyrenees; and on the banks of the river Urbicus, about twelve miles from Astorga, he was encountered by Rechiarius; but the fortune or the numbers of the Suevi were unequal to the contest; a people whose dexterity and

and valour had challenged the admiration of the
firſt Cæſar, and whoſe arms the immortal gods
themſelves had been deemed incapable of reſiſt-
ing, ſcorned readily to yield; and ſuch were the
bloody conſequences of their reſolution, that
their name and kingdom appeared for a while
extirpated by the victory of the Goths. Braga,
their metropolis, was compelled to open her gates
to the victor; and though the lives of her citizens, and the chaſtity of her virgins were reſpected, the moderation which fettered his cruelty and luſt was incapable of reſtraining avarice.
The greateſt part of the clergy and people were
ſold into ſervitude; and the churches and the altars were confounded in the general pillage.
From the former renown, and the ſubſequent
conduct of Rechiarius, it is not to be ſuppoſed
that he quitted ingloriouſly the diſaſtrous field;
and his flight to one of the ports of the ocean,
might be ſtimulated by the hopes of returning
from the ſtore-houſe of the north with new ſwarms
of martial adventurers to avenge the fate of his
ſlaughtered ſubjects; but the obſtinacy of the
winds oppoſed his eſcape; he was delivered to
his implacable rival. In the moment of triumph
Theodoric either forgot, or was indifferent to the
domeſtic peace of his ſiſter, in the execution of
Rechiarius; and the latter, without murmuring,

ſub-

submitted to the mortal stroke with a firmness worthy of the nation he had ruled over.

The Suevi had been vanquished in battle, and confined again in obscurity to the mountains of Gallicia; and the natives of Spain neither hoped, nor endeavoured to stop the progress of the conqueror. Without meeting with any resistance, he penetrated as far as Lerida, the principal town of Lusitania; but he was diverted from the entire conquest of Spain, by the intelligence of a new revolution in Italy; Avitus was no longer emperor; and the interest and honour of Theodoric were deeply wounded by the deposition of his friend and ally. He pointed his march again towards the Pyrenees; and in his retreat were displayed the marks of his disappointment. The city of Astorga was doomed again to feel his presence; the Goths gleaned with industry what had escaped them in their former pillage; and they reaped a new and plentiful harvest in the spoil of the wealthy city of Palentia.

A. D. 462, 482. The conquest that had eluded the grasp of Theodoric was seized by the hand of his brother Euric. He was stained with fratricide; but in an age of violence, his martial spirit atoned for his want of moral virtues. He wielded the Gothic sceptre with vigour and success; and Spain was first doomed to feel the weight of his arm. He passed the Pyrenees, at the head of of a numerous hoft; and occupied by force or fraud the powerful cities of Pampeluna and Saragoſſa. But the warlike nobles of the province of Tarraconenſis refuſed tamely to yield to the invader; and in a field of battle they preſumed to maintain with bloody obſtinacy their independence. They were vanquiſhed, rather by the ſuperior numbers, than the valour of their adverſaries; and Euric, animated by victory, penetrated into the heart of Luſitania; but he ſtill reſpected in the mountains of Gallicia the hardy warriors of Saxony; Roſimund, who reigned over the Suevi, had married the daughter of Theodoric; the ties of blood might prompt him to avenge the murder of his father-in-law; but the more powerful dictates of policy and intereſt warned him to decline the conteſt with the Gothic king. A mutual league of amity was projected and ſubſcribed; and the Suevi were ſuffered to remain in the poſſeſſion of Gallicia, whilſt the reſt of the extenſive peninſula of Spain acknowledged the independent authority of Euric.

A country which forms one of the moſt conſiderable ſtates of modern Europe, was incapable of ſatisfying the ambition of Euric; he diſdained to fix the ſeat of his ſovereignty in Spain; he repaſſed the Pyrenees; and the ſouthern provinces of Gaul were the reward of his addreſs and valour. When Odoacer, ſurnamed the

A. D. 472, 475.

the Mercenary, ufurped the kingdom of Italy, he refigned to Euric all the Roman conquefts beyond the Alps as far as the Rhine and the ocean. The prodigal donation was confirmed without any lofs of power or revenue by the fenate; and under their new fovereign, the Gothic king might afpire to the dominion of Spain and Gaul. His court was eftablifhed in the modern city of Bourdeaux; and the crowd of ambaffadors and fuppliants who waited before the gates of his palace, attefted his influence and renown. The Heruli of the diftant ocean, who painted their naked bodies with its cœrulean colour, implored his protection; and the Saxons refpected the maritime provinces of a prince who was deftitute of any naval force; the Burgundians fubmitted to his authority; and the Franks, who had provoked his enmity, received from him the conditions of peace; the Vandals of Africa fought his friendfhip; and it fupported the Oftrogoths of Pannonia againft the oppreffion of the neighbouring Huns. His nod excited or appeafed the favage tribes of the north; the great king of Perfia had recourfe to the wifdom of his counfels, or the weight of his mediation; Rome, fo late the miftrefs of the world, was anxious to conciliate his favour; and the effeminate Italians who dwelt on the fhores of the Tyber, were defended by the

king

king of the Goths who reigned on the banks of the Garonne.

In the full poffeffion of power and profperity, Euric expired; and the throne of the Vifigoths was inadequately filled by the feeble youth of his fon Alaric. The Franks, beneath their monarch Clovis, from the neighbourhood of the Meufe and the Scheld, the Mofelle and the Rhine, had extended their conquefts to the fouthern banks of the Seine. Syagrius, a noble Roman, who ruled with the authority at leaft, if not with the title of king, over the city and diocefe of Soiffons, with Rheims and Troyes, Beauvais and Amiens, had been vanquifhed by them in battle, his dominions feized, and himfelf compelled to feek refuge in the court of Alaric. The timid counfellors of that prince yielded to the menaces of Clovis, and their own fears; and Syagrius was bafely delivered up to the implacable victor.

The unworthy conceffion, inftead of conciliating the friendfhip, ferved only to inflame the ambition of the king of the Franks. The Vifigoths had embraced the doctrines of Arius, who, in the myfterious and abftrufe queftion of the Trinity, reverenced the Son, but denied him to be equal to the Father. The Franks had been influenced by the example of their fovereign, had been purified in the baptifmal font from the errors of paganism, and endeavoured to atone for their tardy conversion by their zeal for orthodoxy. The guilt of Arianism in Alaric was heightened by his possession of the most fertile provinces of Gaul; no ties nor treaties, however sacred, could bind a prince whose ambition was sanctioned by the name of religion; and in the moment of peace and alliance, Clovis rushed forwards to surprise and oppress the king of the Visigoths.

A. D. 507. Though Alaric was destitute of military experience, in personal courage he was not inferior to his aspiring rival. The Visigoths, long disused to war, resumed their arms, and ranged themselves round the standard of their youthful king; but their valour was in vain opposed to the discipline and veteran intrepidity of the Franks. The decisive battle was fought on the banks of the Clain, about ten miles to the south of Portiers; the Goths were totally routed, and pursued with cruel slaughter. Alaric, disdaining to fly, rushed against his royal antagonist, and obtained an honourable death from the hand of Clovis. Aquitain submitted to the victor; his winter quarters were established at Bourdeaux; in the ensuing spring Thoulouse surrendered; and the siege of Arles was formed and closely pressed by the Franks. The kingdom of the Visigoths in Gaul was shaken to its founda-

foundations; and its total overthrow was folely averted by the policy or generous pity of Theodoric, the Oftrogoth; who, with the concurrence of the Roman emperor of the eaft, had delivered Italy from the ufurpation of Odoacer the Mercenary, and erected in it the feat of his own independent fovereignty. The Oftrogoths marched with alacrity to refcue from deftruction the kindred warriors encompaffed in Arles; with the lofs of thirty thoufand men, Clovis was compelled to retire from the walls of that city. Theodoric declared himfelf the protector and guardian of the infant fon of Alaric; the weighty mediation was refpected by Clovis; yet he ftill retained the greateft part of his late acquifitions; and from the Garonne to the Loire, the ample province of Aquitain was indiffolubly united to the French monarchy.

Amidft the tempeft which had agitated Gaul, Spain had enjoyed a tranfient fufpenfion from hoftility; but her peace was wounded by the unhappy fate of Alaric; and after the fiege of Arles, the chiefs of the Vifigoths conveyed with faithful care their infant monarch Amalaric acrofs the Pyrenees, and eftablifhed his court in Spain. But the authority of Amalaric was difputed by the ambition and mature years of his baftard brother Gefalaic. It was in Gaul that Gefalaic firft erected the ftandard of oppofition;

A. D. 509, 512.

opposition; defeated and expelled by the Burgundians, with a martial band of barbarians, whom his personal qualities, or splendid promises, had attached to his cause, he explored the passes of the Pyrenees, and occupied the city of Barcelona. He was driven thence by the general of Theodoric, who had followed on his steps to defend the throne of Amalaric. Vanquished in battle, he escaped with difficulty to Carthagena; and with a few adherents passed over into Africa. He was enabled, by the liberality of the Vandals, again to penetrate into Spain; and within four miles of Barcelona, a battle was fought which finally extinguished his hopes and life. His death on the field, or in the pursuit, left Amalaric without a rival; but his feeble years were incapable of sustaining the weight of government; and the virtues of Theudes, a noble Ostrogoth, were confessed by the Visigoths themselves, who committed to him the protection of their youthful king, and the administration of Spain.

A. D. 513, 530. During the time that the reins of government were held by the hand of Theudes, the prosperity of Spain attested his justice and ability; but no sooner had Amalaric attained to manhood, than Theudes retired from the high station he had occupied, probably not without a sigh, but certainly without a struggle.
The

The marriage of Amalaric with Clotilda, the daughter of Clovis, seemed to secure the amity, and soon provoked the hostilities of the Franks and Visigoths. The orthodox Clotilda despised her Arian consort; and her intemperate piety summoned her brother to the invasion of her husband's dominions in Gaul. The Visigoths who had attempted to stem the torrent of the Franks, were overwhelmed by its fury; and de-. feated in battle, Amalaric himself escaped with difficulty to the city of Narbonne. It is doubtful whether he perished by the cruelty of the victors, or, on his return to Barcelona, the contempt of his subjects prompted his assassination; but his death finally closed the line of the first and great Alaric. The throne of the Visigoths in Spain, which hitherto had been considered as hereditary, must hereafter be regarded as elective; and a people who had already experienced the illustrious qualities of Theudes, were impatient to avail themselves again of his justice and moderation; and, by their unanimous suffrages, proclaimed him their sovereign.

Even the wisdom and firmness of Theudes were unequal to the difficulties and dangers that arose on every side. The sons of Clovis had pursued their victorious career from the banks of the Garonne to the foot of the Pyrenees; those mountains which separate Spain from

A. D. 530, 548.

from Gaul, were incapable of protecting the former; the passes were either forced or betrayed; and the Franks penetrated to the walls of Saragossa. The inhabitants of that city ransomed their lives with their wealth; and the invaders, encumbered with spoil, slowly pointed their march back towards the Pyrenees. The prudence of Theudes had resisted the ardour of his subjects; and he had refused to commit to the chance of battle the independence of Spain; but he watched and improved the moment of retreat: his squadrons hung upon, and repeatedly assailed the rear of the Franks; and it was only by the sacrifice of the greatest part of their plunder, that the sons of Clovis were permitted to repass in safety the Pyrenean mountains.

While Theudes was occupied in repelling the invasion of the Franks, a revolution, as sudden as extraordinary, had overthrown the kingdom of the Vandals in Africa, and restored that opulent province to the obedience of the Roman emperor. The king of the Vandals had in vain solicited the assistance of Spain, against an enemy whose pretensions might extend to all that once was comprised under the name of the Roman world; and the refusal of Theudes, which has been ascribed to supineness, may be accounted for by the hostile enterprise of the Franks. But no sooner was Spain delivered

from

from the Gallic inundation, than the eyes of Theudes were turned on Africa. On the opposite point to Gibraltar, the fortress of Ceuta, in the kingdom of Fez, is still maintained by modern Spain. In the time of Justinian, it had either been acquired by treaty or by force by the Visigoths; but when the Roman genius prevailed over that of the Vandals, it had been reduced by Belisarius, the renowned general of Justinian, and whose victories have entitled him to the appellation of the *third* Africanus. The recovery of Ceuta was the object of the preparations of Theudes; a narrow strait of about twelve miles, through which the Atlantic flows into the Mediterranean Sea, divides alone the continent of Africa from the peninsula of Spain; the expedition was conducted by the king in person; and Ceuta was invested by the joint forces of the Spaniards and Visigoths. But though an Arian, the piety of Theudes was displayed in the strict observance of the sabbath as a day of rest and devotion; the besieged, less scrupulous, availed themselves of the holy forbearance of their adversaries; they sallied from their walls, and spread terror and slaughter through the camp, which was engaged in fervent prayer. The loss of the Goths must have been considerable, since it induced Theudes to raise the siege and return into Spain; he did not long survive his

his disgrace; he was stabbed in his own palace by an assassin, whose motives have eluded the diligence of history; he languished a few days after he received the wound; and maintained in his last moments, the character of Christian resignation and forgiveness, by freely subscribing the pardon of the guilty author of his death.

A. D. 548, 549. The Visigoths, on his decease, again asserted their right of free election; and their suffrages filled the vacant throne with Theodigild, who had distinguished his valour in the invasion of the Franks; but the renown of the soldier was stained by the lust of the tyrant; and the wives and daughters of his most illustrious subjects were violated by his brutal passion. He fell a victim to a conspiracy of jealous husbands, after having exercised or abused the regal authority about a year and five months.

A. D. 550, 567. The conspirators, in a tumultuous assembly, raised to the throne Agila, who was probably associated in their injuries and resentment; but great part of Spain refused to ratify their choice. The city of Cordova was the first to arm against the partial election; and her inhabitants sallying from their gates, attacked and defeated Agila, who, at the head of a numerous army, had advanced to besiege them. The flame of discontent was fanned by the breath of Athanagilde, a noble Goth, who improved to his own

own advantage the rising disaffection. But his haste to wrest the sceptre from the hand of his rival, betrayed him into a measure unworthy of his own fame, and injurious to the interest of his country; he solicited the assistance of Justinian; and engaged, in return for his support, to cede to him several cities on the shores of the ocean and the Mediterranean; the Roman troops that were dispatched to his aid, enabled him to triumph in battle over Agila; the latter had sought refuge after his defeat, within the fortifications of Merida; but he soon experienced the fate of unfortunate princes; and the citizens of Merida secured the pardon and favour of Athanagilde, by presenting to him the head of Agila.

In the city of Toledo, Athanagilde fixed the seat of the royal residence; and, by a just and lenient administration, reigned in the hearts of his subjects. The tranquillity of his government was interrupted by the rapacity of those he had invited to his protection. The Romans, from their fortresses, oppressed the country round; and the cries of his people summoned Athanagilde to arms. It is probable that he prepared with reluctance to march against an enemy to whose valour he was indebted for his crown; yet no sooner was the war commenced, than he acted in it with vigour and ability; he wrested several of their fastnesses from the Romans; but the latter

ter were fortified, in many of their impregnable stations, by perpetual supplies from Africa. Opposite to that continent they still maintained their ground, and waited an opportunity to inflame the civil and religious factions of the barbarians. Seventy years elapsed before this painful thorn could be extirpated from the bosom of the monarchy; and as long as the emperors retained any share of these remote possessions, their vanity might number Spain in the list of their provinces.

Two daughters, Brunchant and Goisvintha, who were married to the princes of Austrasia and Soissons, and became famous for their vices or misfortunes, were the only issue of the nuptial bed of Athanagilde; his reign had continued eighteen years, when in his palace of Toledo he breathed his last; and the zealous wishes of the orthodox writers of that age have asserted, that before his death he abjured the errors of Arianism, and embraced the pure doctrines of the catholic church.

A. D. 567, 585. Five months of anarchy served to endear to the natives of Spain the advantages of a temperate monarchy; the eyes of the nobility, in the choice of a successor to Athanagilde, were directed across the Pyrenees. Some remains of the Gothic kingdom in Gaul had yet eluded or withstood the ambitious enterprises

prises of the Franks; and Luiva, to whose government they were entrusted, must, in the arduous station, have discovered no common abilities, since at a distance, and without intrigue, they recommended him to the throne of Spain. The moderation with which he received the intelligence of his election, was the best proof that he deserved it; he still remained to watch over the safety of the provinces of Gaul; and he proposed, and obtained the consent of his subjects, to associate in the royal dignity his brother Leovigild. Fraternal affection might first have prompted his choice; but Spain confessed that the virtues of Leovigild deserved a crown; and after Luiva was no more, the whole dominions of the Visigoths were united under the sway of a prince who in peace merited the love of his people, and in war extorted the admiration of his enemies.

The moment of enterprise had been seized and improved by the Romans; and during the suspense and confusion of an interregnum, their arms had advanced from the shores of the sea into the inland country. Their banners were displayed on the walls of Medina Sidonia, in the province of Andalusia, and from the towers of Cordova which overshadow the stream of the Bœtis. But their pride was soon broken by the vigour of Leovigild. After an obstinate resistance,

ance, he entered Medina Sidonia as a conqueror; and the flaughter of the rebellious inhabitants ftruck terror throughout the principal cities of Spain. Yet Cordova, confident in the ftrength of her walls, and the valour of her citizens, ventured to brave the refentment of her fovereign. It was not until after a long fiege, and that the dexterous introduction of gold had cooled the ardour, and diftracted the inclinations of her inhabitants, that the gates were opened to Leovigild. But the furrender of Cordova determined the fubmiffion of the other cities; the imperial garrifons were expelled; and the Romans were again confined to their fortreffes on the coafts of the fea.

It was the natural defire of Leovigild to perpetuate the crown in his own family. To fortify his title, he had efpoufed Goifvintha, the widow of Athanagilde; but his hopes were repofed on Hermenigild and Recared, his two fons by a former marriage. He intimated the neceffity of providing againft the fame anarchy as Spain had experienced after the death of Athanagilde; his wifhes were underftood and gratified; and Hermenigild and Recared were called to the certain fucceffion by the title of princes of the Goths.

In the hilly country of Bifcay, and in the mountains of Orofpeda, which, with the modern
name

name of Sierra Morena, envelope the sources of the Bœtis, an hardy race of freebooters, the descendants of the Cantabrians, still preserved the manners and tone of independence. They were reclaimed to civil life and obedience by the persevering courage of Leovigild; and the Suevi, who had presumed to pass their limits in their support, were compelled to appease the resentment of the victor by their immediate submission.

But the satisfaction which Leovigild derived from the success of his military labours was imbittered by female passion and religious rancour. His eldest son, Hermenigild, who, with the royal diadem, had been invested by his father with the principality of Bœtica, had contracted an honourable and orthodox alliance with a Merovingian princess, the daughter of Sigebert, king of Austrasia, and of the famous Brunchaut. The beauteous Ingundis, who was no more than sixteen years of age, was received with respect, but was soon exposed to the persecution of the Arian court of Toledo. Her grandmother, Goisvintha, who, by her second marriage with Leovigild, was doubly bound to her protection, became her most implacable enemy. The Gothic queen is represented as deformed in her person, blind of one eye, fierce, vindictive, and inexorable; and to her aversion to the religious

principles

principles of Ingundis, might be added her envy of a young and charming princess, whose features and person were the objects of universal admiration. Ingundis refused to sacrifice the faith she had been educated in to the menaces of Goisvintha; who, incensed by her resistance, seized her by the hair, inhumanly dashed her against the ground, kicked her till she was covered with blood, and at last gave orders that she should be stripped and thrown into a bason, or fish-pond. Love and honour might excite Hermenigild to resent this injurious treatment of his bride; and he was gradually persuaded that Ingundis suffered for the cause of divine truth. Her tender complaints, and the weighty arguments of Leander, arch-bishop of Seville, accomplished his conversion; and the heir of the Gothic monarchy was initiated in the Nicene faith by the solemn rites of confirmation.

The bigoted spirit of Goisvintha allowed not Hermenigild to hope that he might cultivate the new doctrines he had espoused in humble security; and it is probable that the zeal of the Catholics of Spain urged him to violate the duties of a son and a subject. He drew the sword against his sovereign and his father; and his rebellion was supported by the powerful and orthodox nation of the Vascones, who inhabited the modern kingdom of Navarre. Yet Hermenigild

menigild was perfuaded foon after to fubmit, by the remonftrances of his brother Recared; he was fent a prifoner to Toledo; and Leovigild entered in arms the country of the Vafcones. His fuccefs is attefted by the city of Victoria, which he founded; and his feverity may be conjectured from the numbers of the inhabitants who quitted their native feats; the country was indeed recovered by Leovigild; but the people ftill refufed to fubmit to his government; they paffed the Pyrenees; poffeffed themfelves of, and multiplied in, part of Aquitain; and, with fome little corruption, ftill preferve their origin in the appellation of Gafcons.

While the martial Vafcones occupied the attention of Leovigild, his fon Hermenigild had eluded the vigilance of his guards, and efcaped from Toledo. He had perhaps flattered himfelf, when he furrendered to his father, that he fhould have been foon reftored to his confidence and affection; but he found himfelf a prifoner in the midft of a city which he might regard as his future capital; and expofed to the infults, and deadly machinations of his mother-in-law, Goifvintha. He had no fooner regained his freedom, than he prepared to defend it by the fword. Notwithftanding the emigration of the Vafcones, the Catholics of Spain were yet numerous; the cities of Merida, Cordova, and Seville, ftrenu-
ouſly

ously espoused the party of Hermenigild; and he invited to his assistance the orthodox barbarians, the Suevi, and the Franks; but the formidable confederacy was broken by the active vigour of Leovigild; the passes of the Pyrenees were strictly guarded against the Franks; the march of the Suevi was intercepted by the Gothic king in person; and they were constrained to retire within their own limits. The sieges of Merida, Seville, and Cordova, were successively formed, and pressed with ardour. Their obstinacy long protracted the civil war; and it was not until they had experienced the extreme misery of famine, that they consented to open their gates. The walls of Cordova had been the last resource of Hermenigild; and when that city surrendered, he became the captive of an exasperated father. Leovigild was still mindful of that sacred character; the life of his son was spared; and he was conveyed in chains to Tarragona. From the place of his imprisonment he contrived to keep up a dangerous correspondence with the court of Constantinople; his ambassador was the arch-bishop Leander, who had been the instrument of his conversion; he solicited the Romans, who possessed Africa, and a part of the Spanish coast, to the conquest of his native land; his negociation reached the ears of Leovigild; and the restless prince was removed from Tarragona,

to

to a strong tower in the city of Seville; an Arian bishop was sent to him, to persuade him to embrace once more his former faith; but the constancy of Hermenigild was inflexible; and he refused to accept the Arian communion as the price of safety and freedom. In his declining years, Leovigild might be jealous of the future spiritual welfare of his people; his holy fears might be improved by the address of Goisvintha; he commanded the execution of his Catholic son; if his rigour was fatal to the life, it was favourable to the fame of Hermenigild; and the stubborn rebel, and undutiful son, was, by the admiration of the orthodox clergy of his age, translated into a martyr and a saint.

The tardy repentance of the parent was drowned by the sound of the trumpet. The Suevi had often provoked and appeased his resentment; but the hour of clemency was passed; and the monarch who had sternly resisted the emotions of nature, was not likely to yield to the suggestions of pity. Policy and ambition fortified Leovigild against the submissive professions of the Suevi; and the latter, distracted by domestic faction, were incapable of withstanding the torrent of the Goths. Their hereditary prince, Eboric, had been deposed by the enterprising genius of Andaca; and the usurper Andaca was in his turn overthrown by the stronger

arm

arm of Leovigild. His head was shaved; and that restless spirit which could not be satisfied in the condition of a subject, was for ever confined within the walls of a monastery. But the power of the Suevi in Spain was finally broken and extinguished; Braga, their capital, averted the horrors of an assault by a timely capitulution; and, with the exception of a few fortresses on the coast, which were held by the Romans, the whole Spanish peninsula was united under the dominion of Leovigild.

The conquest of the Suevi of Spain, was the last of the military labours of Leovigild. But it was not only in war, that his administration was entitled to praise; and in the hour of peace, his subjects confessed and dreaded his severe and equal justice. He revised the laws that had been neglected from the death of Alaric; repealed such as had become useless; and promulgated new ones, adapted to the temper and genius of his people. He introduced discipline into his armies, and regularity into his finances; and watched with jealous care over the regal dignity. He endeavoured to subdue the bold and free imagination of his subjects by a studied ostentation; and Leovigild was the first of the Visigoth kings who was distinguished by the splendour and magnificence of his robes; but whatever state he might assume in public, in private

vate he maintained his wonted fimplicity; and his frugality and temperance were the fources of his wealth, and his vigour in old age. A fhort time before his death he is reported to have reconciled himfelf to the catholic church; and Leander, arch-bifhop of Seville, who had been fo inftrumental in the converfion of the fon, is faid to have influenced that of the father. The rumour was readily embraced by the policy of Recared; but the improbable tale has been rejected by the moft judicious hiftorians; the rebel ambaffador to the court of Conftantinople would fcarcely have been chofen by the fovereign of the Goths as his fpiritual director; nor is there fufficient reafon to doubt but that Leovigild, in the eighteenth year of a profperous reign, expired of difeafe, in his capital of Toledo, in the firm and fteady perfuafion of the truth of Arianifm.

Chapter the Third.

Reign of Recared.—The Catholic church is established.—His victory over the Franks.—Councils of Toledo. His death.—Reigns of Liuva, Witeric, and Gondemar.—Accession of Sisebut.—He persecutes the Jews.—He is succeeded by his son Recared the second.—Death of Recared, and succession of his brother Suintilla.—He expels the Imperialists.—He is dethroned by Sisenand.—Election of Chintila to the throne.—Persecution against the Jews renewed.—Reigns of Tulga, Chindesuintho, and Recesuintho.—Wamba is chosen king.—His exploits.—He regulates the national councils.—Triumph over the Saracens by sea.—Singular manner of his deposition.—Usurpation of Erviga.—He resigns the sceptre to his son-in-law Egiza.—New code of laws promulgated by the Visigoths.

A. D. 585. 610.

THE prudence of Leovigild had smoothed the ascent to greatness for Recared; the Gothic nation respected their former obligation, and ratified it by acknowledging their

their new monarch; but the edifice of Arianism which the deceased king had cemented by the blood of Hermenigild, was overthrown by his favourite son and successor, and on its ruins the Catholic church was firmly established throughout Spain.

More cautious or more scrupulous than his brother, Recared had in silence concealed the orthodox faith he had imbibed; and instead of revolting against his father, he patiently expected the hour of his death; instead of condemning his memory, he piously supposed that the dying monarch had abjured the errors of Arianism, and recommended to his son the conversion of the Gothic nation. An invasion of the Franks delayed the execution of the design; but no sooner had he repelled the foreign enemies of the state, than he turned his thoughts to the care and regulation of its religion. To accomplish that salutary end, Recared convened an assembly of the Arian clergy and nobles, declared himself a Catholic, and exhorted them to imitate the example of their prince. The laborious interpretations of doubtful texts, or the curious pursuit of metaphysical arguments, would have excited an endless controversy; and the monarch discreetly proposed to his illiterate audience two substantial and visible proofs, the testimony of earth, and of heaven. The earth had submitted to the Nicene synod; the Romans,

the

the Barbarians, and the inhabitants of Spain, unanimoufly profeffed the fame orthodox creed; and the Vifigoths refifted, almoft alone, the confent of the Chriftian world. A fuperftitious age was prepared to reverence, as the teftimony of **Heaven**, the preternatural cures, which were performed by the fkill or virtue of the Catholic clergy; the baptifmal fonts of Offat, fituated on the northern banks of the Bœtis, oppofite to Seville, which were fpontaneoufly replenifhed each year on the vigil of Chrift; and the miraculous fhrine of St. Martin of Tours, which had already converted the Suevic prince, and the people of Gallacia. Thefe proofs of Recared were probably fupported by an obedient and Catholic army; the Arian clergy appeared convinced; and the general eftablifhment of the Catholic religion in Spain was applauded and decreed.

Yet the prejudices of mankind are not eafily eradicated; and thofe of religion have been found by experience more deeply rooted than any other. The Arians in fecret lamented the fall of their faith; their indignation was probably increafed by the infulting triumph of the victorious Catholics; and an open infurrection, and fecret confpiracy were the immediate confequences of their difcontent; the firft was broken by the vigour of Recared and his generals; the laft was difconcerted by the timidity or treachery of the confpirators.

tors. Yet the Arians foon after refumed their projects of revenge and dominion; and they were fupported by the riches, and animated by the exhortations of Goifvintha, the widow of Athanagilde, and Leovigild.

The perfecution of Hermenigild might have recoiled on the head of Goifvintha, had not Recared been influenced more by generofity than refentment; but the Gothic king refpected the widow of his two immediate predeceffors; he buried every hoftile or jealous emotion in the affiduous duty of a fon-in-law; and his behaviour towards Goifvintha was not only the admiration of his own fubjects, but was the theme of praife among the neighbouring nations. Could the heart of the Arian princefs have been fufceptible of gratitude, it muft have been penetrated by the kindnefs of Recared; but fhe had been accuftomed only to indulge the fterner paffions of hatred and revenge; and every gift feemed polluted by the hand of the Catholic donor. She had confented to embrace in appearance the orthodox faith; and fhe was readily perfuaded by Ubila, an Arian bifhop, and the affociate of her treafonable defigns, that her guilty compliance could only be effaced by the deftruction of him who had extorted it. The confederates feized the moment when the irruption of the Franks into the provinces of the Vifigoths on the other fide the Pyrenees, embar-

raffed

raffed the counfels of the court of Toledo. But the intention of Goifvintha and Ubila were revealed by the remorfe or perfidy of one of her affociates; rage or defpair at the detection of her crime, extinguifhed the feeble remains of the life of the Gothic queen; yet the fubfequent conduct of Recared proves that fhe ftill might have hoped for pardon. He remembered with refpect the holy character of Ubila; and the Arian bifhop in the mild fentence of exile, muft have lamented his own guilt, and applauded the clemency of his fovereign.

From the detection of domeftic treafon, the attention of the Gothic king was recalled to check the progrefs of foreign invafion. Sixty thoufand Franks deluged the dominions of the Vifigoths in Gaul, and had difplayed their hoftile ftandards in the neighbourhood of Carcaffone, at a fmall diftance from Narbonne. As they indulged in fecurity and intemperance, they were fuddenly attacked and routed by a martial band of Vifigoths; and fix thoufand Franks were flaughtered by three hundred Vifigoths. Such indeed are the partial and exaggerated accounts of feveral of the Spanifh hiftorians; it is poffible the vanguard of the army of Recared might amount to no more, and the honour of the victory might be afcribed to thofe who led the attack; but we learn from the teftimony of a more accurate writer,

ter, that the Franks were deluded by a feigned
flight to purfue with inconfiderate ardour; and
that in the moment of tumultuous triumph they
were fuddenly affailed by the trefh troops of their
adverfaries, and were incapable of rallying, or
retrieving the effects of their imprudence.

Inftead of being elated with his victory and
afpiring to new conquefts in Gaul, the king of the
Vifigoths, in the hour of his fuccefs confented to
negociate an honourable and equal treaty with the
Franks. The internal regulation of his kingdom
ftill claimed his unremitting attention; and the
firm eftablifhment of the Catholic church was the
conftant object of his peaceful labous. While
the laurels of Carcaffone were ftill frefh in the eyes
of his fubjects, he fummoned a general council at
Toledo; the five metropolitans of Toledo, Seville,
Merida, Braga, and Tarragona, prefided in it according to their refpective feniority. The affembly was compofed of their fuffragan bifhops, who
appeared in perfon, or by their proxies, and a place
was affigned to the moft holy, or moft opulent of
the Spanifh abbots. The ftability of the Catholic
church was fecured by new canons or decrees,
and the moderation and wifdom of the affembly
gradually recommended it to the fupreme influence
in the adminiftration of Spain. From the reign
of Recared to the irruption of the Moors, fixteen
national councils were fucceffively convened; and

the

the regular discipline of the church introduced peace and order into the government of the state. During the three first days of the convocation, as long as they agitated the ecclesiastical questions of doctrine and subjection, the profane laity were excluded from their debates, which were conducted however with decent solemnity. But on the morning of the fourth day, the doors were thrown open for the entrance of the great officers of the palace, the dukes and counts of the provinces, the judges of the cities, and the gothic nobles; and the decrees of heaven were ratified by the consent of the people. The same rules were observed in the provincial assemblies, the annual synods which were empowered to hear complaints, and to redress grievances; and a legal government was supported by the prevailing influence of the Spanish clergy. The bishops might labour to exalt the mitre above the crown; yet the national councils of Toledo, in which the free spirit of the Barbarians was tempered and guided by episcopal policy, established some prudent laws for the common benefit of the king and the people.

The vacancy of the throne was supplied by the choice of the bishop and the palatines; and, after the failure of the line of Alaric, the regal dignity was still limited to the pure and noble blood of the Goths. The clergy, who anointed their lawful

ful prince, always recommended, and sometimes practised, the duty of allegiance; and the spiritual censures were denounced on the heads of the impious subjects who should presume to resist his authority, conspire against his life, or violate, by an indecent union, the chastity of his widow. But the monarch himself, when he ascended the throne, was bound by a reciprocal oath to God and his people, that he would faithfully execute his important trust. The real or imaginary faults of his administration were subject to the controul of a powerful aristocracy; and the bishops and palatines were guarded by a fundamental privilege that they should not be degraded, imprisoned, tortured, nor punished with death, exile, or confiscation, unless by the free and public judgment of their peers.

After the conversion of Recared had removed the prejudices of the Catholics, the coasts, both of the ocean and Mediterranean, were still possessed by the eastern emperor, who secretly excited the people to reject the yoke of the Barbarians, and to assert the name and dignity of Roman citizens. Their intrigues provoked the resentment of Recared; and they were taught by the arm of a warrior to respect in future the sanctity of their treaties. But the moderation of the Gothic king was satisfied with protecting his dominions from insult, without aspiring to extend them by conquest.

quest. He stopped in the middle of his career of victory; he solicited Gregory the Great, who had been raised, both by his liberality, and his rude but pathetic eloquence, with the holy title of pope, to the independent administration of the desolated city of Rome, to negociate a new treaty between the Greeks of Constantinople and the Goths of Spain. The same conditions which had existed between Justinian and Athanagilde were the basis of the alliance between Maurice and Recared; and if the cautious Spaniards might applaud the prudence of their sovereign who delivered his country from the calamities of war, the more daring spirit of the Visigoths accused the patience of their prince whose forbearance suffered them still to be insulted by the sight of the rival banners of imperial power.

Yet however Recared might be desirous of peace, when it was no longer to be maintained on just and honourable terms, he invariably asserted the qualities of fortitude and vigour in war. The Gascons might remember with secret indignation the persecution they had sustained under the administration of Leovigild. But the accession of a Catholic king must have extinguished their religious enmity; and it was the desire of reclaiming their fertile fields on the southern banks of the Ebro, which impelled them across the Pyrenees to the invasion of Spain. They were encountered

countered and defeated by Recared; but the mercy of the victor was again difplayed; and the Gafcons who had efcaped the fword on the field of battle, were permitted to repafs in fafety the Pyrenean mountains.

The reign of Recared, though characterized by juftice, by wifdom, and firmnefs, was gloomy and tempeftuous. The Arian clergy neither defired to forget nor to forgive the humiliation of their fect; and the name of Argimond, who was chamberlain to the king, ftamps the third confpiracy againft Recared. The clemency of the monarch was unequal to thefe repeated inftances of revolt and ingratitude; he might feel as a man, but he punifhed as a fovereign; the head of the traitor Argimond was fhaved, a mark of the deepeft infamy among the Vifigoths and Barbarians; he was publicly whipped, his right hand cut off, and on a mule he was expofed to the derifion of the city of Toledo; his fufferings were terminated by his execution; and the affociates of his defigns were condemned to expiate their guilt by death.

This laft act of neceffary feverity clofed the adminiftration and life of Recared; A. D. 610, 612. three fons by different and doubtful mothers were the iffue of his marriage or his amours. The pretenfions of primogeniture were acknowledged by the reft in the election of Luiva; but his fubjects had fcarce time to contemplate with pleafure sure the opening virtues of their new monarch, before he was defpoiled of his crown, his liberty, and his life. The particulars of the confpiracy are involved in obfcurity; but the author of it was Witeric, a Gothic nobleman, whofe treafonable ambition had been pardoned by the father, and was now fatal to the fon. The murderer ufurped the throne; but he was permitted only to enjoy a fhort time the harveft of his guilt. The indignation of his Catholic fubjects was inflamed by the fufpicion that he had privately embraced, and intended to reftore the herefy of Arianifm; he was fuddenly attacked and affaffinated in his palace; and his mangled body, after having been expofed to the infults of the populace, was thrown amongft thofe of the common malefactors.

Of the Gothic chiefs whom refentment for the fate of Luiva, or concern for the Catholic church had excited to the punifhment of Witeric, the name of Gondemar was moft diftinguifhed. His pious zeal was confeffed in a national affembly by the orthodox clergy; and the crown was the tribute of their gratitude. His virtues fanctioned their choice. The imperialifts who had attempted to avail themfelves of the late revolution, and to extend their narrow territories, were broken by his valour, and driven within their former boundaries; but whilft his age and abilities promifed a long and profperous reign to his people, he was
feized

seized and carried of by an epidemic diftemper, the fecond year after his elevation to royalty.

The fuffrages of the Goths were united by the merits of Sifebut, and the fceptre was again placed in the hand of an hero. He refumed or furpaffed the defigns of his predeceffor; and afpired to the glory of expelling the Greeks of Conftantinople from Spain. After quelling fome domeftic commotions in Afturia, he marched in perfon to the conteft; in two decifive engagements the forces of the imperialifts were routed and almoft deftroyed; amidft the carnage of the field the generous and compaffionate mind of Sifebut lamented the confequences of his own victory. The impaffioned exclamation, "Unhappy man that I am " to fee fo much blood fpilt through my means!" will be the fubject of more juft admiration than his martial atchievements, however fplendid; even thefe may be confidered as reftoring the independence of his country. The throne of Conftantinople was fhaken by the formidable hofts of the Perfians and the Avars; and Heraclius, oppreffed by the great king and the chagan, was incapable of affording any fuccour to his fubjects in Spain. He readily fubfcribed a peace that was dictated by Sifebut; the imperial forts and territories on the coafts of the Mediterranean were re-united under the authority of the Vifigoths; and

A. D. 612, 621.

and on the fide of the Atlantic ocean the pretenſions of the eaſtern empire were compreſſed within the modern province of Algarvè.

The triumph of Siſebut over the enemies of his country had been chaſtened by pity, but his heart was fortified againſt the cries and lamentations of the Jews, by ſuperſtition. If we may credit the aſſertions of that miſerable people, they had been firſt introduced into Spain by the fleets of Solomon, and the arms of Nebuchadnezzar. They had been multiplied in that country by the policy of Hadrian, who is reported to have tranſported thither forty thouſand families of the tribe of Judah, and ten thouſand of the tribe of Benjamin. The wealth which they accumulated by trade, and the management of the finances, invited the avarice of their maſters; and they might be oppreſſed without danger, as they had loſt the uſe and even the remembrance of arms; yet the general character of Siſebut allows us to ſuppoſe that he was rather influenced in his perſecution by religious, than avaricious motives. Ninety thouſand Jews to preſerve their wealth or lives, conſented to receive the ſacrament of baptiſm; the fortunes of the moſt obdurate infidels were confiſcated, their bodies tortured; and it ſeems doubtful whether they were permitted to abandon their native country. The exceſſive zeal of the Catholic king was moderated, even by the clergy

of

of Spain, who solemnly pronounced an inconsistent sentence; *that* the sacraments should not be forcibly imposed; but that the Jews who had been baptized, should be constrained for the honour of the church to persevere in the external practice of a religion which they disbelieved and detested.

The persecution of the Jews is the only error which tarnishes the glory of the reign of Sisebut. Though he might detest the calamities of war, the glory or interests of his nation prompted him to carry his arms beyond the natural confines of his kingdom. He passed the straits of Gibraltar and reduced the fortress of Ceuta, and the city of Tangier. He had scarce returned to Spain before he was seized by a mortal disease. And the Visigoth writers of a superstitious age, who have passed with indifference or dwelt with satisfaction on the massacre of so many thousand Jews, have ascribed his death to the judgment of heaven, for his having presumed to depose the profligate but orthodox bishop of Barcelona.

The renown of Sisebut secured the tranquil succession of his son Recared the Second; but the young prince, who is supposed to have resembled his father, had scarcely received the crown before he expired, and the national council was summoned to a new election. In an assembly which consisted of Catholic clergy, the

A. D. 621.
631.

the memory of Recared the First was still revered; and their pious gratitude was displayed in raising to the vacant throne Suintilla, the second son of that monarch. The valour of Suintilla as a subject, had been approved against the rebellious Asturians; and in the condition of a king, it was not suffered to languish in the luxury of the palace. A few months had hardly been devoted to the works of peace, and the revisal of the laws, before the formidable irruption of the Gascons summoned the new monarch to arms. The province of Biscay and the kingdom of Navarre were blasted by their presence; and their hostile progress to the stream of the Ebro was marked by devastation. On the banks of that river they were astonished and awed by the presence of the Gothic king, who at the head of a numerous and disciplined army had pressed forwards to the relief of his people. Dismayed by his activity and vigour the Gascons endeavoured to retreat; in a tumultuous march they reached the foot of the Pyrenees; but the passes of those mountains were already occupied by the forces of Spain which had assembled in their rear. Their camp was assailed by famine, and clouded by despair; their deputies prostrated themselves at the feet of Suintilla, confessed their temerity, and implored his clemency. The compassion of the king might induce him to spare the effusion of blood; and his prudence must

have

have suggested the uncertainty of battle, and the vicissitudes of war. A safe retreat was allowed to the Gascons; but it was purchased by the restoration of the spoil they had acquired; their march across the Pyrenees was gently pressed by the squadrons of Spain; and a strong fortress was erected by the caution of Suintilla to prevent their return. The ground on which it arose is variously supposed to be covered by the modern town of Fontarabia, and the city of Valladolid; but the situation of the former on the coast of the sea, and the edge of the Pyrenees, marks the spot which nature neglected, and which art has constructed as the barrier of Spain against the ambition of France.

Within the narrow limits of the province or kingdom of Algarve, the imperialists had lamented their decreasing influence and waining strength; yet even the sense of the danger which impended over them could not suspend their domestic dissensions. Their little territory was divided between two governors, whose jealous and rival sway distracted their own councils, and invited the arms of their enemies. If the hostile ensigns of Suintilla enforced their tardy union, their rashness precipitated their destruction. They ventured to quit their fortifications, and to encounter the superior numbers of the Goths in an open field of battle; a bloody defeat was the consequence of their presumption;

sumption; and Suintilla improved the advantage with ardour and dexterity. Most of the imperial fortresses were surprised or submitted. A new governor who was dispatched by Heraclius to retrieve the errors of his predecessors, found scarce any thing left to defend. Yet the Grecian band that he commanded might have remembered in the hour of battle that they once had been distinguished by the name of Romans. The effects of military pride or despair were eluded by the address of Suintilla. He proclaimed his unwillingness to destroy so many gallant men, whose valour still might be useful to their country. He offered them a safe retreat, and vessels to transport them to Constantinople; in the interval of negociation the ardour of the soldiers evaporated; the love of life again revived in their bosoms; their general probably participated in their emotions, or yielded to their wishes; he subscribed the treaty, embarked his followers, and the peninsula of Spain was united under the sole authority of Suintilla.

A grateful nation listened with alacrity to the request of their victorious monarch. The son of Suintilla was by the suffrages of the Gothic nobles associated in the royal dignity of his father. But the very measure which promised to establish more firmly the throne of Suintilla, and to transmit it to his posterity, was the cause of its rapid subversion. Success had either changed or revealed his
natural

natural difposition ; and the counfels of his confort and his brother Gailan united to inflame his pride, and ftimulate his rapacity. Haughty, voluptuous, and avaricious, from the protector he became the fcourge of his people; the renown of his former achievements was ftill remembered with terror; and he might long have trampled on the patience of a proftrate nation, had not compaffion or ambition excited Sifenand, who was intrufted with the government of the Gothic territories in Gaul, to erect the ftandard of revolt. Thofe territories could furnifh but a flender band of warriors for the relief or invafion of Spain; and the liberal promifes of Sifenand prevailed on Dagobert, the king of France, to contribute his aid to the overthrow of the tyrant. At the head of a promifcuous army of Goths and Franks, Sifenand croffed the Pyrenees; and Suintilla with the approach of danger refuming his wonted vigour, advanced to engage him in the neighbourhood of Saragoffa. But he was deferted by his troops, his courtiers, and his brother Gailan; he heard the name of Sifenand proclaimed in his camp; and abandoning all hopes of refiftance, by an hafty flight he endeavoured to preferve his life.

With liberal gifts and a promife to fulfil the conditions he had fubfcribed, Sifenand difmiffed the Franks who repaffed the Pyrenees; and ftrong in the affections of his countrymen,

A. D. 631, 635.

trymen, pursued his peaceful progress to the royal city of Toledo. He was there solemnly acknowledged, and anointed as king; but the life of Suintilla was guarded by the memory of his former services; and the arm of resentment was checked by gratitude.

The succour of Dagobert had been purchased by the promise of a fountain of massy gold, the gift of the patrician Ætius to Torrismond the king of the Visigoths, when the valour of the latter wrested the victory from the Scythian host and their celebrated monarch Attila, in the bloody plains of Chalons. It had acquired a double value with the Goths, as the sacred testimony of their glory; but Sisenand had hardly seated himself in the throne before the golden fountain was demanded by the ambassadors of Dagobert; the menaces of the king of France prevailed over the murmurs of his own subjects, and the costly memorial of Gothic fame was delivered to the French envoys. The indignation of the Goths was not confined to vain complaints; the ambassadors were way-laid, attacked in their return, and compelled to surrender the precious object of their mission. A long negociation ensued; and the resentment of Dagobert was at length appeased, and the wishes of the Goths gratified, by the payment of a sum of money equal in value to the monument of the courage of their ancestors.

It

It was not until three years after Sifenand had exercifed the regal authority, that in a national council at Toledo, the depofition of Suintilla was formally confirmed, and his pofterity with that of the perfidious Gailan deemed incapable of ever afcending the Gothic throne. Two years afterwards the death of Sifenand himfelf fummoned the Gothic clergy and nobles to exert their judgment in the choice of a new fovereign.

The name of Chintila is firft revealed by his promotion to the throne; and his reign of fix years is only marked by his edict for the total expulfion of the Jews from Spain. A. D. 638. 639. It is not eafy to difcern at this diftance what event provoked the fury of the king and the people againft that unhappy race. But it is probable that the ufurious advantage which they might derive from their wealth, expofed them to general hatred. The royal decree of Chintila which commanded all his fubjects to profefs the Chriftian faith, was the fignal of perfecution and exile to the Jews. Yet the Goths were unwilling to deprive themfelves of the induftrious flaves, over whom they might exercife a lucrative oppreffion. The Jews ftill continued in Spain under the weight of the civil and ecclefiaftical laws, which in the fame country have been faithfully tranfcribed in the code of the Inquifition. The Gothic kings and bifhops at length difcovered that injuries will produce hatred, and that hatred will find the opportunity of revenge. A nation the secret or professed enemies of Christianity still multiplied in servitude and distress; and the intrigues of the Jews promoted the rapid success of the Arabian conquerors.

A. D. 639, 672. Yet however one sect might complain of the severity of Chintila, we may suppose from the vows of his subjects for his life and prosperity, that the general tenor of his administration was mild and beneficial. Even when he was dead, and flattery was no more, they acknowledged his virtues in filling the vacant throne with his son Tulga. The feeble youth appears to have been incapable of sustaining the weight of royalty; his character presents a blameless void, unmarked by vice or virtue; the bold and restless Goths required the sway of a more firm and nervous arm; by a confederacy of the principal nobles, the sceptre was transferred from the hand of Tulga to that of Chindisuintho; the life of the former was respected; but the ceremony of shaving his head precluded him according to the custom of the Barbarians, from re-ascending the throne; and an obscure and tranquil existence was permitted him within the walls of a monastery.

Age had not chilled the ambition or vigour of Chindisuintho; and the new monarch vindicated

dicated in arms his pretenfions to the crown. The chiefs who prefumed to oppofe his election were crufhed in the field, or executed on the fcaffold; his authority was recognized in a general council at Toledo; his fon Recifuintho was received as the partner of, and the fucceffor to, his power; and after a reign of eleven years, diftinguifhed equally by the praife of the warlike, the learned, and the pious, the death of Chindifuintho dropped the reins of government into the hands of his fon.

During the life of his father the abilities of Recifuintho had been difplayed in quelling a domeftic infurrection, and in chaftifing the Gafcons who had again paffed the Pyrenees; and on his acceffion to the undivided adminiftration of Spain, thofe who had been intimidated by the valour of the prince, were conciliated by the addrefs and clemency of the king. Twenty-four years his fubjects felt and applauded his wifdom, his juftice, and his moderation; and his deceafe at the expiration of that term fummoned them to the melancholy and arduous tafk of providing a fucceffor, who might not fuffer from the remembrance of Recifuintho's virtues.

The fuperior talents and qualities of Wamba united in his favour the fuffrages of his Gothic peers; but the power which A. D. 672. 680.
was

was the ambitious hope of many was slighted by the only person who appeared worthy of it. Wamba long refused to accede to the wishes of the assembly; and his subsequent conduct attests the sincerity of his reluctance. He yielded to the patriotic reproach, that he preferred his own peace to the interest of his country; but when he consented to wear the crown, he desired the council to recollect, that he complied with their, and not his own, inclinations. He had scarce received it before he was sensible of the cares to which it exposed him. The turbulent inhabitants of Navarre and Asturia refused their contributions, and armed against the state; and across the Pyrenees, Hilderic, Count of Nismes, assumed the ensigns of royalty, and aspired with the title of king, to the independent government of the Gothic provinces of Gaul. While Wamba prepared to march against the rebels of Navarre and Asturia, he directed Paul, a veteran and skilful general, to pass the Pyrenean mountains, and reduce the revolted Hilderic. The abilities of Paul were worthy of, but his fidelity was unequal to, the important trust. In a secret council of the chiefs of Catalonia, his ambition was inflamed by the assurances of their support. The timid Hilderic shrunk at his approach, and consented to rank himself among his dependents; the city of Narbonne received him as her sovereign; and his

his ufurpation was protected by the formidable alliance and fuccours of the Franks.

It was on the frontiers of Navarre that Wamba was informed of the perfidy of Paul, and the revolt of Catalonia. His officers advifed him to return to Toledo, and affemble the ftrength of the Gothic nation. But he rejected their dilatory counfels; and his reluctance in afcending the throne was not more fignal than his refolution in the poffeffion of it. Depending lefs on the number of his forces than the celerity of his motions, he penetrated into and laid wafte the rebellious countries of Afturia and Navarre. His rapid and deftructive progrefs ftruck the inhabitants with terror; they implored his clemency; and their pardon was fealed by a folemn oath to arm their martial youth in his defence. Strong in this reinforcement, Wamba haftily traverfed Arragon, entered Catalonia, prefented himfelf before, and was received into Barcelona, and halted before the walls of Gironne. Paul might either have confided in his own activity, or have been unwilling to expofe that city to the calamities of a fiege, when he inftructed the bifhop to acknowledge of the competitors the firft who appeared before the gates. Three days repofe recruited the ftrength of the followers of Wamba; and in four divifions his army attempted and forced the paffes of the Pyrenees, and united

under

under the walls of Narbonne. The garrison of Narbonne were animated by the presence of Witimir, the friend and favourite general of Paul; and in the cause of rebellion they displayed a valour the most obstinate; the gates were at length burst open, and the walls thrown down by the impetuous assailants; a church was the last retreat of Witimir; but he entered it as a warrior and not as a suppliant; yet he was incapable of obtaining the honourable death he sought; he was stunned by the fragment of a beam; was taken alive, and publicly scourged through the streets; but the ignominious punishment was the immediate effects of the resentment of the lieutenants of Wamba, who, however he might himself secretly approve, was far from publicly authorizing their conduct.

Within the walls of Nismes, Paul anticipated the consequences of unsuccessful rebellion. But instead of consuming the hours in vain lamentations, he employed them in preparations for a vigorous defence. The fortifications were repaired, the magazines replenished, and the spirits of his followers revived by assurances that a numerous host of Franks and Germans were ready to march to their relief. But if such were really the hopes of Paul, they were disappointed by the ardour of the generals of Wamba. The machines which had lately overthrown the

walls

walls of Narbonne, battered with inceffant fury thofe of Nifmes; the French mercenaries who had been allured into the fervice of Paul, confulted their fafety rather than their honour; they urged the impoffibility of further refiftance; and their impatience kindled a civil war within the diftracted city. The befiegers improved the opportunity; fcaled the ramparts; and difplayed throughout the ftreets the royal banner. The ample fpace of an ancient amphitheatre received the moft defperate or the moft faithful of the adherents of Paul, and refifted for fome time the tide of conqueft. The interval was improved by negociation; and Wamba to the holy mediation of Argaband arch-bifhop of Narbonne, granted the lives of the namelefs crowd, and only excepted from his promifed mercy, Paul, and the moft guilty leaders of the rebellion.

The feelings of an injured monarch might have juftified the inftant execution of the perfidious rebel. But on every occafion the refentment of Wamba was reftricted by his regard for juftice. In the prefence of the army he demanded of Paul whether he had experienced from him any mark of oppreffion or contempt; the reply of the captive acknowledged the favour and confidence of his fovereign had been ever extended to him, and accufed his own ingratitude. The judges were called upon to pronounce the fentence of the law

againft

againſt traitors, and Paul and his aſſociates were condemned to death. The deciſion was ſoftened by the clemency of Wamba; and the rebels were permitted to lament their fortune, or implore the forgiveneſs of their crime in the perpetual ſecluſion of a monaſtery.

After viſiting and confirming the tranquillity of the Gothic provinces of Gaul, Wamba repaſſed the Pyrenees, and entered in triumph the city of Toledo. The minds of the vulgar had been dazzled by his ſucceſs in war, but the judgment of the more ſagacious ſtamped the merit of his regulations in peace. The luxury of the clergy, the frequent, perhaps the invidious, complaint óf every age and clime, excited the attention of the Gothic king; and in a general aſſembly at Toledo, new canons were promulgated to reſtore the ancient ſimplicity of the church. It is not probable that the meetings of the unpoliſhed conquerors of Spain were conducted with the greateſt regard to decorum; and the firſt law of the aſſembly of Toledo was calculated to repreſs the tumultuous clamours, or licentious harangues which too frequently diſgraced it; the words are remarkable: " Such " as are members of this, or any other council, " ſhall behave with the utmoſt modeſty, and " ſpeak with the greateſt decency, obſerving at " other times a perfect ſilence, and, by a ſtrict " atten-

"attention testifying their respect of the place
"they are in. Whenever they are called upon
"for their opinions, they shall deliver themselves
"with much circumspection, without any va-
"riation from truth, without any sarcasms, with-
"out needless repetitions that create confusion,
"and without indulging an unseasonable wit
"amidst serious and important business." The
regulation may have originated among an unci-
vilized people, and in a period of barbarism;
but the polite legislators of modern France and
Britain, must confess it neither unworthy of, nor
unnecessary in, their own times.

The authority of Wamba had been vindicated from a powerful and perfidious rebel, and the glory of his country was asserted against a formidable and infidel enemy. In the rapid growth of less than a century, the faith of Mahomet from the distant region of Arabia had overshadowed the provinces of the east; had penetrated into and subdued the greatest part of Africa; and from the ports of that continent their piratical squadrons had menaced or ravaged the coast of Andalusia. Their progress had alarmed the declining age of Recisuintho; and it excited the jealousy and warlike preparations of Wamba. To protect the repose of Spain, and to chastise the pride of the ferocious Saracens, a numerous fleet was diligently prepared by the Gothic king; and though the

Visi-

Visigoths, accustomed only to combat at land, might at first regard the new theatre of action with terror, they soon vanquished their fears, and from a variety of desultory conflicts, returned home with spoil and victory. The bold and persevering disposition of the Saracens allowed them not readily to renounce the hopes of plunder and conquest; their squadrons were collected; and when they reviewed the prodigious number of their vessels, they might justly advance in the full confidence of certain success. From the coast of Andalusia might be beheld the hostile ensigns of Christ and Mahomet; from the former renown and subsequent achievements of the Mahometans, we may be assured that the Christians did not exult in a bloodless victory; but the proof of it was as decisive as glorious. Two hundred and seventy vessels of the Saracens were towed in triumph into the ports of Spain. The musselman pride was humbled; their naval strength broken; the conquest of Spain was for some time abandoned; and had the successors of Wamba imitated the vigour and vigilance of that prince, their country, secure in its natural situation, might have braved the host of the faithful, and never have been bowed beneath the Mahometan yoke.

But the kingdom of the Visigoths was rent by the kindred passions of jealousy, of resentment, and ambition. The reign of Wamba had been

distin-

distinguished by a series of great and illustrious actions; it had been acknowledged as the æra of wisdom and justice. Yet amidst the affection of his subjects and the admiration of his neighbours, the king of the Visigoths was deprived of the crown his virtues had adorned. It might naturally have been expected that the reign of the conqueror of Paul and the Saracens could only have expired with his life; that he either perished by the dagger of an assassin, or was overwhelmed by an hostile confederacy of rival sovereigns. Yet the fate of Wamba is not related without hesitation, and the concurrence of various historians; nor can it be read without exciting a smile. A strong opiate was administered to him by the treachery of a domestic, and as he laboured beneath the effects of the stupifying potion, the opportunity was improved by Erviga, an ambitious Goth who boasted his descent from Athanegilde; his long and silver locks, the symbol of his dignity, were severed by the daring hand of Erviga; his head was shaved; and Wamba, for he was a king no more, awoke to the full sense of his injury. He dissembled his surprise; assumed the language of voluntary retirement; and stifled the emotions of revenge to promote the tranquillity of Spain. He recommended as his successor the traitor who had defrauded him of royalty; and within the holy walls of a monastery heard, without exulting in, the

the abdication of Erviga. In that peaceful retreat he could reflect without remorse or regret on the measures he had pursued, and the station he had occupied; the last years of his life were certainly the most happy, though not the most splendid; and the indifference with which he bore the loss of a crown, proved how truly he was worthy to possess it.

A.D. 680, 693. The testimony of Wamba, united the suffrages of the national council of Toledo, in favour of Erviga; and a kingdom that had been obtained by treachery, was governed with justice and wisdom. Some suspicions had escaped of his treason towards Wamba; but the murmurs of the people were appeased by the address of their sovereign, who, to extinguish the embers of faction, neglected the pretensions of his own sons; and with the hand of his daughter Cixilona, called the nephew and heir of Wamba to the certain succession of the throne. In the dark and confused legends of the Spanish historians, some words are dropped of domestic insurrection; and a victory of Erviga is variously supposed to have been over the Gascons who invaded Spain, or the Visigoths who revolted in Gaul. But this appears to have been the only instance of foreign or civil war; and during the eight years that he held the sceptre of Spain, that country was preserved in peace and security by his vigour and prudence.

prudence. At the expiration of that term he was seized with a dangerous indisposition; and during the suspension of disease he scrupulously observed the solemn vow that he had made, to quit the robes of royalty for the habit of a penitent. He declared, or prevailed on the Gothic nobles to receive, Egiza as his successor; and in return for the crown he bestowed, he exacted an oath from Egiza to repair any wrongs that he himself had inadvertently occasioned. Satisfied with this stipulation, his head was shaved, and he assumed the garb of a monk; but he was not long suffered to edify his subjects by the example of repentance; and he breathed his last a few days after he resigned the sceptre.

In the possession of a throne the peace of Egiza was invaded by a pious scruple. He had sworn to repair the injustice of Erviga, and he had bound himself by a solemn oath to protect his widow and children; yet Luivagotona, the consort of Erviga, had availed herself of her influence over that prince to usurp the demesnes of several of his subjects; and justice demanded the restitution. In a council of the clergy Egiza stated the irreconcileable obligations he had accepted; his doubts were solved by the answer of that assembly; policy or interest recommended them to release Egiza from his first oath; and to recommend the resumption of the demesnes that Luivagotona had usurped.

It was in one of the legislative assemblies of Toledo during the reign of Egiza, that the code of laws which had been compiled by a succession of Gothic kings from the fierce Euric to the sagacious Eryiga, was examined and ratified. As long as the Visigoths themselves were satisfied with the rude customs of their ancestors, they indulged the subjects of Gaul and Spain in the enjoyment of the Roman law. Their gradual improvement in arts, in policy, and at length in religion, encouraged them to imitate, and to supersede those foreign institutions; and to compose a code of civil and criminal jurisprudence, for the use of a great and united people. The same obligations, and the same privileges were communicated to the nations of the Spanish monarchy: and the conquerors, insensibly renouncing the Teutonic idiom, submitted to the restraints of equity, and exalted the Romans to the participation of freedom. The code of the Visigoths has been treated by the president de Montesquieu with excessive severity. He has lavished on it the epithets of puerile and ridiculous; he has declared it to have been incapable of attaining its end; to have been frivolous in substance, and turgid in style. The language it is

con-

conveyed in may indeed juftly have deferved his cenfure; and the fuperftition which pervades it may fubject it to reproach; yet according to the teftimony of a more modern, and much efteemed writer's judgment, it poffeffed the merit of impartial policy, and deferved the praife of wifdom and moderation.

It foftened at leaft the condition of the fubjected; and while throughout the fpacious realms of Gaul and Italy the vanquifhed native funk into the abject flave of the conqueror, the Spaniard was permitted to ranfom his freedom, and not unfrequently to redeem his property, by the payment of a fmall fine or annual rent; the feudal fyftem which has been fo often, and by an hiftorian of our own country fo elegantly defcribed, prevailed indeed from the ftraits of Gibraltar to the mountains of the Pyrenees; but the harfhnefs of its features were meliorated by prudence or humanity; and although in war the vaffal was obliged to follow the ftandard, in peace he might with confidence appeal from the arrogance and oppreffion, of his lord.

Chapter the Fourth.

Conspiracy of the Jews with the Mahometans of Africa.—War with the Franks and Gascons.—Death of Egiza, and accession of Witiza.—The Pope's claim of supremacy is rejected in the council of Toledo.—Tyranny of Witiza.—Revolt and elevation of Roderic.—Treachery of Count Julian.—Invasion of the Saracens.—Battle of Xeres.—Flight and death of Roderic.—Exploits of Tarik.—Of Musa.—Of Abdalaziz.—The greatest part of Spain conquered.—Recall of Musa.—Government of Abdalaziz.—His marriage with the widow of Roderic.—He is assassinated.—Rival factions of the Abbassides and Ommiades.—Abdalrahman appears on the coast of Spain.—His victory over the Abbassides.—He establishes his independent throne at Cordova.—The æra of Arabian splendour in Spain.—Reign of the third Abdalrahman.—His wealth and magnificence.—Town and palace of Zehra.—His revenue.—Trade and natural productions of Spain.—Character of Alkalem the second.—His justice.—He is succeeded by his infant son Hassem.—Renown of Almanzor, the vizir of Hassem.—Overthrow of the house

houſe of the Ommiades.—Degeneracy and diſſenſions of the Moors of Spain.

In the generous policy of an equal and impartial code of laws, Egiza might juſtly have hoped that the reign of the Gothic princes in Spain would have been prolonged through ſucceſſive centuries by the union of their Chriſtian ſubjects. Yet he was not long permitted to indulge the pleaſing illuſion; his mind was diſtracted by the rapid progreſs of the Saracens on the oppoſite coaſt of Africa; he dreaded the enthuſiaſtic valour and rapacious myriads of the general enemies of Chriſtianity; and his apprehenſions were kept awake by the reſentment of a ſect, whom he had perſecuted and deſpiſed. *A. D. 683, 709.*

The decree which had commanded the expulſion of the Jews from Spain had been eluded by avarice; and that wretched people by the connivance of the governors of the provinces, and of the ſucceſſors of Chintila, had been permitted to purſue and improve the arts of trade and commerce. But without a legal eſtabliſhment, the fruits of their ingenuity or labour, and even their lives, were expoſed to the caprice or covetouſneſs of their rulers. They might ſometimes complain of wanton cruelty; but they could always, and with justice, accuse the insatiate demands of the hungry Visigoths; they were suffered to accumulate only to swell the coffers of their masters; the thirst of revenge became more strong in proportion as it was necessary to cherish it in silence; they exulted in the victories of the Mahometans; they continued a dangerous and hostile correspondence with their brethren, who under the administration of Chintila had sheltered themselves from persecution in Africa; and on their assurances of support, and with the secret hope of more effectual succour from the Saracens, they fixed the day to erect the standard of revolt.

Before the appointed time arrived, their preparations had alarmed, or their intentions had been betrayed to, Egiza. In a national council the Gothic king unfolded the conspiracy, and ratified the punishment of the Jews. The public exercise of their religion was prohibited under the most severe penalties; their children under seven years of age were directed to be taken from them, and to be educated in the Christian faith; and those who presumed to conspire against their sovereign, or who, after having been purified in the baptismal font, returned to their ancient heresy, were deprived of their property and liberty.

The premature discovery of the conspiracy of the

the Jews, might disconcert, but did not deter the Saracens from aspiring to the conquest of Spain. Their numerous squadrons issued from the ports of Africa, and menaced again the coasts of Andalusia. But their pride was chastised by a second naval defeat; and the victory which dispelled the immediate apprehensions of the Visigoths, was ascribed to the valour and conduct of the youthful Theodomir, the son-in-law of Egiza.

A short but bloody war with the Franks or Gascons was terminated by the mutual weakness and losses of both nations; and Egiza in the moment of tranquillity might, in establishing the succession to the crown, equally consider the happiness of his people, and the aggrandisement of his family. In a national assembly at Toledo his son was associated with him in the regal dignity; and soon after the death of Egiza, devolved on Witiza the undivided administration of Spain.

During the first months of his reign, Witiza might be considered as the protector and father of his people; during the last years he was the scourge and tyrant of his subjects. The advantages which his country derived from a short affectation of virtue, were few and transient; the evils with which she was afflicted from the indulgence of his passions and vices were numerous and lasting. Yet one instance of firmness marks

his

his accession: with the title of Pope, and as the successor of St. Peter, the patriarch of Rome, claimed an absolute dominion over the Christian states of Europe; but in the eighteenth council of Toledo, a spirit of ecclesiastical freedom was kindled by the eloquence of the metropolitan Gundaric. He vindicated the independence of the church of Spain: his piety and blameless manners gave weight to his arguments; and the extravagant pretensions of the see of Rome were encountered with decent and manly opposition.

If justice or virtue had taken root within the bosom of Witiza, they were soon eradicated by the flattering language of a licentious train of courtiers, who successfully insinuated that youth was the season for pleasure and enjoyment, and that the sovereign was to be distinguished from his subjects by his more ample privilege of luxury and prodigality. The pleasing doctrine was readily preferred to the distasteful admonitions of the holy Gundaric; the court of Witiza was disgraced by scenes of shameless excess and debauchery; and the wives and daughters of the most illustrious of the Gothic nobles were violated by his lusts. To a vicious tyrant, virtue must ever become the object of hatred and jealousy; to intemperance succeeded cruelty; and those whose qualities and descent from the most honoured of his predecessors recommended them to popular favour,

favour, were, as diftruft or caprice prevailed, sentenced to banifhment or death.

Yet the deteftation of the tyrant has been indulged by the hiftorians of his reign beyond the bounds of truth or probability. We may fafely reject the law that he is reported to have framed, and which gratified the amorous inclinations of his fubjects, by unlimited polygamy. We may diftruft the regulation which enjoined the deftruction of all offenfive weapons throughout Spain; and the invafion of the Moors, and the fieges they encountered, convince us how falfely he is accufed of difmantling, with the exception of Toledo, Tuy, and Aftorga, all the cities throughout his dominions.

However exaggerated or perverted may be the chronicles of thofe times, it may be pronounced with certainty that the follies and vices of Witza were glaring and numerous, fince they at length provoked the open indignation of his fubjects, and confummated his deftruction. Among the noble fufferers from his jealoufy was Theodofred, who is defcribed as the brother, but who moft likely was the nephew of Recifuintho; he was deprived of his fight, and fent a prifoner to Cordova; but the hours of darknefs and captivity were beguiled by the filial affection of the fon Roderic; in their free converfe their murmurs againft their oppreffor were gradually inflamed to an

hope

hope and a project of revenge. His father's wrongs, and the memory of Recisuintho pleaded powerfully for Roderic; he erected the standard of revolt; and the thousands who in themselves or their connexions had either felt or dreaded the lust or cruelty of the tyrant, joined him with alacrity; a civil war was kindled and raged for some time with doubtful violence; but was at length terminated by the deposition or death of Witiza, and the elevation of Roderic to the throne of the Visigoths.

By the fall of Witiza, and his own accession to royalty, Roderic had gratified the emotions of revenge and ambition; but he was not long in possession of the crown of Spain before he was instructed that his ascent to greatness was equally dangerous to himself and his country. Across the narrow channel which divides Europe from Africa, the fortress of Ceuta had been defended by the valour and skill of count Julian against the host of the Saracens; and while Musa, the leader of the faithful, revolved his disappointment with indignation, his hopes were awakened, not only to the entire reduction of Africa, but to the conquest of Spain, by the proffered alliance of the chief, and the surrender of the fortress from which he had so lately retired with disgrace.

In extenuating or accounting for the treachery of Julian, the Spanish historians repeat the popular story

story of his daughter Cava violated by the guilty passion of Roderic; but the tale, romantic in itself, is ill supported by external evidence. Some doubts have occurred whether it was the wife or daughter of the Gothic general whose honour was profaned. It has even been insinuated that the injury was offered by Witiza, and not by Roderic; nor are there wanting critics who have totally rejected the suspicious narrative. A more probable reason for the revolt of Julian has been assigned by the luminous historian of the Decline and Fall of the Roman Empire, who has described with elegance and concisenefs the invasion of Spain by the Saracens, and whose account of that memorable revolution is preserved in the succeeding pages. The voice of the nation had indeed placed the sceptre in the hand of Roderic; but the sons of Witiza, impatient of a private station, waited the moment to assert their hereditary pretensions in arms. Their followers were excited by the remembrance of favours and the promise of a revolution; and their uncle Oppas, the archbishop of Seville, possessed an equal influence in the church and state. It is probable Julian had little to hope and much to fear from the new reign; his merit and popularity rendered him an useful or formidable subject; his estates were ample, his adherents numerous and bold; and it was too fatally shewn that by his Andalusian and Mauri-

tanian

tanian commands, he held in his hands the keys of the Spanish monarchy. Too feeble however to meet his sovereign in arms, he sought the aid of a foreign power; and his rash invitation of the Moors and Arabs, produced the calamities of eight hundred years. In his epistles, or in a personal interview, he revealed the wealth and nakedness of his country; the weakness of a disputed throne; the degeneracy of an effeminate people. The Goths were no longer the victorious Barbarians who humbled the pride of Rome, despoiled the queen of nations, and penetrated from the Danube to the Atlantic ocean. Secluded from the world by the Pyrenean mountains, the successors of Alaric had slumbered in a long peace. The walls of the cities were mouldered into dust; the youth had abandoned the exercise of arms; and the presumption of their ancient renown would expose them in a field of battle to the first assault of the invaders. The ambitious Saracen was fired by the ease and importance of the attempt; but the execution was delayed till he had consulted the commander of the faithful; and his messenger returned with the permission of Walid, to annex the unknown kingdoms of the west to the religion and throne of the Caliphs. In his residence of Tangier, Musa, with secrecy and caution continued his correspondence and hastened his preparations. But the

the remorse of the conspirators was soothed by the fallacious assurance that he should content himself with the glory and the spoil, without aspiring to establish the Moslems beyond the sea that separates Africa from Europe.

In two successive attempts the naval force of the Saracens had been broken by the Gothic fleet; but Roderic, either distracted by civil war and intent on revenge, or confiding in the vigilance and fidelity of Julian, neglected the natural means of defence; the unguarded coast invited the descent of the Moslems. Yet before Musa would trust an army of the faithful to the dangers of a foreign and Christian land, he made a less dangerous trial of their strength and veracity. In the year seven hundred and ten after the birth of Christ, one hundred Arabs, and four hundred Africans passed over in four vessels from Tangier or Ceuta; the place of their disembarkation on the opposite shore of the strait is marked by the name of Tarif, their chief; from their first station, they marched eighteen miles through an hilly country to the castle and town of Julian; the appellation of the green island, which from a verdant cape that advances into the sea, they bestowed upon it, is still perpetuated by a corruption from the Arabic, in the name of Algezira. Their hospitable entertainment, the Christian vassals of Julian who joined

A. D. 710, 755.

their

their standard, their inroad into a fertile and unguarded province, the richness of their spoil, and the safety of their return, announced to their brethren the most favourable omens of victory. In the ensuing spring five thousand veterans and volunteers were embarked under the command of Tarik, a dauntless and skilful soldier, who surpassed the expectations of his chief. The necessary transports were provided by the industry of their too faithful ally. The Saracens landed at the pillar or point of Europe; the corrupt and familiar appellation of Gibraltar (*Gabal al Tarik*) describes the mountain of Tarik; and the intrenchments of his camp were the first outlines of those fortifications which in the hands of Great Britain have resisted the art and power of the united house of Bourbon.

Roderic had slumbered over the preparations and first attempt of the Saracens, he was awakened by the magnitude of their second invasion; yet instead of collecting his whole force and advancing in person to rush the rash intruders, he contented himself dispatching his lieutenant Edeco, at the head of some select troops, to arrest their progress. The Visigoths, enervated by luxury, were incapable of withstanding the martial enthusiasm of the Moslem fanatics; and the flight of Edeco revealed to Roderic the approach of the enemy, and his own danger.

The

The Visigoths were still capable of great and formidable efforts; the standard of their sovereign was unfurled; and at the royal summons, the dukes and counts, the bishops and nobles of the Gothic monarchy assembled at the head of their followers. The host that marched under the conduct of Roderic consisted of ninety or an hundred thousand men, and must have insured victory, had their discipline and fidelity been adequate to their numbers. But the Visigoths long unaccustomed to, were oppressed by the weight of armour; and the sons of Witiza, who consented to range themselves under the royal banner, remembered the condition and fate of a father and a kinsman, and their own ambitious hopes blasted by the promotion of Roderic.

Yet even the fanaticism of the Moslems could not be insensible to the preparations of the Goths. The promise of Paradise was weighed against the danger of the unequal field; and the prudence of Tarik was displayed in his timely retreat, while he solicited and obtained the assistance of his African brethren. By the diligence of Musa the Saracens were augmented to twelve thousand; and to these were joined a promiscuous crowd of Christian malecontents who were attracted by the influence of Julian, and of Africans greedy to taste the temporal blessings of the Koran. About two leagues from Cadiz, the town of Xeres, has been illuſtrated by the encounter which determined the fate of the kingdom; the ſtream of the Guadalato, which falls into the bay, divided the two camps, and marked the advancing and retreating ſkirmiſhes of three ſucceſſive and bloody days. On the fourth day the two armies joined a more ſerious and deciſive iſſue; but in the moment when they were moſt neceſſary, Roderic ſeems to have been deprived of the qualities which had raiſed him to a throne; Alaric would have bluſhed at the ſight of his unworthy ſucceſſor, ſuſtaining on his head a diadem of pearls, incumbered with a flowing robe of gold and ſilken embroidery, and reclining on a litter, or car of ivory, drawn by two white mules. Notwithſtanding the valour of the Saracens they fainted under the weight of multitudes; and the plain of Xeres was overſpread with their dead bodies. "My brethren," ſaid Tarik, to his ſurviving companions, "the enemy is before you, "the ſea is behind; whither would ye fly? fol- "low your general: I am reſolved either to loſe "my life, or to trample on the proſtrate king "of the Viſigoths." Beſides the reſource of deſpair, he confided in the ſecret correſpondence, and nocturnal interviews of count Julian, with the ſons and brother of Witiza. The two princes and the archbiſhop of Seville occupied the moſt

import-

important post; their well-timed defection broke the ranks of the Christians; each warrior was prompted by fear or suspicion to consult his personal safety; and the greatest part of the Gothic army were scattered or destroyed in the flight and pursuit of the three following days. Amidst the general disorder, Roderic started from his car, and mounted Orelia, the fleetest of his horses. Some credulous Spaniards believed that in an hermit's cell he concealed his disgrace, and eluded the search of his enemies; but it is more probable that he escaped a soldier's death to perish ignobly in the waters of the Bœtis or Guadalquivir. His diadem, his robes, and his courser were found on the bank; but as the body of the Gothic prince was buried in the waves, the pride and ignorance of the Caliph must have been gratified with some meaner head, which was exposed in triumph before the palace of Damascus. " And such," continues a valiant historian of the Arabs, " is " the fate of those kings who withdraw themselves from a field of battle."

The fortifications of Eciga, a strong town situated on a branch of the Guadalquivir, and not far from the theatre of their defeat, afforded a temporary asylum to the fugitive Visigoths. But the walls were soon encompassed and assaulted by the victorious Saracens; and if the besieged were confirmed in their resistance by despair, the besiegers

siegers were animated in their attacks by the double hope of plunder and of Paradise. After a short but bloody struggle, the standard of Mahomet was displayed on the ramparts; the garrison was overpowered; and the defenceless inhabitants were involved in the promiscuous slaughter by the inexorable victors.

Count Julian had plunged so deep in guilt and infamy, that his only hope was in the ruin of his country. After the battle of Xeres, and the capture of Eciga, he recommended the most effectual measures to the Moslem invaders. " The " king of the Goths is slain; their princes are " fled before you; the army is routed; the na- " tion is astonished. Secure with sufficient de- " tachments the cities of Bœtica; but in per- " son, and without delay, march to the royal " city of Toledo, and allow not the distracted " Christians either time or tranquillity for the " election of a new monarch." Tarik listened to his advice. A Roman captive and proselyte who had been enfranchised by the Caliph himself, assaulted Cordova with seven hundred horse. He swam the river, surprised the town, and drove the Christians into the great church, where they defended themselves above three months. Another detachment reduced the sea coast of Bœtica, which in the last period of the Moorish power, has comprised in a narrow space the populous

pulous kingdom of Grenada. The march of Tarik from the Bœtis to the Tagus might confift of near two hundred miles, and was directed through the Sierra Morena, that feparates Andalufia and Caftille, till he appeared in arms under the walls of Toledo. The moft zealous of the Catholics had efcaped with the relics of their faints; and if the gates were fhut, it was only till the victor had fubfcribed a fair and reafonable capitulation. The voluntary exiles were allowed to depart with their effects; feven churches were appropriated to the Chriftian worfhip; the archbifhop and his clergy were at liberty to exercife their functions, the monks to practife or neglect their penance; and the Goths and Romans were left in all civil and criminal cafes to the fubordinate jurifdiction of their own laws and magiftrates.

But if the juftice of Tarik protected the Chriftians, his gratitude and policy rewarded the Jews, to whofe fecret or open aid he was indebted for his moft important acquifitions. Perfecuted by the kings and fynods of Spain, who had often preffed the alternative of banifhment or baptifm, that outcaft nation embraced the moment of revenge. The comparifon of their paft and prefent ftate was the pledge of their fidelity; and the alliance between the difciples of Mofes and of Mahomet, was maintained till the final æra of their common expulfion.

From the reduction or submission of Toledo, the sons and brother of Witiza found themselves no longer necessary to the victors; they had consented to be considered as the confederates, and they sunk into the dependents of the enemies of their country and religion. From the royal seat of Toledo, the Arabian leader spread his conquests to the north over the modern realms of Castille and Leon. The prostrate cities opened their gates and surrendered their treasures on his approach. The celebrated table of one single piece of solid emerald, encircled with three rows of fine pearls, supported by three hundred and sixty-five feet of gems and massy gold, and estimated at the price of five hundred thousand pieces of gold, acquired by the Goths among the spoils of Rome, was presented by the Arabs to the throne of Damascus. Beyond the Asturian mountains the maritime town of Gijon bounded the progress of the lieutenant of Musa, who had performed his victorious march of seven hundred miles from the rock of Gibraltar to the Bay of Biscay. Spain, which in a more savage and disorderly state had resisted two hundred years the arms of the Romans, was over-run in a few months by those of the Saracens; and such was the eagerness of submission and treaty, that the Governor of Cordova is recorded as the only chief who fell, without conditions, a prisoner

into

into their hands. The cause of the Goths had been irrevocably judged in the field of Xeres; and, in the national dismay, each part of the monarchy declined a contest with the antagonist who had vanquished the united strength of the whole. That strength had been wasted by two succesive years of pestilence and famine; and the governors who were impatient to surrender, might exaggerate the difficulties of collecting the provisions necessary to sustain a siege. To disarm the Christians, superstition likewise contributed her terrors; the subtle Arab encouraged the report of dreams, omens, and prophecies; in the palace of Toledo, an ancient tower had been regarded as the structure of magic; and the tradition, that whenever it was opened the Gothic monarchy should be extinguished, had been respected by the successors of Alaric. The mind of Roderic was inflamed by the hope of an immense treasure, and his avarice impelled him to tempt the charm. The gates were unlocked or burst open; and a massy chest in an inward apartment was the object of his eager curiosity. Instead of gold and silver, it was found to contain on a long roll of linen the ferocious features of the Saracens, with an inscription that such was destined to be the conquerors of Spain. The historian who has preserved the tale, has apologised for his insertion of it; but if it was eagerly received by the Goths and Spaniards, the belief of it contributed to produce the consequences it was supposed to have predicted; and an army already impressed with the presage of defeat, could but faintly aspire to the glory of victory.

From Gijon, Tarik had been recalled to Toledo, to excuse his presumption of conquering a kingdom in the absence of his general. The intelligence of his rapid success had converted the applause of Musa into envy; and he began, not to complain, but to fear that Tarik would leave him nothing to subdue. At the head of ten thousand Arabs and eight thousand Africans he passed over in person from Mauritania to Spain. The first of his companions were descended from the most noble tribe of Arabia; his eldest son was left to command in Africa; the three younger brethren were of an age and spirit to second the boldest enterprises of their father. At his landing at Algezire he was respectfully entertained by count Julian, who stifled his inward remorse, and testified both in words and actions, that the victory of the Arabs had not impaired his attachment to the cause. Some enemies yet remained for the sword of Musa. The tardy repentance of the Goths had compared their own numbers and those of the invaders; the cities from which the march of Tarik had declined, considered themselves as impregnable; and the bravest patriots

defend-

defended the fortifications of Seville and Merida. They were fucceffively befieged, and reduced by the labour of Mufa, who tranfported his camp from the Bœtis or Guadalquivir to the Anas or Guadiana. When he beheld the works of Roman magnificence, the bridge, the aqueducts, the triumphal arches, and the theatre of the ancient metropolis of Lufitania, "I fhould imagine," exclaimed he, " that the human race muft have " united their art and power in the foundation of " this city; happy is the man who fhall become " its mafter." He afpired to that happinefs, but the Emeritans fuftained on this occafion the honour of their defcent from the veteran legionaries of Auguftus. Difdaining the confinement of their walls, they gave battle to the Arabs on the plain; but an ambufcade rifing from the fhelter of a quarry or a ruin, chaftifed their indifcretion, and intercepted their return. The wooden turrets of affault were rolled forward to the foot of the ramparts; but the defence of Merida was obftinate and long; and the *caftle of the* martyrs was a perpetual teftimony of the loffes of the Moflems. The conftancy of the befieged was at length fubdued by famine and defpair; and the prudent victor difguifed his impatience under the names of clemency and efteem. The alternative of exile or tribute was allowed; the churches were divided between the two religions,

gions, and the wealth of thofe who had fallen in the fiege, or retired to Gallicia, was confifcated as the reward of the faithful.

The adventurous fpirit of Tarik had firſt explored in Spain the road to conqueſt; yet in an interview between Mufa and his lieutenant, a rigid account was demanded from the latter of the fpoils of victory. His character was expofed to fufpicion and obloquy; he was impriſoned, reviled, and ignominiouſly fcourged by the hand, or the command of Mufa. Yet fo ſtrict was the difcipline, fo pure the zeal of the primitive Moſlems, that after this public indignity, Tarik could ferve and be trufted in the reduction of the Tarragoneſe province. The gates and treaſures of Saragoſſa were delivered up to Mufa; and by the pious liberality of his companions a mofch was erected within the walls of that city; the port of Barcelona was opened to the veffels of Syria; but the flight of the Goths beyond the Pyrenean mountaints was moſt probably refpected by the Saracen general; and the beſt hiſtorians poftpone the invaſion of Gaul by the Moſlems, to above twenty years after that of Spain.

While Mufa purfued his victorious career to the foot of the Pyrenean mountains, his fon Abdelaziz chaſtiſed the infurgents of Seville; and penetrated along the fea-coaſt of the Mediterranean from Malaga to Valentia. In the diſtricts of Murcia

cia and Carthagena, whose plains are fertilized by the waters of the Segura, he was opposed by an adversary worthy of the arms of the Moslems. Theodomir was the son-in-law of Egiza, and had in the reign of that monarch, rendered his name terrible to the Saracens, by the defeat and almost the destruction of their fleet. Under the administration of Roderic his counsels were neglected, and his valour probably unemployed. But when that prince was no more, he started from obscurity; and his former renown collected to his standard a band of martial Christians; at their head he waged with success a desultory war; and even the enthusiastic valour of the Saracens seems to have sunk before his genius; Abdelaziz communicated his difficulties to, and invoked the assistance of his father; the rapid squadrons of Arabia rushed to his relief. Theodomir was surrounded on every side; and the pious enmity of the Moslems might have been gratified by the slaughter of several thousand Christians, had not the sanguinary counsels of the former been tempered by the prudence or generosity of Abdelaziz; his original treaty with Theodomir will represent the manners and policy of the times. *The conditions of peace agreed and sworn between Abdelaziz the son of Musa, the son of Nassir, and Theodomir prince of the Goths.* " In the name of the most merciful " God, Abdelaziz makes peace on these condi- " tions; *that* Theodomir shall not be disturbed in
" his

"his principality; nor any injury be offered to
"the life or property, the wives and children, the
"religion and temples of the Chriftians; *that*
"Theodomir fhall freely deliver his feven cities
"Orithwell, Valentola, Alicant, Mola, Vacafora,
"Bigerra, *now* Begar, Ora or Opta, and Lorca;
"*that* he fhall not affift or entertain the ene-
"mies of the Caliph, but fhall faithfully com-
"municate his knowledge of their hoftile de-
"figns; *that* himfelf, and each of the Gothic
"nobles, fhall annually pay one piece of gold,
"four meafures of wheat, as many of barley,
"with a certain proportion of honey, oil, and
"vinegar; and that each of their vaffals fhall
"be taxed at one moiety of the faid impofition.
"Given the fourth of Regab in the year of the
"Hegira ninety-four, and fubfcribed with the
"names of four muffulmen witneffes." In the
conditions of peace Theodomir and his fubjects
muft have confeffed the lenity of their conquerors;
the articles were ftrictly obferved; and four hundred years after the death of Theodomir, his territories of Murcia and Carthagena, according to
the Nubian geographer Edrifi, preferved the remembrance of his adminiftration and his name in
the corrupt appellation of Tadmir.

It was not only the natives of Murcia and Carthagena who were compelled to acknowledge the
moderation of their Mahometan mafters. Many
partial

partial calamities were doubtlefs inflicted by the carnal or religious paffions of the enthufiafts; fome churches were profaned by the new worfhip; fome relics or images were confounded with idols; the rebels were put to the fword; and one town, an obfcure place between Cordova and Seville, was razed to its foundations; yet in general the footfteps of the Saracens were far from being marked with blood or devaftation; they exacted the rights of conqueft, but they exacted them with temperance; and the rate of the tribute which they impofed appears to have fluctuated from a tenth to a fifth, according to the fubmiffion or obftinacy of the Chriftians.

The poffeffion of Spain was confidered by Mufa only as the firft ftep to the monarchy of Europe. With a powerful armament by fea and land he was preparing to transfer the war beyond the Pyrenees, to extinguifh in Gaul and Italy the kingdoms of the Franks and Lombards, and to preach the doctrines of Mahomet on the altar of the Vatican. From thence fubduing the Barbarians of Germany, he propofed to follow the courfe of the Danube from its fource to the Euxine fea, to overthrow the Greek or Roman empire of Conftantinople, and returning from Europe to Afia, to unite his acquifitions with Antioch and the provinces of Syria. But he was only permitted to revolve the vaft enterprife; and the vifionary conqueror

queror was soon reminded of his dependence and servitude. The friends of Tarik had effectually stated his services and wrongs at the court of Damascus, the proceedings of Musa were blamed, his intensions suspected, and his delay in complying with the first invitation was chastized by an harsher and more peremptory summons. An intrepid messenger of the Caliph entered his camp at Lugo in Gallicia, and in the presence of the Saracens and Christians arrested the bridle of his horse. His own loyalty, or that of his troops, inculcated the duty of obedience; and his disgrace was alleviated by the recall of his rival, and the permission of investing with the government of Spain his son Abdelaziz. His long triumph from Ceuta to Damascus, displayed the spoils of Afric and the treasures of Spain. Four hundred Gothic nobles, with gold coronets and girdles, were distinguished in his train; and the number of male and female captives, selected for their birth or beauty, was computed at eighteen, or even at thirty thousand persons. As soon as he reached Tiberias in Palestine, he was apprised of the sickness and danger of the Caliph, by a private messenger from Soliman his brother and presumptive heir, who wished to reserve for his own reign the spectacle of victory. Had Walid recovered, the delay of Musa would have been criminal; he pursued his march, and found an

enemy

enemy on the throne. In his trial before a partial judge, againſt a popular antagoniſt, he was convicted of vanity and falſehood; and a fine of two hundred thouſand pieces of gold, either exhauſted his poverty or proved his rapaciouſneſs. The unworthy treatment of Tarik was avenged by a ſimilar indignity; and the veteran commander, after a public whipping, ſtood a whole day in the ſun before the palace gate, till he obtained a decent exile under the pious name of a pilgrimage to Mecca.

The puniſhment of Muſa may accuſe the juſtice of the Caliph; yet where the perſonal reſentment of Soliman interfered not, he appears to have been ſenſible of equity and capable of humanity. Among the few Viſigoths who accompanied, without wearing the chains of Muſa, Theodomir was the moſt diſtinguiſhed for his merit, the ſons of Witiza were moſt conſpicuous for their birth; the former was received with reſpect by the commander of the faithful; his treaty with Abdelaziz was ratified; and his return in ſafety inſtructed his countrymen that they might repoſe with confidence on the faith of the Moſlems. The ſons of Witiza were reinſtated in the private patrimony of their father; but on the deceaſe of Eba the elder, his daughter was unjuſtly deſpoiled of her portion by the violence of her uncle Siſebut. The Gothic maid pleaded her cauſe before the Caliph Haſham, and obtained the reſtitution

tution of her inheritance; she was given in marriage to a noble Arabian, and their two sons, Isaac and Ibrahim, were received in Spain with the consideration that was due to their origin and riches.

The guilt of Julian, if we may credit the doubtful historians of that age, was expiated by an end more deservedly wretched. After betraying the cause of his country and his religion, he could not expect to share the confidence of the infidel victors. His counsels were slighted, his services coldly acknowledged or tardily rewarded; and an hasty murmur of discontent that escaped him was greedily received, and improved into the project of a new revolution; his vast estates were confiscated; he was thrown into a deep dungeon; and the contempt of his masters suffered him to languish out the wretched remnant of his life in chains and darkness. The calamities his ambition or resentment had inflicted on his country recoiled on his own head; yet it was not from the hands of the Saracens that he merited his unhappy destiny; and his fate reveals the jealousy or ingratitude of Abdelaziz.

The son of Musa was himself soon destined to experience the vicissitudes of fortune; the administration of Spain had been delegated to him by his father, and in the arduous station, above the condition of a subject, and below that of a sovereign, his active vigilance had challenged the praise

praise of the victors and the vanquished. But the happy effect of his abilities and his virtues were effaced by one injudicious and ill-fated paffion. His heart was fenfible to the charms of Egilona, the widow of Roderic, and his marriage with her offended the prejudices both of the Chriftians and Moflems. His new confort might firft have inflamed him with the defire of independent fovereignty; and the injurious treatment of his father muft have fortified him in the defign of erecting his throne at Cordova. But the minds of the Moflems were not yet ripe for rebellion; they ftill revered in the Caliph the holy fucceffor of Mahomet; and no fooner was a fufpicion of the intentions of Abdelaziz diffufed, than a powerful confpiracy was cemented againft him. The deftruction of the fon of Mufa could not, it was juftly fuppofed, prove unacceptable to the court of Damafcus. But the manner of his death was a reproach to the fanctity of the Moflems. As at the hour of prayer, with the primitive fimplicity of the Arabs, he repaired alone to the mofch of Cordova, he was attacked and murdered by the confpirators. His death was heard with indifference by the Goths and Saracens; his head was tranfmitted to the Caliph; and by a refinement in cruelty was prefented to the father with the infulting queftion, whether he acknowledged the features of the rebel? " I know his features,"

he exclaimed with indignation. "I affert his in-
"nocence; and I imprecate the fame, a jufter fate
"againſt the authors of his death." But the age
and defpair of Mufa raifed him above the power
of kings, and he expired at Mecca of the anguiſh
of a broken heart.

On the affaffination of Abdelaziz, Ayub, the
moſt guilty or the moſt zealous of the confpirators, affumed the adminiſtration of Spain; he
was foon removed by the fuperior favour or merit
of Alahor; and the new lieutenant of the Caliph,
after feverely chaſtiſing the rapacity, prepared to
exercife the valour of the Moſlems, by leading an
army of the faithful acrofs the Pyrenees. The
diffenfions of the Franks and the weaknefs of the
Vifigoths facilitated the enterprife; the remnant
of the Gothic monarchy beyond thofe mountains
was overwhelmed by the torrent of the Saracens.
The ſtandards of Mahomet were difplayed along the
gulf of Lyons beyond the ſtream of the Garonne;
the cities of Carcaffone, Narbonne, Beziers, and
Nifmes, opened their gates or were carried by
affault. But the invaders feem to have been impelled by the thirſt of glory and of fpoil; and fa-
tiate with flaughter and plunder, they abandoned
their conqueſts, and repaffed the Pyrenees. Yet
the poffeffion of Spain often tempted the Saracens
to afpire to the total conqueſt of the Weſt; their
defeat under the walls of Thouloufe, inflamed in-
ſtead

stead of chilling their ardour; the south of France was blasted by their presence; and under Abderame, one of the successors of Alahor, they pitched their camp in the fruitful plains between Poitiers and Tours. They had been suffered to advance, they neither wished, nor would have been permitted to retreat. The warriors of the West were united under the command of Charles, the illegitimate son of Pepin; who, with the title of mayor, governed France with absolute power under the sanction of the Merovingian name. The banks of the Loire was the theatre of a conflict as memorable for its consequences, as for the number and renown of the combatants. During the six first days of desultory action, the horsemen and archers of the East maintained their wonted superiority; but on the seventh the host of the Saracens was in a close engagement broken by the robust stature and nervous courage of their adversaries. On that immortal day, the weighty strokes of Charles first acquired him the surname of *Martel*, the Hammer; the bloody field was strewed by Abderame himself, and, if we credit the Monkish writers, three hundred and seventy-five thousand Mahometans. But though this number is doubtless exaggerated, the victory was complete. The chiefs of the Saracens, amidst the terror of the night, provided each for his separate safety; a second irruption into Provence served only

only to expose them to a second defeat; and they were instructed by experience to restrain their ardour within the limits of the Pyrenees, and to guard, instead of passing, the strong posts of those mountains.

A province is assimilated to the victorious state by the introduction of strangers, and the imitative spirit of the natives; and Spain, which had been successively tinctured with Punic, with Roman, and with Gothic blood, imbibed, in a few generations, the name and manners of the Arabs. The first conquerors, and the twenty successive lieutenants of the Caliphs, were attended by a numerous train of civil and military followers, who preferred a distant fortune to a narrow home. The private and public interest was promoted by the establishment of faithful colonies; and the cities of Spain were proud to commemorate the tribe or country of their Eastern progenitors. The victorious though motley bands of Tarik and Musa asserted, by the name of Spaniards, their original claim of conquest; yet they allowed their brethren of Egypt to share their establishments of Murcia and Lisbon. The royal legion of Damascus was planted at Cordova; that of Emesa at Seville; that of Chalcis at Jaen; that of Palestine at Algezire and Medina Sidonia. The natives of Arabia Felix and Persia were scattered round Toledo, and the inland country; and the

fertile

fertile feats of Grenada were beftowed on ten thoufand horfemen of Syria and Irak, the children of the pureft and moft noble of the Arabian tribes.

A fpirit of emulation, fometimes beneficial, more frequently dangerous, was nourifhed by thefe hereditary factions. The patient and fubmiffive fpirit of the Moflems which has been fo well delineated in the example of Tarik, had evaporated in the gradual acquifition of wealth and influence. The rival houfes of Ommijah, and of Abbas the uncle of Mahomet, convulfed the Eaft by their pretenfions from the Indus to the Euphrates. On the banks of the Zeb the important conteft was decided; Mervan the fourteenth, and laft caliph of the houfe of Ommijah, animated his army by his prefence and his example; but he was forced to yield to the enthufiafm of the Abbaffides, conducted by Abdallah, the uncle of his competitor. The vanquifhed Caliph croffed the Euphrates; and, without halting in Paleftine, pitched his laft camp on the banks of the Nile; he was purfued and attacked by Abdallah; and the lance of an Abbaffide terminated the reign and life of Mervan.

At a diftance from the fcene of action, and fecured by feas and mountains, the Moflems of Spain had liftened to the revolution which had agitated the Eaft. Their zeal foon involved them in the consequences of it. In the proscription of the Ommiades a royal youth of the name of Abdalrahman alone escaped from the rage of his enemies, and gained the shelter of the vallies of mount Altas. His presence in the neighbourhood of Spain revived through that peninsula the hopes of the party who had deplored the ruin of his house. They invited and received him on the coast of Andalusia with open arms. The white standard, the distinction of his faction, was unfurled; and the chiefs who reverenced the memory of the immediate successors of Mahomet, drew their sabres in his support. The defeat of the Zeb was avenged on the banks of the Guadalquivir; that river was swelled with the bodies of the slaughtered Abbassides; and the throne of the victorious Abdalrahman was established at Cordova.

A. D. 755, 912. It was then arose the age of Arabian gallantry and magnificence, which exalted the Moors of Spain above their contemporaries, and rendered Cordova the seat of the rival arts, and arms. Near thirty years the reign of Abdalrahman was prolonged amidst the acclamations of his people; and an hero who was indebted for the sceptre to his sword, as a sovereign encouraged and extended the mild influence of agriculture and commerce. He had solicited against the fleet and army of the caliph Almansor,

the

the aid of the Christians; and after victory, in his edict of pacification, he was not forgetful of their assistance; the modest imposition of ten thousand ounces of gold, ten thousand pounds of silver, ten thousand horses, as many mules, one thousand cuirasses, with an equal number of helmets and lances, rather asserted his sovereignty, than marked the ability of his subjects. The country, from a scene of desolation, rapidly assumed under his impartial government the features of wealth and prosperity. Cordova became the centre of industry, of politeness, and of genius. The bold and noble strove in tilts and tournaments; the prize of address and valour was disputed in the capital of the Ommiades by the most illustrious knights from every part of Europe; and Spain was the only kingdom of the West where the influence of music was felt, and the studies of geometry, astronomy, and physic, were promoted and regularly practised.

Hassam the son and successor of Abdalrahman, was not inferior to his father in his thirst of glory and his passion for architecture. He applied the plunder of the southern provinces of France to the holy purpose of completing the mosch which had been begun by his predecessor. He was not only a patron of, but a proficient in the arts; and the bridge which he planned, and threw over the

the Guadalquivir, remains a lasting monument of his skill.

Beneath the second Abdalrahman, new structures supplied the wants of the citizens, and augmented the magnificence of Cordova; a perpetual supply of pure water was conducted through pipes and aqueducts into the heart of the city; and the erections of numerous moschs admonished the inhabitants where their gratitude was due for the prosperity they enjoyed. The protection of learning and the learned illustrates the reign of Alkaham the second. The university of Cordova was founded and endowed by his munificence. The birth-place of the Senecas and the Lucans asserted again its pretensions to literary fame; and might boast a library of six hundred thousand volumes, forty-four of which were employed in the mere catalogue.

A. D. 912. 961. Yet these may be considered as faint and imperfect sketches of the wealth, the power, and the magnificence of the caliphs of Spain; and the pomp and profusion of the third Abdalrahman, who reigned about a century and a half after his house was first established at Cordova, must have excited the wonder and envy of his contemporaries, and has almost surpassed the belief of posterity. His seraglio, with his wives, his concubines, and black eunuchs, amounted to six thousand three hundred persons;

and

and he was attended to the field by a guard of twelve thousand horse, whose belts and scimitars were studded with gold. The presents that were laid at his feet by his favourite Aboumalik, when preferred to the post of grand vizir, consisted of four hundred pounds of virgin gold, ingots of silver to the value of four hundred and twenty thousand sequins, five hundred ounces of ambergris, three hundred ounces of camphire, thirty pieces of gold tissue, so rich as to be worn alone by a Caliph, ten suits of khorasan sables, and one hundred suits of less valuable fur; forty-eight sets of gold and silk trappings for horses, four thousands pounds of silk, fifteen coursers of the purest breed of Arabia, and caparisoned worthy of the master that was to mount them; a promiscuous heap of Persian carpets and coats of mail, of aloes, of shields, and lances; and the long and splendid procession was closed by forty youths, and twenty girls of exquisite beauty, whose collars and bracelets sparkled with gems of inestimable value. Yet to Abdalrahman the most precious gift of his minister was the poem which celebrated, and perhaps justly, his virtues; he listened with attention; claimed at least the praise of liberality; and rewarded the merit or artful flattery of the bard with a pension of one hundred thousand pieces of gold, or upwards of forty thousand pounds sterling.

The

The monarch who could thus acknowledge the influence of verse, was not likely to be insensible to the power of beauty; and Abdalrahman it must be confessed, loved at least with magnificence. Three miles from Cordova, the city, the palace, and the gardens of Zehra, or Arizapha, were constructed in honour of, and designed to perpetuate the name of his favourite sultana. The most celebrated architect of Constantinople was invited to draw the plan; the most skilful sculptors and artists of the age were attracted by the munificence of the Caliph to execute it. The edifice was supported by near twelve hundred columns of Spanish and African, of Italian and Greek marble; the latter were the pledges of alliance and friendship from the emperor of Constantinople. The richness of the hall of audience exceeded the bounds of credibility. The walls were incrusted with gold and pearls; in the centre was a bason with curious and costly figures of birds and quadrupeds; above it hung a pearl of inestimable price, the tribute of the fears or gratitude of the emperor Leo. Twenty-five years, and above three millions sterling, were consumed in constructing and adorning the favourite residence. Within, and sequestered from view, were the apartments of the envied females who shared, or were reserved for the embraces of Abdalrahman. The charms of Zehra shone above the

name-

nameless multitude, and might defy the eye of malignant criticism; over the principal entrance to the palace, her statue extorted the admiration of the crowd; yet while the enraptured Moslems gazed with ardour on the symmetry of her form, their piety was wounded by the boldness of their sovereign, whose amorous passion had presumed to violate the express mandate of the prophet, which provided against the danger of idolatry by the interdiction of images. Their murmurs probably never reached the ears of Abdalrahman, who when satiated with the delights of love, or fatigued with the toils of the chace, reposed in a lofty pavilion, situated in the midst of a garden, which was adorned with a fountain replenished, not with water, but with the purest quicksilver.

In our imperfect estimation of the lot of human life, there are few who would not willingly accept the cares, with the comforts of royalty. Yet the name of Abdalrahman may be added to the list of those who from the time of Solomon to the present age, have complained that the possession of a throne could never afford any lasting satisfaction. An authentic memorial, which ought to temper the ardour of ambition, was found in the closet of the Caliph after his decease; was transcribed, and carefully preserved, as an instructive lesson to posterity. "I have now " reigned above fifty years in victory or peace;
" beloved

" beloved by my subjects, dreaded by my ene-
" mies, and respected by my allies. Riches and
" honours, power and pleasure, have waited on
" my call, nor does any earthly blessing appear
" to have been wanting to my felicity; in this
" situation I have diligently numbered the days
" of pure and genuine happiness which have
" fallen to my lot: they amount to *fourteen*: O
" man! place not thy confidence in this present
" world." The admonition was probably read,
admired, and neglected; the successors of Mahomet seem to have forgotten the spiritual rewards that had been promised by the prophet; they disdained the abstinence and frugality of the first Caliphs, and aspired to emulate the magnificence, and condescended to indulge in the luxury of the Persian kings.

The vanity of regal splendour may exercise the fancy of the moralist, the means which supply it are the objects of the historian's enquiry. Besides the structures of private pleasure and public utility, a formidable army and regular naval establishment awed the enemies and secured the prosperity of the faithful. The master of the richest provinces of Spain reaped the harvest of a wise and equitable administration. The royal city of Cordova contained six hundred moschs, nine hundred baths, and two hundred thousand houses; eighty large cities, and three hundred of

the

the second order confessed the authority of the Caliph; the banks of the Bœtis, which under the Moors assumed the name of Guadalquivir, were embellished by twelve thousand villages; every hour presented to the traveller a new hamlet; and in the course of a day's journey he might number three or four considerable towns; these were inhabited by an industrious race occupied in agriculture and manufactures. The soil which was ungrateful to the plough teemed with the most valuable minerals; copper, quicksilver, and iron, were exported from the ports of Spain to Barbary, Egypt, and the East. Ambergris, sulphur, saffron, ginger, and myrrh, were classed among her natural productions; the coast of Andalusia was celebrated for coral, and that of Catalonia for pearls; the rubies of Malaga and Bajar, and the amethysts of Carthagena were highly esteemed; the admirable temper of the Spanish steel recommended it to a warlike age; and the Moslems of Africa eagerly purchased their cuirasses, their helmets, and their scimetars from their brethren of Spain. The silk manufactures of Grenada, and the woollen cloths of Murcia, were sought after with avidity, and were sold at an immense profit in the ports of Alexandria and Constantinople. The policy of the Ommiades was displayed in an amicable intercourse with the Byzantine court, which they regarded as their strongest

strongest barrier against the enmity of their rivals the Abbassides, and as the most ready market for the industry of their subjects. All the havens of the Grecian dominions were open to the Spanish traders, who imported rich cargoes of merchandize adapted to the capital of opulence and luxury, and in the advantageous commerce attracted to Spain the treasures which had been accumulated by a long series of conquest. But it is probable that the chief source of the wealth of Abdalrahman was derived from the mines of gold and silver with which the country abounded; the value of these it is impossible to appreciate; but the tribute which he exacted from his people has been preserved by an Arabian historian, and amounted annually, exclusive of the imposts which were paid in kind, to twelve million nine hundred and forty-five thousand dinars, or near six millions sterling; a sum which, in the tenth century, most probably surpassed the united revenues of the Christian monarchs; and when the difference of the value of silver between that age and the present is computed, certainly exceeds in a six-fold proportion the revenue of modern Spain; though the neglect of her mines in Europe may have been replaced by the produce of those of America.

In the full possession of wealth and power Abdalrahman had been disappointed of happiness; but

but he might indulge a natural hope that his magnificence would be perpetuated in the splendour of his edifices; and that a throne which was protected by powerful armies, and opulent provinces, might long be filled by his descendents; yet the glories of Zehra have crumbled into a duft; not a trace remains to mark the spot where stood the palace erected with such a waste of treasure; and in less than fifty years from his decease, the kingdom of Cordova was diffolved, and the house of Ommijah overwhelmed.

The name of his son and successor Alkaham the second, is still dear to learning; in the luxury of building he resembled and rivalled his father; and his foundation of the university of Cordova, and the immense library he collected, are honourable proofs of his taste and liberality; but he was not only known by the works of art; and in the exercife of virtue, and the diftribution of juftice, he fought, and acquired the efteem of his people. A fimple ftory attefts his character open to reproof, and paints beyond laboured pages the manners of the times. A poor woman at Zehra poffeffed a fmall fpot of ground contiguous to the royal palace; the Caliph, defirous of extending his gardens, had in vain tempted her to part with the land for a fum of money; a regard for the patrimony which had

A. D. 961, 976.

been

been rendered sacred by the birth of her ancestors, induced her to reject every proposal; and the head gardener abused the authority of his master, and seized by force what she refused to yield for gain. The woman in an agony of despair flew to Cordova to implore the protection of Ibu Bekir, the chief cadi of the city. This magistrate immediately mounted on his ass, taking with him a sack of an extraordinary size, and presented himself before Alkaham, who was then sitting in a magnificent pavilion on the very ground in question; the arrival of the cadi, and the appearance of the wallet, surprised the prince; Bekir having prostrated himself, intreated Alkaham to allow him to fill his sack with some of the earth they were then upon. This request granted, and the sack filled, the cadi desired him to help him to lift it upon his ass. The last demand appeared still more extraordinary than the preceding; the Caliph however consented; but upon putting his shoulder to it, could not help complaining of the excessive weight of the load. "Sir," replied the
" cadi, this sack, which you find so heavy, con-
" tains but a small portion of the earth which
" you have unjustly taken from a poor woman;
" how then do you expect to be able at the day
" of judgment to support the weight of the
" whole field you have had so little scruple in
" usurping." Far from being incensed at the bold
rebuke

rebuke, the Caliph generoully acknowledged his fault, and ordered the land to be reftored to the proprietor with every thing he had caufed to be erected upon it; and the tale is an inconteftable evidence, that though the generality of the conquerors of Spain had felt the influence of a luxurious and degenerate age, fome ftill cherifhed the fimple virtues of the primitive Moflems.

A feeble infant of the name of Haffem was the fon and fucceffor of Alkaham; but the reins of adminiftration were intrufted to the hand of the celebrated vizir Mahomet Abenamir, who from his valour and vigilance deferved and acquired the furname of *Almanzor*, or the *Defender*. He fuccefsfully ftruggled againft the tempeft of civil and foreign commotion; and fix campaigns that he fucceffively took the field, he returned crowned with victory and covered with glory; the character of *invincible*, was wrefted from him in an obftinate and bloody conflict with the Chriftians; and from a doubtful or difaftrous field he retired to Medina Cœli; his haughty fpirit allowed him not to brook difgrace; the deftruction of one hundred thoufand of the faithful was imbittered by the reflection that they fell by the fwords of the enemies of their religion; Almanzor deplored or envied their fate, and afhamed to furvive, or impatient

A. D. 976.
1492.

patient to join them in paradise, he plunged a dagger in his bosom.

The renown of Almanzor was respected in his descendants; the office of vizir became hereditary in his family; and his sons ruled with power as absolute as that of the Caliphs; but their usurpation urged the ambition of other chiefs and emirs; the exclusive pretensions of the house of Ommijah were no longer regarded; and we may discern through the gloom of history, that the grandson of the great Abdalrahman was plunged into a dungeon by his rebellious Moslem subjects, and was released and restored to his throne by a Christian ally; the victorious Saracens in little more than two centuries run the same career as the Visigoths they had vanquished; they abused their prosperity; abandoned themselves to luxury; and exhausted in domestic dissensions that strength which might have enabled them to have resisted or to have overwhelmed the common enemy. Their ancient glory was overshadowed by a long night of darkness; the limits of their dominions gradually receded; and were at length confined within the boundaries of Grenada. On that ground the Moors however still displayed the traces of that warlike spirit which had shone conspicuous in the field of Xeres; and according to the Spanish historians, near eight centuries of almost uninterrupted war elapsed, and three thousand fand feven hundred battles were fought, before the laſt of the Mooriſh kingdoms in Spain ſubmitted to the Chriſtian arms.

Chapter the Fifth.

The Goths maintain their independence in the Asturian mountains.—Reign and achievements of Pelagius.—Death of his son and successor Favilla.—Election of Alfonso, surnamed the Catholic.—Reign of Froila.—He regulates the Catholic church.—His victories over Abdalrahman.—His severity.—His assassination.—Succession of Aurelio, and Silo.—Usurpation of Mauregato.—Election of Bermudo.—He resigns the crown to Alfonso, the Chaste.—Glorious administration of Alfonso.—He is succeeded by his son Ramiro.—Reign of Ordogno.—Of Alfonso, surnamed the Great.—Of Garcias.—Of Ordogno the second.—Of Froila the second.—Of Alfonso the fourth.—Of Ramiro.—He wrests the city of Toledo from the Moslems.—Administration of Abdalrahman the third.—Prudence of Ramiro.—His victory over the Moors.—He is succeeded by his son Ordogno the third.—Reign of Sancho.—He is deposed.—Accession of Ordogno the fourth.—Restoration of Sancho.—He is poisoned.—Election of Ramiro the third.—Of Bermudo the second.—Of Alfonso the fifth.—Of Bermudo the third.—His death unites

in

in his brother-in-law Ferdinand the crowns of Leon and Castille.

IN our admiration of the rapid victo- A. D. 718, ries of the Mahometans, the scanty 737. remnant of Christians who still rejected their yoke are almost lost to our sight; after the disastrous field of Xeres, and the reduction of Seville and Merida, an illustrious band of fugitives cherished the flame of liberty in the Asturian vallies. In a life of poverty and freedom their former virtues revived; their nerves were braced by the keen air of independence; in many a bloody encounter they asserted against the fanatics of Arabia their descent from the hardy warriors of the North; and in the severe school of adversity they courted and deserved the return of prosperity.

Amidst their trackless retreats the Christian Spaniards preserved with care and affection their ancient laws and customs; the noble birth, distinguished courage, and acknowledged ability of Pelagius recommended him as their leader; yet it was not until six years after the defeat of Xeres that in a national assembly of his countrymen he received the title of king; the narrow territory that he was elected to reign over was confined within the district of Liebana, and extended about nine leagues in length, and about four in breadth; but it was broken by steep and frequent mountains; and was inhabited by an undaunted race, who might justly aspire to conquer, since they feared not to die.

Descending from their craggy abodes, these iron mountainiers presumed again to try their valour in the open country; their bold incursions were planned with judgment and executed with success; and their election of Pelagius awakened the Moors from the illusion, that all resistance to their dominion in Spain was extinguished. Across the Pyrenees, amidst his career of victory, the exultation of Alahor was checked by the intelligence of their achievements; at his command, an army of the faithful was drawn from the garrisons of Seville, Toledo, and Merida; they were joined by a select detachment from the Arabian forces in Gaul; and under the command of the valiant Alahaman, and the treacherous Oppas, they directed their march to the Asturian mountains to trample out the last spark of liberty.

At the head of his brave associates, fortified by the love of freedom and the contempt of death, Pelagius heard without dismay the approach of the numerous host of the invaders; he suffered them to traverse the rough and lofty mountains of Auseba, and to descend into the valley beneath.
But

But with the eye of a general he marked that narrow spot for the scene of his own glory and their destruction. While they triumphed in the full assurance of success, they were suddenly assailed from the neighbouring heights with stones, with arrows, and with javelins. Their numbers only served to increase their confusion, and to swell the tide of slaughter; they were incapable of avoiding the ponderous fragments of rocks which were precipitated from above on their heads; an ambuscade of Christians started from the hollow caverns of the mountains; and their swords completed the bloody labour which had been begun by the missile weapons of their brethren. Oppas in chains was reserved to meet the just reward of his perfidy; Alahaman fought and obtained a soldier's death; the vale is said to have been heaped with the bodies of one hundred thousand Moslems; and though we may distrust the number, we may safely assert that where religion and revenge combined to edge the sword of the victors, the slaughter was urged with cruel diligence and without mercy. The remnant that escaped from battle traversed with fearful steps the mountain Auseba, and on the banks of the Deva halted from the pursuit of the conquerors, and hoped they had reached the term of their misfortunes; but a less glorious fate impended over them; as they attempted to pass the stream of the Deva, a neighbouring mountain was overthrown by an earthquake; the river was agitated by the concuſſion and ſwelled by the maſſy fragments; the greateſt part of the fugitive Moſlems were overwhelmed in its waters; the convulſion of nature in a ſuperſtitious age was attributed to the preternatural interference of providence; and the courage of the pious Chriſtians was confirmed by the belief that heaven warred on their ſide.

One defeat had not effaced in the minds of the Moſlems a long ſeries of victory and plunder; on the intelligence of the national calamity, Mumuza the Mooriſh governor of Gijon marched forth with his garriſon to check the pride and chaſtiſe the temerity of the Chriſtians. In the valley of Olalles, about three leagues below the modern city of Oviedo, his preſumption was reproved by the martial followers of Pelagius. Two thirds of the Moors periſhed in the action or purſuit; the ſtrong town of Gijon capitulated or was reduced by force; vanquiſhed in two trials, the Moors tacitly relinquiſhed for ſome time the unprofitable conteſt. More intent on ſpoil than on propagating the faith of their prophet, they turned from a wild and barren country overſhadowed with woods and mountains, defended by a fearleſs race, whoſe ſwords and freedom were almoſt their ſole poſſeſſions, to breathe the genial climate, and to revel in the plenty of the ſouthern

southern provinces of Gaul; their succefs acrofs the Pyrenees was productive of a double advantage to the independent Spaniards; it allowed them a fhort repofe from war to eftablifh order in their new government; and in the abufe of profperity and the indulgence of luxury, it relaxed the nerves and gradually foftened the ferocious fpirit of their enemies.

Nineteen years Pelagius fwayed with fuccefs the fceptre he had formed; and a territory above forty leagues in length acknowledged his authority; in that fpace he exercifed the virtues which had raifed him to fovereignty; his fubjects were taught to revere his juftice, and his neighbours to refpect his valour; his end is involved in obfcurity; but it is more than probable amidft a turbulent and fanguinary age, a peaceful death was the reward of his merits.

The gratitude of Spain, and of Chriftianity, have embalmed the memory of Pelagius, and elevated to the vacant throne his fon Favilla; two years of royalty were not fufficient to difplay the ambiguous character of Favilla; and he is varioufly reprefented by the Spanifh hiftorians as indolent and luxurious, as active and enterprifing; his fubjects foon deplored or exulted in his premature fate; and as he eagerly purfued the chace in the mountains of Afturia, he was thrown to the ground, and mortally wounded

A. D. 737, 739.

wounded by a bear before his attendants could interpose in his defence.

A. D. 739, 758. His brother-in-law Alfonso was by the suffrages of a free people called to the succession; the surname of the *Catholic* was the tribute to his zeal for religion; and the esteem of his subjects was the reward of his valour and wisdom. New churches arose on the ruins of the moschs of the infidels, and new boundaries were prescribed to the ambition or usurpation of the Saracens. The Moslems, exhausted by domestic factions and the rival pretensions of the houses of Ommijah and Abbas, were inattentive to, or incapable of opposing his progress. He penetrated into Gallicia; reduced Lugo, which had beheld the glory and disgrace of Musa; and turning to the north, pitched his camp in the plains of Leon and Castille; the gates of Astorga, Saldagna, and Victoria, were burst open by his arms, or were unbarred by the secret inclinations of the inhabitants; he presented himself on the borders of the modern kingdom of Portugal, and he pursued his victorious march through *old* Castille to the range of mountains which divides it from the *new*. Yet his enterprises, though conducted with vigour, were tempered with prudence; at the conclusion of each campaign he retired within the craggy district of Asturia; his retreat was marked by devastation; he prudently interposed

posed a wide and desert frontier between his narrow territories and the populous dominion of the Moors; but the fame of his exploits and the liberal distribution of his spoil, attracted from every quarter of Spain a crowd of bold or hungry Christians, who had long borne with indignation the yoke of the Mahometans; the latter were exhausted by famine and civil commotion; yet it was not until the evening of his reign that Alfonso ventured to quit his native fastnesses, and to rebuild the walls of, and to occupy the cities of Leon and Astorga.

His son Froila succeeded to his crown and his abilities in war, but he possessed not his generosity and magnanimity in peace. His disposition was stern and sanguinary; and he commanded the obedience, without deigning to conciliate the affections of his subjects. His first reform has been applauded by the writers of a monkish age; the clergy had availed themselves of the general distraction after the death of Roderic, to gratify the impulse of nature, and several had contracted themselves in marriage with the objects of their honourable passion; but the laity, who had regarded with indifference their promiscuous amours, were scandalized in their violation of the canons of the church by the forms of a legal union. The austerity of the sovereign happily accorded with the wishes of his subjects;

A. D. 758, 768.

subjects; the authority of the Catholic church was vindicated by Froila; and throughout Spain, its ministers were confined to celibacy without being restored to chastity.

The victory of Abdalrahman on the banks of the Guadalquivir had established in Spain the house of the Ommiades; and a prince who had triumphed over the kindred valour of the Moslems, endured not without indignation the hostile progress of the Christians; the expectation of spoil, and the promise of paradise, assembled between the Duero and Tagus a numerous host of the Saracens; they passed the confines of Portugal, and the name of Pontumo marks the spot in Gallicia where they descried the ensigns of the Christians. The inferiority of numbers was supplied by the skill and valiant example of Froila; fifty-four thousand Moslems were extended lifeless on the field; their general was amongst the slain; the moment of success was improved by the address of Froila; and the city of Oviedo, which he destined for his new capital, was, with the spoils of the vanquished, erected at a small distance from Gijon, on the banks of the Aste, which is formed from the confluence of the waters of the Ova and Deva.

A second attempt of Abdalrahman to retrieve his honour, served only to augment his disgrace; another army of the Moslems was lost in the mountainous

HISTORY OF SPAIN.

mountainous districts of old Castille; and the Caliph in an honourable truce confessed his dread of his Christian adversary. But Froila was not less the terror of his enemies than of his subjects. In the last invasion of Abdalrahman, the natives of Gallicia had neglected or refused to join the standard of their sovereign; and no sooner had he concluded peace with the Saracens, than at the head of an obedient army he entered Gallicia, and by the execution of the most illustrious or most rebellious of the inhabitants, taught them to dread the resentment of an offended monarch. The neighbouring provinces beheld with dismay and discontent the tremendous example; the guilt and danger of disobedience were forgotten in the excess of the punishment; and Froila, who had never possessed the love, was now exposed to the hatred of his people; his mind was probably irritated by the ingratitude of the multitude and consciousness of his services; and his brother, except himself the only legitimate son of Alfonso, was the victim of his jealousy. Bimarano inherited, or was supposed to inherit, the popular qualities of his father; the esteem of his countrymen was the signal for his death; and in a perfidious conference he was stabbed by the hand of Froila. The safety of the tyrant, for such is the name that he hereafter deserves, was undermined by his own crime; his nobles repressed their abhorrence of his unnatural deed; and patiently

tiently waited for the moment of retaliation. The dagger of an affaffin was whetted againft the life of Froila; and he fell without being lamented by the people whom he had defended.

A.D. 768, 770. The feeble claims of an infant fon, the only fruits of the marriage of Froila with his beautiful captive Monina, were loft in the deteftation of the father, or were deferred from the debility of his years; and Alfonfo, who afterwards arofe the father and the glory of his country, was fet afide for Aurelio, the coufin of, and probably one of the confpirators againft the late king; a confederacy of the Moorifh flaves to avenge their fufferings in the blood of their Chriftian mafters, but which was early detected and quelled, marks alone the reign of Aurelio; his brother Bermudo had entered into the pale of the church, and feemed precluded from the cares and comforts of royalty; and Aurelio, deftitute of offspring, fought a fucceffor amongft the moft illuftrious nobles of his court. The addrefs or virtues of Silo fecured him the preference; he received the hand of Adofinda, the kinfwoman of his fovereign; was intrufted with a confiderable fhare in the adminiftration; and on the death of Aurelio, was declared his fucceffor by the fuffrages of the nobility and with the approbation of the people.

A.D. 774, 783. The judgment of Aurelio was approved in the meafures of Silo; during a reign a reign of nine years an obscure rebellion in Gallicia alone interrupted the public tranquillity. The new monarch promoted with ability the happiness of his people, and watched with honourable care over the education of the youthful Alfonso. On his death that prince was, with the consent of several of the nobility, and under the protection of the dowager queen Adosinda, declared king; but the sceptre was ravished from his hand by a mature and unexpected competitor.

The piety of Alfonso the Catholic, had not fortified him against the frailty of human nature; a Moorish captive had shared his embraces; and the issue of their illicit intercourse had obtained from the mother the name of Mauregato. In the humble condition of a subject, he remembered the rank of his father; and his ambition suggested to him the means of ascending to the same station. He was not ignorant of the secret dread lest Alfonso should inherit the austerity of Froila; he improved the fears of the multitude by dark and subtle rumours; and at length openly assumed the crown. It is probable Alfonso in a field of battle might have substantiated his previous election; but a civil war might have proved fatal to the infant strength of the Christians; and the son of Froila proved himself worthy of a throne by refusing to hazard his country's welfare in the defence of it. He retired to his patrimonial

A. D. 783, 788.

trimonial estate in Biscay; that popularity which had been denied him in the palace, accompanied him to his retreat; and whatever might be the secret wishes of Mauregato, he engaged to respect, and he feared to violate the safety of his magnanimous rival; but he disgraced by weakness the crown he had obtained by perfidy; to support his title he introduced into his dominions the enemies of his country and his religion; an army of Moors awed the rising discontents of his subjects; but while they protected him from the indignation of the Christians, they held him in dependence on the will of the Moslems. The invidious tale of his furnishing to the seraglio of the Caliph the annual tribute of an hundred virgins, has been rejected by the most impartial critics; yet it is certain he was exposed both to the suspicion and hatred of his people; and his death, after an unpopular reign of six years, was considered as a national deliverance.

A. D. 788, 791. On his decease, it might naturally have been expected that the former forbearance of Alfonso would have united in his favour the voice of the nation; yet we read with surprise, that Bermudo the brother of Aurelio was drawn from the cloister to exchange his cowl for a crown. The election of Bermudo cannot be suspected of intrigue; and the goodness of his heart was evinced in the first measure of his reign;
he

he fent for Alfonfo, introduced him into his councils, and as foon as the public prejudice was fubfided, intrufted him with the principal military command. The ambition or fanaticifm of the Moors had again impelled them to invade the Chriftian territories; and Bermudo, accompanied by Alfonfo, marched to oppofe the infidel hoft. Buraba, a fmall town in the neighbourhood of Burgos, was the fcene of their bloody encounter; and the ftream of the river Aranzon was purpled with the blood of the combatants. The Moors were broken and defeated; and amidft the tumult of the day the valour of Alfonfo was confpicuous above that of his countrymen. The generous Bermudo feized the moment of admiration and gratitude; he refigned the crown; and Alfonfo the fecond, who from the purity of his life and manners was furnamed the *Chafte*, was elected in his place.

The grateful affection of Alfonfo fuffered not Bermudo to efcape to retirement; though he had refigned the title, he was ftill regarded by his fucceffor as a king, and lodged with every mark of refpect in the palace. But while Alfonfo divided the honours, he fupported alone the cares of fovereignty. Gallicia was deluged by a fecond inundation of the Moflems, and their deftructive progrefs claimed the prefence of the new monarch. He marched at the

A. D. 791.
845.

the head of the companions of his former victory; and near Lodos attacked the infidels, who by their own temerity or the treachery of their guides, had been betrayed into a morafs. Sixty thoufand of the Moflems were either flaughtered by the Chriftians or loft in the bog. The domeftic diffenfions of the Moors fufpended for a fhort time their hoftile enterprifes; and Alfonfo neglected not to avail himfelf of the favourable opportunity; he repaired the walls, and re-peopled the city of Braga on the banks of the Cavado; he penetrated in arms through the heart of Portugal to the mouth of the Tagus; he reduced the city of Lifbon, whofe ancient name of Olifippo, was in an age of fable fuppofed to have been derived from Ulyffes; and with the fpoil he enriched the new citizens of Braga.

The advantages which Alfonfo had gained in arms, he endeavoured to preferve by negociation; Charlemagne, the potent emperor of the Weft, had during the diffenfions of the Moors, been invited into Spain by a powerful emir of the name of Ibinala, and who appears to have abufed the independent authority he had exercifed over the city of Saragoffa. Driven thence by the general indignation of the inhabitants, in the diet of Paderborn he implored the affiftance of Charlemagne; the influence of the exiled Arabian was re-eftablifhed by the arms of the Chriftian

tian monarch, who carried by affault Pampeluna, traverfed the Ebro, and fuccefsfully invefted the city of Saragoffa. The rebellious followers of Chrift and Mahomet were impartially crufhed by the protector of infulted fovereignty; but in the fidelity of an ally, Charlemagne neglected not his own aggrandifement; he occupied in his own name the countries he penetrated through; and the *march* of Spain which he inftituted, extended from the river Ebro beyond the Pyrenees, and included the country of Rouffillon. Barcelona was the refidence of a French governor, whofe jurifdiction was confeffed through the province of Catalonia, and the kingdoms of Navarre and Arragon. But in his retreat the rear-guard of Charlemagne was expofed to difgrace and lofs; and it is this action which has been fo much celebrated in romance for the death of the famous Roland.

The fituation and religious communion of Charlemagne pointed him out to Alfonfo as his natural ally. In a fplendid embaffy the king of Oviedo fought and obtained the friendfhip of the powerful emperor of the Weft; the Moors dreaded, and were cautious of provoking the refentment of the latter; but they ftill hoped to overwhelm the former. A new hoft of infidels laid wafte the country round Burgos, and purfued their diforderly march through the mountainous diſtrict of Biſcay; as they advanced incumbered with ſpoil, and careleſs of diſcipline, they were attacked and cut to pieces by Alfonſo. So many illuſtrious exploits ought to have rendered the king of Oviedo the idol of his ſubjects; yet it is with aſtoniſhment we find that in the moment of victory he was ſeized, dethroned, and impriſoned, by a formidable faction; the whole tranſaction is involved in obſcurity; but if we may credit the Spaniſh hiſtorians, the army which he led againſt the Moors, was compoſed chiefly of malecontents, who remembered the ſeverity of Froila, and waited to avenge it on his ſon; they betrayed the confidence that had been repoſed in them; ſuddenly ſurrounded his tent, and though they violated the dignity, they reſpected the life, of Alfonſo; the monaſtery of Abalia became his priſon; but his diſgrace was of ſhort duration; the ingratitude he had experienced was reſented by the majority of his people; the name of Theudes is preſerved as the illuſtrious chief who firſt animated the multitude to arms in defence of their injured ſovereign; the rebels were compelled to yield to the torrent of loyalty; and from Abalia Alfonſo was conducted in triumph to Oviedo. By his clemency he extinguiſhed the embers of faction; and the conſpirators who were pardoned by his magnanimity, ever afterwards ſerved him with zeal and fidelity.

In

In three succeffive actions the renown of Alfonso was confirmed, and the superiority of the Christians established over the infidels; but on a throne the son of Froila, was not suffered to taste repose; and the perfidy of a Moorish chief whom he had protected against Abdalrahman the second, and intrusted with the defence of the frontiers of Gallicia, summoned him again to arms; Mahomet, for such was the name of the traitor, to purchase the pardon of the court of Cordova, consented to betray his trust; and Gallicia was suddenly desolated by the Moslems; the aged limbs of Alfonso were once more clothed in steel; and at Lugo the adversaries of his faith and country were taught that years, though they had impaired his strength, had not chilled his ardour; the field was strewed with fifty thousand lifeless infidels; and the head of the perfidious Mahomet was presented to the victor.

The last moments of the reign of Alfonso were gilded by victory; but his infirmities warned him of his approaching end; a disposition naturally serious might, between the cares of royalty and the grave, wish to employ some short interval in pious meditation; the king of Oviedo might be desirous of placing his glory beyond the reach of fortune, or of committing the protection of his subjects to a more vigorous arm. In the choice of a successor he is asserted to have been influenced

enced by the power and splendid reputation of Charlemagne; and it has been supposed that he only yielded to the unwillingness of his subjects to exclude from the throne the house of Pelagius; the idea which has been hastily adopted and adorned by the lively pen of the Abbé Vertot, is effaced by a reference to the dates of the most accurate historians; the emperor of the West had expired near thirty years before the king of Oviedo abdicated the throne; the ties of gratitude and consanguinity more powerfully pleaded for Ramiro the eldest son of Bermudo; the young prince had already signalized his valour in the victory of Lugo; and to his hand, with the approbation of his people, Alfonso resigned the sceptre of Oviedo. Fifty years of foreign war and domestic commotion were succeeded by four of private tranquillity; divested of the authority, he still displayed the magnificence of a monarch; the numerous churches he erected were the monuments of his piety; and in the seventy-eighth year of his age, he breathed his last amidst the lamentations of his subjects.

A. D. 845. 851. His death exposed his kingdom again to the storms of civil discord; the absence of Ramiro on the frontiers of Navarre, encouraged the presumption of Nepotian, whose birth or situation is marked by the title of count; at the head of a powerful army he advanced

vanced towards Bifcay, and compelled the new monarch to vindicate his title in arms; but before the encounter, the minds of the followers of Nepotian were vanquifhed by fear or remorfe; they delivered their leader in chains to their king; his life was fpared; but he was deprived of his eye-fight, and he was confined ever after within the walls of a monaftery.

The adminiftration of Ramiro was fhort, ftormy, but glorious; a fecond rebel, whofe rank of count of the palace reveals his ingratitude, fucceeded to the hopes, and fhared the fate of Nepotian. A daring race of adventurers defcending from the fnowy mountains of Norway, explored every fhore that promifed fpoil or fettlement; their veffels were moored in the haven of Corunna; and their predatory incurfions commanded the prefence of the king himfelf; the northern pirates were routed with confiderable flaughter; part of their fleet was deftroyed; and for fome time the kindred fquadrons of Norway fhunned the inaufpicious coaft. The fecond Abdalrahman proved a more formidable adverfary; and in Afturia the number of Moflems who at his command overfhadowed the land, were compared to a cloud of locufts. Yet the long array was broken by the martial Chriftians; and the valour of Ordogno the fon of Ramiro, proved him worthy of the crown of Oviedo; in a fecond invafion invasion Abdalrahman might deplore the degeneracy of the Moslems, or the rising virtue of the Christians; and the plains of Clavigo were fertilized with the blood of the infidels. It was on this occasion that St. James, the patron of Spain, mounted on a milk-white steed, was supposed to have animated by his presence the warriors of Christ; his assistance was repaid by the endowment of the church of Compostella; and long after the Spaniards complained that the yoke of the infidels could not have been more heavy than the tribute of gratitude which had been imposed in the name of the saint.

A. D. 851.
862.

After a turbulent reign of six years, Ramiro was dismissed to the grave; and the sceptre of Oviedo dropped into the hands of his son Ordogno, who from the victory over the Moors, had been associated with his father in the toils of government. Yet the first moments of accession were disturbed by the revolt of the natives of Biscay; and he had scarce quelled by his vigour the insurgents, before he was informed that the forces of the Caliph had penetrated into the heart of his dominions. His march was conduct with secrecy and celerity; and before the infidels had intelligence of his approach, they were astonished by his presence in their camp; the remnant that escaped the sword, consulted their safety in a precipitate retreat; their intestine

tine diffenfions fufpended for fome time their hoftile incurfions; and the rage of the contending factions was fomented by the policy of Ordogno, who beheld and rejoiced in their mutual deftruction.

The profperity of his people was the beft reward of his addrefs; yet Ordogno was not exempted from the murmurs of his fubjects; the bifhop of Compoftella had been accufed of a crime as degrading to nature, as offenfive to religion; in the manly abhorrence of Ordogno, he forgot that the accufers of the prelate were his flaves, who might be influenced by private refentment; he commanded the bifhop inftantly to be expofed in the circus to a wild bull; but the furious beaft inftead of deftroying, gently approached the holy culprit; an event that might be derived from a thoufand caufes, and which probably was the effect of the natural afcendancy of man over the brute creation, was in a fuperftitious age improved into a miracle; the bifhop was however content to elude his danger; and to conceal his fhame, or cherifh his indignation in an hermitage; and he was followed to his cell by the acclamations of the unthinking crowd, whofe reproaches accufed the juftice of their fovereign.

The angry clamours of the multitude at the fentence of Ordogno, may ferve to difplay the fuperftitious veneration of the age for the mini-

fters

sters of the church; but they were soon drowned in the loud applause which was extorted by the martial achievements of the king of Oviedo. The Moors again invaded his dominions, and their temerity was again chastised by the aged arm of the royal warrior. Near Albaga, Muza, who with the title of emir, ruled with independent authority over the district of Saragossa, was defeated with the loss of ten thousand Moslems; his son-in-law was amongst the slain; and Muza himself escaped with difficulty the chains of the victors to expire of his wounds in his capital. The Normans whose incursions had again violated the tranquillity of Gallicia, were repulsed, and compelled to seek shelter in their ships; and the infidels, after a second irruption into Asturia, were obliged to retire with disgrace; a formidable fleet that had been assembled by the Caliph for the conquest of Portugal, was dispersed by tempests, or destroyed by the squadrons of Oviedo. Animated by victory, Ordogno aspired beyond the glory of a defensive war; and he besieged and wrested from the caliph Mahomet the important cities of Salamanca and Coria. The difficulty of preserving any acquisitions beyond the stream of the Duero, probably influenced Ordogno to abandon his new conquests; the walls were dismantled; the Mahometan inhabitants were swept away into slavery; and their spoils enriched the capital of Oviedo.

The

The victorious career of Ordogno was checked by the increasing infirmities of age, and it was the natural desire of the father to transmit to his son the sceptre which he himself had wielded with so much vigour and success. In a national council the wishes of Ordogno were gratified; Alfonso was associated with him in the royal dignity; and soon after, in the full possession of the admiration and esteem of his subjects, the veteran monarch breathed his last.

Alfonso the third, who from his exploits deserved and obtained the surname of *Great*, was in his eighteenth year when he ascended the throne of his father; but the dawn of his future glory was overcast by the clouds of domestic commotion; he had scarce received in his capital the oath of allegiance from his subjects, before he was astonished by the approach of a formidable army, conducted by Froila, who had been intrusted with the government of Gallicia; and whose ambition aspired to the crown. Incapable of resisting the presumptuous rebel, Alfonso quitted Oviedo, and retired into the mountains of Castille; he was accompanied in his retreat by the most illustrious of the nobles, who acknowledged in their attachment to the son, the services and friendship of the father; the success of the usuper had been rapid, but his authority was transient; he was incapable of sustaining with mode-

A. D. 862, 910.

moderation the favour of fortune; and in the abuse of his power, he quickly degenerated into a tyrant. His arrogance offended those who had contributed to his elevation; his cruel jealousy was dreaded by the party who secretly repined at his grandeur; obnoxious to all, he was soon the victim of his temerity; a conspiracy was silently formed against him; and he was assassinated in the palace that he had so lately seized.

The fate of the tyrant was rapidly conveyed to the mountains of Castille; Alfonso quitted his retreat, and entered Oviedo amidst the acclamations of his subjects; even the troops which had promoted the usurpation of Froila, joined in the general joy. A prudent amnesty quieted their fears, but might encourage the presumption of other pretenders; and the revolt of the counts of Alava, claimed the presence of the new monarch in the province of Biscay; the rebels, astonished by his celerity, deprecated his wrath by submission; but no sooner had he pointed again his march towards Oviedo, than they derided and violated their engagements, and again assembled in arms; without hesitation Alfonso turned his face once more towards Alava; the revolt was crushed by his vigour; but the traitors could no longer hope for mercy; and the natural disposition of Alfonso yielded to the claims of justice and the resentment of an injured sovereign.

It

It was on his own subjects that the first trophies of Alfonso were erected; but the more splendid and acceptable monuments of his fame were founded on his victories over the enemies of his faith and country. In the nuptial bed he had scarce tasted the charms of the fair but turbulent Ximené, before he was summoned to the field; and the surname of *Great* was earned in near thirty laborious but prosperous campaigns. Two Mahometan armies which had endeavoured to penetrate into his dominions by the opposite routes of Leon and Gallicia, were successively encountered and defeated; the victor passed in arms the Duero; overthrew, and restored the walls of Coimbra; re-peopled the cities of Braga and Porto; repaired those of Lamego and Viseo, and occupied the district of modern Portugal between the Minho and the Duero. Yet in extending his dominions he was exposed to fierce and frequent conflicts; and it was not until the pride of the king of Cordova had been humbled by repeated defeats, and his son Almundar had been obliged to retreat before a Christian hero, that he consented to subscribe an honourable truce for six years, which confirmed to Alfonso the districts he had conquered.

While Alfonso was feared and admired abroad, his throne was assailed, and his authority resisted at home. Three successive rebellions in Gallicia

Gallicia are diftinguifhed by the names of their leaders, Ano, Hermegild, and Witiza; the motives of revolt are concealed from our view; but the punifhments of the rebels are recorded; the eftate of the firft was confifcated; the fecond atoned with his life for his treafon; and the third was condemned to perpetual imprifonment. Yet clemency and feverity feemed to produce the fame effects; the reign of Alfonfo was deftined to inceffant warfare; and one rebellion was fcarce extinquifhed before another broke out.

In Caftille a fecond Froila afpired to feize the crown of Oviedo; his extraction was probably illuftrious; but the fuppofition of Mariana, that he was a fon of Ordogno, is deftroyed by the evidence of a contemporary hiftorian, who afferts Alfonfo to have been the only iffue of that monarch. His three brothers Nugnez, Odoair, and Veremond, were impelled by affection or feduced by ambition to fhare his hopes and danger; but their counfels were betrayed; and before they could affemble a fufficient army to maintain their pretenfions in the field, they were alarmed by a fummons to appear before their fovereign. Their flight proclaimed their guilt; they were purfued, overtaken, and brought back in chains; and the lofs of their eyes was the confequence of their prefumption.

After an year of darknefs and confinement, the chains of the blind Veremond were unlocked

by

by a friendly hand; and from his dungeon of Oviedo he efcaped to the ftrong city of Aftorga. His flight revived the drooping fpirits of his faction; and the walls of Aftorga were defended againft Alfonfo by a numerous and defperate party; the caufe of Veremond was fupported by the king of Cordova; who ftrove to extend the flames of civil commotion, and retorted on the Chriftians the arts which they had practifed on the Moflems; a Moorifh army marched to the relief of Aftorga; they were joined by the garrifon; and in the plains which are fertilized by the river Ezla, the rebels with their infidel allies hazarded, and were vanquifhed in a decifive engagement; part fell by the fword; part perifhed in the waters of the Ezla; but amidft the tumult of defeat, the life and liberty of Veremond was preferved by the care of his attendants; from the field he was conveyed into the Moorifh dominions; and found an afylum in the policy or generofity of the caliph Abdallah.

A new truce between the Chriftians and Moflems was foon fucceeded by war; and the banks of the Duero, in the neighbourhood of Zamora, were diftinguifhed by the laft victory which Alfonfo achieved as a king. In every foreign or domeftic conteft that monarch had refifted or vanquifhed his enemies; and during a long and tempeftuous reign his labours had been cheered by by the remembrance of former exploits, and the hopes of future fuccefs. But his declining years were expofed to a ftruggle which even conqueft could not reconcile; the magnificence of his buildings and the length of his wars had compelled him to impofe new taxes on his fubjects; and an ungrateful and inconfiderate people murmured at the expences which had contributed to their fplendour and fecurity. Their difcontents were fecretly inflamed by Garcias, the eldeft fon of the king, whofe impatient and rebellious hand grafped at a fceptre, which in a fhort time muft have defcended to him without guilt; the confederacy was fwelled by Ximené, who repined in the arms of an old and infirm hufband. But the unnatural defign of Garcias had not entirely eluded the obfervation of Alfonfo; the prince was feized and ftrictly confined; and Ximené, after having in vain folicited his releafe, prepared to obtain it by force. She was fupported by Nugnez Fernandez, one of the moft powerful nobles of Caftille; and a civil war was kindled throughout the kingdom. The prudence of Alfonfo taught him to prevent or terminate a conteft which muft have been fatal to his houfe, and deftructive to his people; he difdained to reign by force; he abhorred the effufion of Chriftian blood; and in a national council at Oviedo he declared his intention to refign the crown to his fon; more truly great in the moment

of

of his abdication than in the meridian blaze of profperity, he retired from the palace; even the ftubborn fpirit of Garcias was vanquifhed by his generofity; and in the poffeffion of the throne, he difplayed that duty and reverence for his father, while he had defpifed or neglected in the condition of a fubject.

The Moors were foon taught that notwithftanding the abdication of Alfonfo, the fame counfels prevailed at Oviedo. Garcias penetrated into the heart of Caftille, defeated an army of the infidels, and made their general prifoner. In a fecond incurfion the van guard was led by Alfonfo himfelf; and the Chriftians and Mahometans beheld with mutual aftonifhment a fon truft the father whom he had dethroned, and a father ferve the fon by whom he had been betrayed. The country beyond the Duero was fwept by their united arms; the cities of Meda, Corunna, Ofma, and Coca, on the banks of that river rofe from their ruins and were ftrengthened by new fortifications; but the royal veteran was incapable of fuftaining the fatigue of this laft expedition; and on his return within the walls of Zamora, death clofed the long and glorious toils of Alfonfo the Great. *A. D. 910, 913.*

Bold and enterprifing in the field, Garcias was the terror of his enemies; but ftern and inexorable in the capital, he never acquired the affections

tions of his subjects; they applauded his valour, but they dreaded his severity; and his premature death after a short reign' of three years, was received with indifference or exultation.

A. D. 913, 923.
The vacant throne was filled by his brother Ordogno the second, who had administered with independence the province of Gallicia during the life of Garcias. He inherited the active valour of his father; and the town of Talavera, and the castle of Alhanges are distinguished by two successive victories over the Moors; the pride of Abdalrahman the last and greatest caliph of that name, was wounded by the rapid success of Ordogno; the ardour of the Moslems was rekindled by the hope of plunder, and the promise of paradise; some partial succour was drawn from their brethren of Africa; and a kindred host of eighty thousand Mahometans devoured the fertile country along the banks of the Duero. The Christian banners summoned them from the indulgence of rapine, to the trial of valour. After an obstinate and bloody struggle their ranks were transpierced, and their arrogance confounded by the hardy warriors of Asturia; the multitude was dispersed, their leaders slain; and their rich armour, their belts enchased with gold, were the rewards of the victors. Leon witnessed the triumph, and more than shared the protection of her sovereign; that city was established

blished by Ordogno as his capital, and the title of king of Oviedo was lost in that of Leon.

Yet prosperity gilded not invariably the administration of Ordogno, and he was soon after reminded of the vicissitudes of fortune; the Spanish march which had been instituted by Charlemagne, had been dissolved in the weakness of his successors; and about fourscore years after his death, the governors of Charles the Simple revolted from his authority, with the title of count confounded that of king, and asserted their independence over their separate districts. The king of Navarre oppressed by the superior numbers of the Moslems solicited the assistance of his nephew Ordogno; and policy or the ties of blood induced the latter to march with a powerful army to the succour of his kinsman and ally. In the valley of Junquera their combined forces attacked the infidel host; but the event of the day was unfavourable to the Christians; the confederates were defeated; with the remnant of his followers Ordogno regained with difficulty his capital of Leon; but the Moors neglected to improve their advantage; and wasted in a fruitless incursion into Gaul the strength that might have restored their ascendancy in Spain.

Some desultory and successful enterprises restored the spirits of the Christians; but the glory of the reign of Ordogno was past; and his last days were stained with cruelty and clouded by domestic uneasiness. The influence and power of the counts of Castille provoked his jealousy; they were summoned to appear before their sovereign; the royal faith was violated by their detention; the forms of justice were disregarded in their execution; and the rumour of conspiracy and rebellion, which was artfully propagated, could not conceal the unworthy fears and bloody injustice of the king of Leon.

The widowed hand of Ordogno had been bestowed on Argonta, who was descended from one of the most illustrious families of Gallicia; but Argonta had scarce excited the envy of her fair companions, before she was entitled to their compassion. A malicious tale was fabricated against her virtue, was communicated to Ordogno, and readily believed; she was repudiated with contempt by a jealous husband who lived long enough to repent his credulity; but Argonta devoted the remainder of her days to devotion; and Ordogno endeavoured to forget her charms in the nuptial bed of Santua, the daughter of the king of Navarre. He had scarce returned with his bride to his capital of Leon before he was surprised by death; the pretensions of his sons Alfonso and Ramiro, the issue of his first marriage, were supplanted by the intrigues of their uncle; and Froila the second, in a national council, was declared king of Leon and Oviedo.

The

The third son of Alfonso the Great   A. D. 923, was unworthy of the blood he sprung   924. from. He received the sacred trust of royalty only to abuse it; and the first months of his reign were stained by the murder of the nobles who had opposed his election; but his cruelty was arrested by disease; a tyranny of an year was terminated by a leprosy; on his death the claims of primogeniture were respected; and his nephew Alfonso was declared his successor.

Alfonso, the fourth of that name,   A. D. 924, had scarce received, before he found   928. himself incapable of sustaining the weight of a crown. His aversion to the cares of government was increased by the death of his consort Urraca, whom he appears to have tenderly loved; and in less than an year after his election he resigned the sceptre of Leon to his brother Ramiro the second. In a private station Alfonso might have enjoyed that happiness which he had never tasted on a throne. But his easy disposition rendered him the instrument of the ambition of others; and while Ramiro assembled his forces at Zamora to march early in the spring against the Moors, he was astonished by the intelligence that Alfonso had quitted his retreat, had re-assumed the ensigns of royalty, and had occupied once more the city and palace of Leon. The siege of Leon was instantly formed by Ramiro, at the head of the army with which he had propofed to attack the infidels; the defence of Alfonfo was obftinate; and in the vain attempt to regain the crown, he difplayed a vigour which would have maintained him in the quiet poffeffion of it. Famine at length compelled him to implore the mercy of his brother; a general pardon was granted to his adherents; but his own confinement was ftrict; and with his victorious troops Ramiro advanced into the Afturias to reduce by arms the three fons of Froila the fecond, who had alfo erected the ftandard of revolt. His fuperior genius or fortune again prevailed; but this fecond rebellion feems to have exafperated the fpirit of Ramiro; his brother and coufins were involved in the fame fate, and the lofs of their eyes was the punifhment of their prefumption. Yet in a ftate of darknefs they were ftill treated with refpect; the humanity of the victor was exerted to alleviate the mifery of kinfmen who were no longer formidable; and when Alfonfo the fourth, who from his misfortunes and devotion was furnamed the *Blind* and the *Monk* expired, his remains were honoured with a royal funeral.

A. D. 929, 952. No fooner were the flames of civil difcord extinguifhed, than thofe of foreign war were kindled. The martial exploits of Ramiro rivalled thofe of the moft illuftrious of his predeceffors; he paffed the Duero; attacked and

and carried by assault Madrid, the present capital of the Spanish monarchy, and insulted by his presence Toledo, the strongest city of the caliphs of Spain. In the plains of Osma the Moors aspired to retrieve their glory and they augmented their disgrace; they were defeated after a bloody struggle by Ramiro; and Ahaga the Moorish chieftain of Arragon was compelled to acknowledge himself the vassal of the king of Leon.

Yet during the glorious career of Ramiro, the sceptre of Cordova was held by no feeble hand; and the pride of the third Abdalrahman stimulated him to exertions worthy of the ancient power and renown of the Mahometans. From the mouth of the Guadalquivir to the source of the Tagus, the descendants of the tribes of Arabia obeyed the summons of the successor of the prophet; one hundred and fifty thousand Moslems were united by their zeal for religion, or their thirst of plunder; the natives of Grenada were distinguished from the crowd; and in the dexterous management of their coursers asserted their origin from the horsemen of Syria and Irak; they overturned in their course the Christian town of Solocuvas, trampled the harvest of old Castille, desolated the flourishing banks of the Duero, and pitched their camp where that river is swelled by the waters of the Puiserga. It was there they awaited or were checked by the appearance of the Christian army;

the plains of Simancas afforded a wide theatre to the skill and rage of the combatants; the battle was obstinately disputed through a long summer's day; and it was not until the close of evening that victory declared for Ramiro; the pursuit was continued by the indefatigable monarch, though the darkness of the night, and eighty thousand Moslems are reported to have fallen by the sword, or to have been precipitated into the waters of the Duero and the Puiserga. So complete and bloody an overthrow Ramiro might have expected would have broken for years the spirit of the Moors; yet the remnant of their forces again united, and was swelled by fresh detachments; and it was not until he had gained a new victory in the neighbourhood of Salamanca, that the king of Leon entered his capital in triumph.

The increase of taxes is the ungrateful, but too often the indispensable duty of the sovereign; nor ought the subject to complain as long as the revenue or service that is exacted, is strictly applied to, or exceeds not the necessity of the state; the conquests of Ramiro had been extended to the mountains that separate old and new Castille; and an heavy expence had been incurred in restoring the towns on the Duero, and erecting a strong barrier against the Moors; the counts of Castille, whose influence rose above that of subjects, and whose station was below that of princes, had long
secretly

secretly aspired to independence; they murmured at the command of Ramiro to repair the fortifications of Osma and Clunia, which had been overthrown by the Moslems; they murmured, but they obeyed; and it was not until they were summoned to join the royal standard against the infidels, that they presumed openly to reject the authority of the king of Leon. The prompt and vigorous spirit of Ramiro was equal to every event; he abandoned the hopes of foreign conquest to extinguish the flames of civil commotion; and with an obedient and well-disciplined army he suddenly presented himself in Castille; he dissipated the hostile league, seized the persons of the counts Ferdinand Goncalez, and Diego Nugnez, the most formidable of the confederates, and conveyed them prisoners to Leon. A less prudent prince might have instantly sacrificed them to his insulted authority; but Ramiro was more jealous of the happiness of his people than of the dignity of his crown; he condescended to remonstrate with his noble captives; he urged that it was alone by union that the Christians in Spain could hope to avert the yoke of Mahomet, or aspire to expel the infidel invaders; Goncalez and Nugnez at least affected to be convinced; they were restored to freedom; and the ties of public were drawn more close by those of private connexion, in the marriage of Ordogno the

son

son of Ramiro, with Urraca the daughter of Goncalez.

With the return of unanimity the king of Leon resumed the martial preparations he had suspended. At the head of a numerous army he passed the mountains of Avila, and near the walls of Talavera he descried the Moorish banners. The conflict was fierce and obstinate; the waters of the Tagus were purpled with the blood of the combatants; and it was not until Ramiro had repeatedly charged his adversaries in person, that he could claim the victory; twelve thousand of the Moors were extended lifeless on the plain; the fertile fields of new Castille were desolated by the Christians; and with an immense booty Ramiro slowly directed his march towards Leon; he was permitted to enjoy but a short time the acclamations of his subjects; he was seized with a mortal disease, and convinced that his end approached, he was desirous before his death of fixing the crown on the head of his son. In a national council the resignation of Ramiro was accepted, and the election of Ordogno unanimously approved; and a few days afterwards, amidst the general lamentations of his people, he closed a glorious reign of near twenty years.

A. D. 952. 957. The elevation of Ordogno the third had been promoted by the wishes and renown of his father; but in the possession of a throne,

throne, his subjects were compelled to acknowledge he deserved it; and though his virtues could not always secure their fidelity, they invariably extorted their admiration. During a short but active reign of five years and an half, he resisted the combinations of his domestic foes, and vanquished the foreign enemies of his country. A civil war was kindled immediately on his accession by the ambition of his brother Sancho, whose pretensions were supported by his uncle the king of Navarre; and Ordogno beheld with surprize and indignation his own father-in-law Goncalez march among the associates of his rival. The confederates were disconcerted by the bold attitude of Ordogno; his dominions were protected by a chain of posts occupied with judgment and maintained with firmness; his adversaries were awed by his genius, and retired; their disappointment was productive of mutual reproaches; and their discontents soon dissolved the unnatural confederacy.

The ascendancy of Ordogno was established by his safe and bloodless victory, but the mind that was superior to danger was not insensible to resentment. He divorced with contempt the daughter of Goncalez, and raised to his bed Elvira, who was descended from one of the most noble families of Gallicia. The arrogance of the kindred of the queen provoked a new insurrection;

tion; and when Ordogno prepared to march against the Moors, he was mortified by the intelligence that the inhabitants of Gallicia were in arms; with a select body of troops he halted on the frontiers of that province; and his offer of a general pardon, and his promise to redress their grievances, reclaimed the malecontents to their allegiance; they ranged themselves under his standard; strengthened by the junction of their forces, he advanced through Portugal without encountering an enemy; and Lisbon was a second time assaulted and plundered by a Christian army; in his return he penetrated into Castille, accepted the submission of Goncalez; and when the territories of that chief were invaded by the Moors, their deliverance was achieved by the arm of Ordogno.

A. D. 957, 967. His career of glory was arrested by a fever, and he expired after a short illness at Zamora; a feeble infant by his last marriage was incapable of stemming the unpopularity of his mother, and the ambition of his uncle; and in a national assembly Sancho was preferred to the throne of Leon. The new monarch, who had attempted to wrest the sceptre from his brother, was incapable of retaining it when legally committed to his hand. His health was oppressed by a dropsy; his authority was shaken by the intrigues of the turbulent Goncalez; he sought a

retreat

retreat in the court of his uncle the king of Navarre; and the crown of Leon was placed by the hand of Goncalez on the head of Ordogno the fourth.

The virtues of three monarchs had endeared the name of Ordogno to the Chriftians, but it was difgraced by an ufurper to whom was juftly applied the epithet of *wicked*. He was the nephew of Ramiro the fecond, and the fon of the unfortunate Alfonfo the Blind; but he neither inherited the genius of his uncle nor the mild virtues of his father; he received the hand of the repudiated Urraca from Goncalez, who twice beheld his daughter feated on the throne of Leon, and who hoped from the gratitude of his fon-in-law to erect his own extenfive demefnes into an independent principality; but the project was blafted by the vices and cruelty of Ordogno. The health of Sancho had been reftored by tranquillity or by the fkill of the Arabian phyficians, who revived in Europe the fcience of medicine; to confult them he had vifited the court of Cordova; and it was there that he was informed of the tyranny of Ordogno and the difaffection of his fubjects; his caufe was efpoufed by the generofity or policy of the caliph Abdalrahman, and was fupported by the kindred bands of the king of Navarre. The confederate armies of Moflems and Chriftians advanced to the frontiers of Leon; the gates of the cities

cities were thrown open on their approach; from the execrations of his people Ordogno fought refuge with the Moorish chief of Arragon; the more intrepid spirit of Goncalez impelled him to try the chance of battle; he was vanquished and taken prisoner in the plains of Aronia; his defeat extinguished the hopes of his faction; and Sancho re-ascended the throne of Leon.

In the school of adversity Sancho had learned to distrust the smiles of fortune; and it was by generosity instead of terror that he endeavoured to disarm his enemies. He prevailed on the king of Navarre to release the count of Castille; and from the obscure records of the times, we may conjecture that he strove to secure the future friendship of Goncalez, by renouncing all claims of homage; gratitude might restrain him from invading the dominions of Abdalrahman; but he repulsed with cruel slaughter the Normans, whose piratical descents had afflicted the coasts of Gallicia. His satisfaction was interrupted by the intelligence that an officer whom he had intrusted with an important command on the frontiers of Portugal, had revolted; he marched against the rebel, defeated, pardoned, and received him into favour. But he was the victim of his own magnanimity; and a poisoned apple which he received from the ungrateful traitor, was attended by his immediate death.

Sur-

Surrounded by active and powerful enemies, the Christians of Oviedo and Leon had in the choice of a sovereign sought the qualities of experience, of wisdom, or of valour; their judgment had rarely been deceived; and during more than two centuries the sceptre of Pelagius had been intrusted, with few exceptions, to a succession of warriors and statesmen; in the full confidence of their strength, or from veneration to the memory of Sancho, they had relaxed from their wonted caution; the son of the late king, though only five years old, was placed on the throne; the reins of government were committed to the hands of his mother Teresa, and his aunt Elvira; a female administration might at first provoke a smile of derision; yet during twelve years that it was continued, it was distinguished by prudence and vigour; a profound peace was maintained with the court of Cordova; but the rapacious adventurers of Norway, who had renewed their depredations, were severely chastised; their retreat was intercepted, their fleet destroyed; and those who escaped the sword were sold into servitude.

A. D. 967, 983.

At the age of seventeen Ramiro the third claimed the authority he was incapable of exercising; his reign was disgraced by the follies, and disturbed by the passions of youth; in the choice of a consort he had consulted the late regents;
but

but whatever virtues Donna Urraca might possess, were more than outweighed by the insolence and rapacity of her relations; a general murmur of disgust was heard; and the eyes of an indignant people were turned on Bermudo, the son of Ordogno the third; his graceful person and affable manners united in his favour the multitude; and the renown of his father recommended him to the nobility; it was in Gallicia that he was invested with the ensigns of royalty; yet Ramiro, it must be confessed, defended his crown with vigour and resolution; a bloody battle that was fought with doubtful success, was only terminated by night; in the slaughter of their brethren, the Christians might deplore the guilt and madness of civil war; and the numbers that were swept away in the bloody conflict of Monterossa, exceeded those who had fallen in any action with the Moors; the opportune death of Ramiro as he was engaged in recruiting his forces, put an end to the contest, and Bermudo the second, without a competitor, ascended the throne of Leon.

A. D. 985, 999. The abilities of Bermudo are acknowleged; yet the difficulties of his situation exceeded his abilities; in his contest with Ramiro the strength of the monarchy had been dissolved; the spirits of the Moors were revived; they were conducted to conquest by the renowned

ed Almanzor, who united with the talents of a general, the addrefs of a ftatefman. The king of Leon beheld without daring to oppofe, the devaftation of the fertile country along the banks of the Duero, the deftruction of the walls Simencas, and the banners of the infidels ftreaming from the towers of Zamora. He was feebly feconded by a laity corrupted by profperity and luxury; he was embarraffed by a proud and turbulent clergy; yet hope never deferted him; he collected with difficulty an army fufficient to face the infidels in the field; and on the banks of the river Ezla he rather confided in the juftice of his caufe, than in the goodnefs or number of his troops. Yet in the heat of action, the Chriftians for a moment afferted their ancient renown; the ranks of the Moflems were broken; and the battle was only reftored by the defpair of Almanzor; his followers were afhamed to abandon a chief, who declared his refolution to conquer or to perifh on the fpot on which he ftood; they returned to the charge, and the efforts of rage and fhame were fuccefsful. The Chriftians were overpowered; and Bermudo retreated, or probably fled towards his capital. The fortifications of Leon were incapable of refifting the ardour of a victorious army; the king was not ignorant of the enterprifing fpirit of Almanzor; he ordered the inhabitants to retire with their moft valuable effects;

he removed with pious care the sacred remains of his predecessors to Oviedo; and after placing a strong garrison in Leon, with the rest of his forces he withdrew to the shelter of the Asturian mountains.

The city of Leon was besieged, carried by assault, and levelled to the ground by Almanzor, who in three successive campaigns reduced or overthrew the walls of Astorga, of Coimbra, Viseo, and Lamago, and penetrated from the source of the Ezla to the mouth of the Duero. The fortifications of Braga awhile resisted his fury; but the obstinacy of the inhabitants was severely chastised by the sentence of slavery, and Braga itself was razed to its foundations. Gallicia was ravaged, Castille menaced; and disease alone checked the progress of the victor; he retired to return more dreadful; but his retreating steps were closely followed by Bermudo; his rear was frequently attacked, and the Christians severely avenged on the straggling Moors the sufferings of their brethren of Leon and Braga.

The threats of Almanzor had been heard throughout Spain; and their common danger united the Christians from the Atlantic Ocean to the Pyrenees, from the extreme verge of Asturia to the banks of the Duero. The various but kindred standards of the kings of Leon and Navarre, and the counts of Castille, were displayed

in

in the spacious plain of Osma. They awaited, but they awaited not long the approach of Almanzor. Though broken with the gout, and incapable of mounting on horseback, Bermudo animated in person his soldiers; both leaders were alike impatient of delay, and both armies rushed to the encounter with equal alacrity; the struggle between the contending hosts was continued long after the close of day; but the return of the dawn revealed to the Christians the extent of their victory; the Moorish camp was abandoned; the plain of Osma was covered with an hundred thousand lifeless infidels; the haughty spirit of Almanzor scorned to survive defeat; and the exultation with which the Christians received the intelligence of his death, may be considered as the strongest evidence of his abilities.

The shattered constitution of Bermudo allowed him not to achieve the entire deliverance of his country; in about a year after the victory of Osma he expired of disease; and the same suffrages that raised to the throne his infant son Alfonso, committed the protection of his dominions to his widow Elvira. In the arduous station Elvira deserved and acquired the general esteem; an army of Moors who had presumed to ravage Leon, was encountered and driven back with disgrace; and the dissensions of the infidels themselves, prevented them

A. D. 999, 1014.

P 2   from

from renewing their hostile enterprises; by negociation the regent obtained from the counts of Castille, and restored to the family of Cabala, the district of Alava, which the former had usurped from them; but the most important care of Elvira was to form the character of the young Alfonso, on whose qualities the happiness or misery of his subjects was ultimately to depend; the happy genius of the royal youth facilitated the labours of his preceptors; and his marriage with the daughter of the wife and virtuous Gonzalez his governor, might be variously ascribed to love or gratitude.

A. D. 1014, 1026.   The voice of a people called Alfonso the fifth to practise on a throne the lessons that he had studied in the cabinet; within the tranquil walls of a monastery, Elvira listened with pleasure to the rising virtues and renown of her son. During twelve years that his reign and life were continued, he laboured, and not unsuccessfully, to restore the glory and felicity of his subjects. Beneath his auspices the walls of Leon rose in fresh strength, and the capital resumed its ancient magnificence; the new fortifications of Zamora protected the Christians, and awed the infidels; the Moors rent by intestine discord were incapable of opposing his progress; with a well disciplined army he passed the Duero, and invested the city of Viseo; it was defended by a strong garrison; the heat of the weather tempted ed Alfonso to lay aside his cuirass; and as he rode round the walls he was mortally wounded by a Moorish arrow; a few hours after he expired in his tent, and left an only and infant son, who was the heir of his crown and virtues.

Bermudo the third, was probably not more than twelve years of age A. D. 1062, 1037. when he was chosen to succeed his father; but the bloody dissensions of the Moors suffered them not to avail themselves of the weakness of a minority; and at the expiration of four years, when Bermudo received from the hands of the queen his mother the reins of government, it was the formidable power of a Christian neighbour that first excited his jealousy. By arms or address, by birth or alliance, Sancho, king of Navarre, had added to his paternal dominions the kingdom of Arragon, and the greatest part of the province of Biscay; under the pretence of avenging the murder of Garcias, count of Castille, who had been basely assassinated, he entered that country with a numerous army, seized and executed the assassins, and converted to his own advantage their crime, by retaining the dominions of the unfortunate Garcias. From the mountains of Sierra Morena to the northern extremity of the Pyrenees his authority was acknowledged. His ambiguous claim to the city Valencia on the frontiers of Asturia was openly resented by Bermudo;

mudo; and a war was kindled between the rival monarchs; the country between the Puiferga and the Cea was over-run by the united forces of Navarre and Caftille; and the ftrong city of Aftorga on the banks of the Ezla, was after a long fiege compelled to furrender. To recover the country that had been wrefted from him, and to retrieve the honour of his arms, Bermudo collected with diligence his forces, and pitched his camp in fight of that of Sancho. The ardour and ambition of the leaders might have prompted them inftantly to have decided their differences in a field of battle; but their fubjects had embraced their quarrel with reluctance; the holy mediation of the bifhops of Navarre and Leon were fuccefsfully employed; and Sancho and Bermudo were perfuaded, perhaps with difficulty, to avert the effufion of Chriftian blood, and to try the effect of a negociation; the king of Navarre confented to refign to his fecond fon Ferdinand, his new acquifition of Caftille; the country between the Puiferga and the Cea was ceded by Bermudo to the latter as the marriage portion of his fifter; and with the hand of Sancha, the name of Ferdinand was infcribed as the firft king of Caftille.

A reconciliation which had been extorted by neceffity, was obferved no longer than intereft dictated; the death of Sancho diffolved that formidable power which had awed the king of Leon.

His

His eldest son Garcias succeeded to the crown of Navarre, with the province of Biscay; the dominions of Ferdinand his second, have been already described; to Gonzalez the third, were bequeathed the districts which under the name of Sobranza and Ribargona stretch along the frontiers of Arragon and Catalonia; and the fertile and populous kingdom of Arragon was the inheritance of Ramiro the fourth. The division which paternal affection suggested, might have proved fatal to all; but it was Ferdinand who first had reason to dread the consequences of it. With a numerous army Bermudo besieged and reduced the city of Palentia, and recovered without a battle, and in one campaign, the country between the Puiserga and the Cea. Incapable of contending alone with the king of Leon, he summoned to his assistance his brother of Navarre. Their combined forces were collected in the valley of Samara near Fromista, when they were informed of the approach of Bermudo. The obscure spot of Carrion has been rendered illustrious for the decisive action; and could the king of Leon have restrained his ardour, the superiority of his numbers would probably have secured to him the victory; but impatient of resistance or delay, he spurred his courser into the thickest ranks of the enemy, and while he darted his eyes around in search of his royal adversaries, his unguarded bosom was transpierced by the lance of an unknown foe. He fell lifeless from his horse; and his astonished troops, without a general, must have been exposed to certain slaughter, had they not been rescued by the prudence and policy of Ferdinand. His voice restrained the martial fury of his followers; the battle ceased, and the crown of Leon was the reward of the forbearance of the victor. The male descendants of Pelagius after reigning three centuries, were extinguished in Bermudo the third; the natural claims of the brother-in-law of that prince were debated and acknowledged in a national council; and the crowns of Leon and Castille were united on the head of Ferdinand.

Chapter

HISTORY OF SPAIN.

Chapter the Sixth.

State of Spain on the union of the crowns of Castille and Leon under Ferdinand the first.—War of that monarch with his brothers, the kings of Navarre and Arragon.—Account of, and exploits of Don Rodrigo, surnamed the Cid.—Death of Ferdinand.—Division of his dominions.—Sancho the second despoils his brothers of Leon and Gallicia.—He is killed in the siege of Zamora.—Accession of Alfonso the sixth.—Disgrace of the Cid.—Establishes himself on the frontiers of Valencia.—Alfonso reduces Toledo.—Is defeated by the Moors.—His peace and marriage with the daughter of the king of Seville.—Invasion of the Almovarides.—Defeat of Ucles.—Death of Alfonso.—His daughter Urraca is acknowledged as his successor.—Civil wars with her husband and son.—On her death, Castille and Leon submit to her son Alfonso the seventh.—His glorious reign.—He receives the title of emperor from the princes of Spain.—Divides his dominions between his sons Sancho and Ferdinand.—Short but prudent reign of Sancho over Castille.—Turbulent minority of his son Alfonso the eighth.—He assumes the administration.—Is defeated by the Moors near Alercon.

con.—*He marries his daughter Beregara to his nephew the young king of Leon.*—*Crusade of the Christians against the infidels of Spain.*—*Gallantry of Alfonso in the battle of Tolofo.*—*Splendid victory of the Christians.*—*Prudent reign and death of Alfonso.*—*He is succeeded by his son Henry.*—*Disputes for the regency.*—*Death of Henry, and accession of Beregara.*—*She resigns the crown to her son Ferdinand the second, who on the death of his father unites the kingdoms of Castille and Leon.*

A. D. 1037, 1067. At the time that Ferdinand united with Castille the crown of Leon, the greatest and most fertile part of Spain acknowledged his own authority or that of his brothers; the eldest, Garcias, reigned over Navarre and part of Biscay; the third, Gonzalez possessed the districts of Sobranza and Ribargona, which projected into or separated Arragon and Catalonia; Arragon was the royal inheritance of Ramiro the fourth, who established in Saragossa the seat of his government. But considerable districts were still occupied by the Moors; from the Pyrenees their territories stretched along the Mediterranean sea to the rock of Gibraltar, and from the point of Tarif coasted the Atlantic to the mouth of the Tagus; beyond that river to the Duero they

they possessed several strong and important towns; and though a few Christian chiefs might confide in the natural or artificial strength of their rocks and castles, they rather disturbed the tranquillity than asserted the independence of Portugal; but Andalusia, Granada, and Murcia, believed in the faith, or obeyed the followers of Mahomet; Toledo, with a portion of new Castille, and all Valencia, were cultivated by the Moors; and a Saracen emir resided in Barcelona, and stimulated the industry of the Catalans. The magnificent cities of Seville and Cordova were inhabited by Moslems; a long tract of sea-coast afforded frequent and spacious harbours, and was propitious to commerce; and the grateful soil of Granada repaid seven-fold the toils of the husbandman; yet these advantages were neglected or abused by the Moors; the same causes as had nearly overwhelmed the Christians, precipitated the downfall of the Moslems of Spain; and while ambition or jealousy pointed their swords against each other, their kindred strength was consumed, and the boundaries of their dominions gradually receded.

The designs of conquest which had been suspended by the death of Alfonso the fifth, were resumed by the martial and active spirit of Ferdinand. He passed the Duero near Zamora, carried by assault, and put to the sword the garrison

of

of Zena; and formed the siege of Viseo; the walls of that city were levelled by his machines; and the execution of the Moor whose skill had been fatal to Alfonso, rather marks his veneration for the memory of that monarch than his regard for justice. The fortifications of Coimbra were superior to force; and in his second campaign, Ferdinand patiently awaited the capitulation of the garrison from the slow but certain effects of famine. A chain of posts occupied with judgment and vigilance, prevented the introduction of all supplies; yet for several months the perseverance of the Moors was displayed, nor did they surrender until hunger had exhausted their vigour, and hope was no more.

In the reduction of Viseo and Coimbra, his subjects might applaud with justice, and exult without remorse in the success of Ferdinand; but the martial trophies of that prince were chiefly erected over his own kinsmen; his victory at Carrion had been stained with the blood of a brother-in-law; he was soon involved in a contest which was only terminated by the destruction of a brother; and though his moderation has been loudly praised by the Spanish historians, yet some suspicions naturally rest on a prince who at least acquired one kingdom by violating the ties of domestic alliance. He listened with alacrity to the intelligence, that in a visit to the court of

Na-

Navarre, he had narrowly efcaped being detained a captive; and when on the indifpofition of Ferdinand, the fraternal affection of Garcias attracted him to Leon, on the recovery of his brother he found himfelf with indignation arrefted and conveyed a prifoner to the fortrefs of Cea. He eluded the vigilance of his guards, efcaped to his own dominions, and returned at the head of a numerous army impatient for revenge. It is probable that Ferdinand was unwilling to depend on force, for thofe advantages which he had endeavoured to obtain by fraud; but every offer of reconciliation was fternly rejected; and nine miles from Burgos, the plains of Atupuerta and Agas were deluged with Chriftian and kindred blood; while the battle raged with doubtful violence, a javelin from a vulgar hand pierced the bofom of Garcias; he fell into the arms of, and was conveyed from the field by, his attendants; but their zeal was vain; the wound was mortal; and he foon after expired. His troops, difmayed by his fate, retired in confufion; the purfuit was checked by Ferdinand; and the forbearance of the victorious monarch has been afcribed to remorfe. But that emotion feldom finds room in the bofoms of ambitious princes; and moft probably Ferdinand feared lefs the reproaches of his confcience than the murmurs of his fubjects; he might dread an union of the other powers of Spain to check his career

of

of conqueft; and he fuffered without a ftruggle the crown of Navarre to defcend, or be placed on the head of the fon of Garcias.

Yet it is doubtful whether the reign of Ferdinand is not marked by the flaughter of another brother; the fate of Ramiro king of Arragon, and his war with Caftille, have been regarded by many critics as entirely fpurious; by fome hiftorians thofe events have been fixed after the death of Ferdinand; a faint light however glimmers through the dark and confufed records of the times; and the monument of Ramiro in the monaftery of St. John de la Pagna, attefts that he died before his brother Ferdinand; the moft general account is, that he attacked the dominions of a Moorifh chief, who was tributary to the king of Leon and Caftille; the latter ordered his forces under the command of his fon Sancho, and under the conduct of his celebrated general Rodrigo, better known from the mufe of Corneille by the name of the Cid, to march to the defence of his vaffal; a battle was fought, Ramiro killed; and the victory which was imputed to the fkill, confirmed the renown of Rodrigo.

Fifteen fummers had not yet matured the ftrength of Rodrigo, when his fearlefs fpirit was difplayed in vindicating the honour of an infulted father. The aged Alfonfo de Vivar had in the prefence of the court received a blow from the count

count de Lozano. He could not truft to his own feeble arm for reparation; and though he had three fons who had attained to manhood, it was to the youthful ardour of the fourth that he confided the indignity, and his hopes of vengeance; his choice was juftified by the alacrity of Rodrigo; and, before the royal palace, Lozano fell by the fword of an adverfary, whofe youth and inexperience he had derided. A martial age approved the deed; and the valour which had avenged the injuries of a father, extended the glory of a people. Rodrigo grew in fame and years; but on his return from a fuccefsful campaign againft the infidels, he was accufed by the filial piety of the daughter of Lozano; fhe found the culprit in full poffeffion of the royal favour and the admiration of his country; fhe was moved to compaffion by his renown, fhe was inflamed to love by his majeftic perfon and graceful addrefs; fhe confented to become the confort of an hero; and the death of a father was forgotten, or atoned in the embraces of a vigorous hufband.

The furname of Cid, is a corruption from the Arabic of *El Seid,* or Lord, which the refpect of the Moors firft conferred on their conqueror, and which was afterwards confirmed to him by the efteem of his king. The exploits of the Cid have been adorned and exaggerated by fancy, yet through the cloud of fable we may difcern that

he

he was an intrepid soldier and skilful captain. To his genius was ascribed the defeat of Ramiro; as the general of Sancho, the son and successor of Ferdinand in the throne of Castille, he wrested the victory from Alfonso of Leon; with his own followers he recovered Valencia; though his integrity exposed him to the ingratitude of a court, he was constantly followed by the esteem of his countrymen; and in the reign of Alfonso the sixth, after near sixty successful years of martial toils, he encountered with the resignation of a Christian that death which he had so often braved as a warrior.

The marriage and victory of Ferdinand had first united the crowns of Castille and Leon; his death separated them; the division of his dominions which he prevailed on a national assembly to ratify, might rather become a fond parent who wished to distribute his favours impartially among his children, than a wise monarch jealous of the happiness and grandeur of his people. To his eldest son Sancho, he assigned Castille; to Alfonso, his second, Leon and the Asturias; Gallicia, with the part of Portugal he had conquered were erected into an independent kingdom for Garcias the youngest; and to his daughters Urraca and Elvira he bequeathed the cities of Zamora and Toro, on the banks of the Duero.

His death was the signal of almost immediate hostihoftilities between his children; the A.D. 1067, ambitious Sancho confidered the rights 1072. of primogeniture as violated by the ungrateful diftribution. He invaded Leon with a formidable army; and was encountered by his brother Alfonfo at Valpallar, near Carrion. The action was maintained throughout the whole day until darknefs parted the combatants; in the lofs of his braveft foldiers, Sancho might repent his rafh injuftice; but his fpirits were revived by the counfels of the Cid; while the troops of Alfonfo were drowned in fleep, or anticipated in revelry the fruits of victory, their camp was fuddenly attacked, and in the confufion of a night affault, they were expofed to the fwords of their more vigilant foe; Alfonfo fled and was overtaken; he was defpoiled of his dominions; but his life was fpared; and the monaftery of Sahagon was affigned as his prifon. The victor entered Gallicia; and Garcias,. attacked by his brother and deferted by his fubjects, fought an afylum in the Mahometan court of the king of Seville.

Yet though Sancho had regained by arms what he conceived himfelf unjuftly deprived of by the partiality of his father, he was not permitted long to enjoy the territories he had ufurped; the flight of Alfonfo from Sahagon awakened his fears; and a fufpicion that the means of efcape had been furnifhed by his fifters, excited his refentment;

VOL. I. Q Toro,

Toro, the inheritance of Elvira, was terrified into submission; but the resistance of Zamora was animated by Urraca herself, who, above the weakness of her sex, derided the menaces and repulsed the attacks of her brother; the length of the siege exhausted the patience or prudence of Sancho; he listened to the insidious promises of an officer of the garrison who proposed to betray to him the gate he commanded at; as Sancho advanced without caution, an ambuscade started from some adjacent ruins; he was encompassed, and slain; his guards arrived only to behold their master weltering in his blood; the siege of Zamora was instantly raised; the army that had formed it dispersed; and the pious care of the Cid conveyed and deposited the remains of the unfortunate Sancho in the monastery of Ona.

A. D. 1072, 1109. In Toledo, Alfonso was informed of the fate of his brother; and whatever hopes the dispatches of Urraca might inspire, were alloyed by the survey of his own precarious situation; his fears were dissipated by the generosity of the Moorish monarch Ali Maimon, who nobly disdained to shackle his illustrious guest with unworthy conditions; and with mutual vows of eternal friendship and honourable alliance, dismissed him to improve the return of fortune. At Zamora Alfonso the sixth received the congratulations of the nobles of Leon and Asturia; but
some

some delay was interposed by the pride of the Castilians; and it was stipulated, that on his arrival at Burgos he should by oath, before he ascended the throne, clear himself of being privy to the murder of Sancho. Yet when the moment came the nobles of Castille were awed by the presence of their future sovereign; their silence was reproached by the honest boldness of Rodrigo; he proposed the sacred obligation; it was accepted by Alfonso; but the Cid was for ever estranged from the counsels and favour of the new monarch. With a train of martial adventurers he quitted Castille; surprised the castle of Alcazar on the frontiers of Arragon; penetrated to the borders of Valencia; and in the pleasant district of Teruel, which is fertilized by the streams of the Guadalquivir and Alhambra, fixed his residence on a craggy height, that still bears the name of *Pena de el Cid,* or the *Rock of the Cid.*

At the same time that Alfonso quitted the court of Toledo, Garcias emerged from his retirement of Seville; in the hour of exile the former had probably deplored the unhappy lot of the latter; but seated on a throne, he indulged the ambition he had so lately been the victim of; Garcias had scarce resumed the government of Gallicia, before he was invited to a conference with Alfonso; he accepted it, hastened to Leon, and became the prisoner of his brother; and Gallicia was united

united under the same authority as Castille and Leon.

The turbulence of the times was favourable to the first enterprises of Alfonso. He availed himself of the revolt of the inhabitants of Navarre, to seize the important province of Biscay. Gratitude might restrain him from disturbing the tranquillity of Ali Maimon; but that monarch was no more; and the sceptre of Toledo in less than a year had passed from the hand of his eldest son Hassam, to his youngest Hiaga. If we may credit the Spanish historians, the citizens of Toledo themselves solicited Alfonso to deliver them from the bloody controul of a tyrant. Yet if the character of Hiaga is stained with cruelty, it appears not devoid of vigour. Though destitute of allies, and harassed by the king of Seville, whom sound policy should have directed to have defended, and not oppressed his Mahometan neighbour, four campaigns were consumed, and many engagements maintained before Alfonso presumed to approach the walls of Toledo. In the fifth year he formed the siege of that city; and the obstinacy with which it was defended for several months by the citizens, may justly entitle us to suspect the impartiality of those writers who represent Hiaga as detested by his subjects. But famine raged within; a bold and numerous enemy were indefatigable in their attacks without; and Hiaga consented to negociate when he was no longer

longer able to refist; he obtained permission, with those who were willing to share his fortunes, to retire in search of new adventures; a solemn treaty promised and ought to have secured to the inhabitants who remained, the free exercise of their religion and the quiet possession of their property; Valencia received Hiaga and his companions; and that life which had been respected by the swords of the Christians, was sacrificed to the daggers of the Moslems.

Toledo was erected by Alfonso into the capital of the kingdom of Castille; and an acquisition which had been made at the expence of so much blood and treasure, was secured by new fortifications. But the success of the Christians had aroused the Mahometans from their supineness. To the powerful king of Seville, was joined the Mussulman prince of Badajoz, who ruled over the province of Estremadura, and they both invoked the assistance of their brethren from Africa. Alfonso, who was not ignorant of the object of their alliance, still confided in his own activity and the valour of his subjects; he penetrated into Estremadura, and extended his ravages to the stream of the Alagon. On the banks of that river he attacked and reduced the town of Corea; but he had scarce taken possession of it before he was informed of the approach of the kings of Seville and Badajoz at the head of the tribes who inhabited

bited the country between the Guadalquivir and Guadiana. He advanced to meet them; and the decisive battle was fought between Badajoz and Merida; but the event of day was unfavourable to the Christians; Alfonso himself was wounded in the leg by an arrow; and escaped with difficulty from a field overspread with twenty thousand of his subjects. Yet it is probable amidst danger and dismay he was not unmindful of his rank and renown; and he would not have presumed at Toledo to have reproached the ignominious speed of his nobles, had he himself first deserted his station.

The honour of the field had been obtained by the Moslems; but it had been purchased at the expence of thirty thousand of their lives; and the kings of Seville and Badajoz, far from being able to act on the offensive, were scarce capable to protect their dominions. While the spirit of Alfonso rose superior to defeat, the courage of his troops was revived by a successful incursion against the Moors of Portugal; he carried Lisbon by assault, and was admitted into Cintra by capitulation; but he resigned in the ensuing year his acquisitions on the banks of the Tagus to Henry of Besançon, who had crossed the Pyrenees from France to his support, had received in marriage the hand of his natural daughter Theresa, and laid the foundation of the Christian kingdom of Portugal.

Alfonso

HISTORY OF SPAIN.

Alfonſo had been defeated; the ſtrength of the infidels had been exhauſted by victory, and both parties inclined to peace; the charms of Zaida, the daughter of the king of Seville, haſtened the negociation; Alfonſo was impatient to receive into his bed a princeſs whoſe beauty and accompliſhments were the theme of general admiration; and to ſhare the throne of Caſtille and Leon, Zaida renounced the faith of her anceſtors. The articles of future alliance between the two kings were eaſily adjuſted; a mutual exchange of ſeveral places was agreed upon, and a tranſient tranquillity was reſtored to Spain.

It was while the war raged with doubtful fury that Hiaga, king of Valencia, was aſſaſſinated in his capital; at the head of his own followers, and a ſmall reinforcement ſent him by Alfonſo, the Cid, diſdaining the repoſe of age, marched to avenge his fate. After a long ſiege Valencia ſubmitted to the genius of an hero; Rodrigo fixed in it his reſidence, defended it againſt an hoſt of Moſlems; and when he expired full of years and glory, his undaunted ſpirit ſeemed to have ſurvived in the boſom of his widow, who maintained Valencia againſt the attacks of the infidels, until the prudence and diſtreſs of Alfonſo prompted him to abandon a diſtant and precarious conqueſt.

In a reign of above thirty years, Alfonſo could reflect

reflect but on a few months of tranquil enjoyment. The storms of war again gathered in the south; the Almovarides, of Arabian extraction, who professed a rigid obedience to the Koran, had possessed themselves of the kingdoms of Fez and Morocco; in their new settlements they retained the native ferocity of the wandering Arabs; they were governed by a king or caliph of the name of Yusuf or Joseph; and it is doubtful whether they were at first invited as allies, or landed in Spain as open enemies; it was against the Moors their immediate attacks were directed; Seville was betrayed by treachery, or reduced by force; and a vigorous war was waged against the Moslems of Murcia; but the artifice did not deceive the vigilance of Alfonso; and he doubted not but the invaders aspired to the entire conquest of Spain; a considerable body of troops that the king of Castille and Leon had detached to the support of his father-in-law of Seville, compelled Joseph to throw off the mask; he attacked and defeated the Christians at Quada in la Mancha, a country that in the romance of Don Quixotte, has been immortalized by the pen of Cervantes. Yet the victor presumed not to await the approach of Alfonso, who on the news of the disaster had advanced to retrieve the honour of his arms at the head of the martial nobles of Castille and Leon. The chiefs of the Almovarides withdrew to
Malaga,

Malaga, reimbarked for Africa, and inflamed their brethren by a diftribution of the fpoil and a defcription of the wealth of the country. The rapacious myriads of Fez and Morocco readily obeyed the voice of their fovereign that incited them to plunder; a confiderable fleet was collected, probably in the port of Velez; a favourable wind foon tranfported them to the coaft of Granada; they were joined by their countrymen who had maintained poffeffion of Seville; and the fertile fields along the Tagus were blafted by their deftructive prefence.

Age and infirmities fuffered not Alfonfo to take the field in perfon; he was deprived by death of his fon-in-law Raymond, to whofe valour and experience he might have confided the command of his forces; and a feeble boy eleven years old, the only fon of Alfonfo, could not animate the Chriftians by his example, but might confirm their efforts by the fenfe of his danger. The *infant* Sancho, for fuch was the title of the prefumptive heir to the crown, was fhielded by the arm of his governor Don Garcia de Cabra, who probably alfo acted as general. At Ucles, near Toledo, the Chriftians defcried the banners of Mahomet and the myriads of Africa; yet they advanced with confidence; and the battle was long difputed with that fury which religious and national enmity naturally infpire. The fquadrons of of the Almovarides penetrated at length or overwhelmed the adverse ranks; the horse of Sancho was killed, his governor slain in his defence, and the prince himself trampled to death; seven counts of the most illustrious families of Spain preserved their honour but lost their lives: and of the nameless crowd near thirty thousand perished in the action or pursuit.

To a discerning eye, the character of Alfonso never appeared to greater advantage than amidst the storms of adversity. On the couch of sickness he still retained the same vigour of mind as had formerly distinguished him in the field of battle; he had no longer a son; but his private loss was forgotten in the public calamity; he levied new forces; secured Toledo by a strong garrison; and still appeared formidable to the invaders; who as they surveyed the field, mournfully acknowledged the loss of the victors had exceeded that of the vanquished; and turned aside from the walls of Toledo to more easy conquests over the infidels of Catalonia.

A. D. 1109, 1126.   Eighteen months after the disastrous battle of Ucles, and in the thirty-seventh year of his reign, Alfonso breathed his last; a short time before his death he had bestowed the widowed hand of his daughter Urraca, on Alfonso king of Navarre and Arragon. To claim the crown of his late father-in-law, that monarch

monarch advanced with a powerful army to the frontiers of Caftille; but he was admonifhed by the nobles that his own dominions were the proper ftation for his troops; and that no force was neceffary, fince the rights of Urraca were undifputed. He yielded to their remonftrances, difmiffed his followers; and in a national affembly the authority of Urraca over the kingdoms of Caftille and Leon was formally recognized.

Alfonfo had flattered himfelf that he fhould have reigned under the name of his confort; but he found it eafier to conciliate the affections of a martial nobility, than to command the obedience or to gain the acquiefcence of an imperious and turbulent woman. Urraca defpifed the authority or influence of her hufband; their domeftic diffenfions ripened into a civil war; the queen was imprifoned by Alfonfo, was delivered by her nobles, who confidered their honour as wounded by her captivity; and in a field of battle prefumed to defend her independence; but they were vanquifhed by the fuperior numbers or fkill of their adverfaries; yet whatever advantage Alfonfo had acquired in the field, he foon loft in the cabinet. The convenient confcience of Urraca was afflicted by her marriage with her coufin; her doubts were imparted to an obfequious clergy; and in the council of Palentia her union with the king of Arragon was formally diffolved by the omnipotent fentence of the Roman pontiff.

Yet

Yet though the subjects of Urraca had espoused the cause, they were far from approving the conduct of that princess. Their eyes were turned on the infant Alfonso, the issue of her first marriage with Raymond count of Burgundy; Gallicia acknowledged him as her sovereign; his title was sanctioned by the holy influence of the archbishop of Compostella; and a new scene of bloody and kindred discord was opened. Tenacious of a sceptre which she had held against the grasp of a vigorous husband, Urraca refused to yield to the pretensions of a youthful son; ten years Castille and Leon were distracted by the rival factions; at the end of that term Urraca expired at Saldagna of indisposition, and Alfonso the seventh, in the twentieth year of his age, was declared king of Castille and Leon,

A. D. 1126, 1157.
The king of Arragon had not been an indolent spectator of the late commotions; notwithstanding the sentence of the Roman pontiff, the cities of Carrion, Nagara, and Burgos, preferred his claims to those of Urraca; but on the death of the queen, they expelled his garrisons and proclaimed Alfonso the seventh. The king of Arragon appeared in arms on the banks of the Lima to chastise their levity; but near the stream of that river he was opposed by his royal antagonist, who with a firm step led on the martial nobles of Castille and Leon to battle. Amidst the

the sanguinary annals of ambitious monarchs, we are pleased to discover some traces of a feeling heart; the king of Arragon confessed his affection for a prince whom he had been accustomed to call his son; he consented to evacuate the few places he still retained in Castille, and to become the ally, instead of the enemy of her youthful sovereign.

A slight revolt that was excited by the house of Lara in Castille, served only to display the vigour, and exercise the clemency of Alfonso; an insurrection in the Asturias was scarce attended with more serious consequences; the ardour of the new monarch accorded with that of his subjects; to efface their disgrace at Ucles, the flower of the nobility repaired to the royal standard. The army in two columns forded the Guadiana; the right, which passed beneath the towers of Badajoz, was intrusted to Roderic de Gonzalez, who had rebelled, been vanquished, and by his subsequent services justified the lenity and confidence of his prince; the left, which penetrated through the mountains of Sierra Morena, was conducted by the king himself; their march was marked by devastation; and so judiciously was the enterprise concerted, and so happily executed, that they arrived the same day by different routes at the castle of Gallalo. The calamities which had been inflicted by the Moors on Castille, might vindicate the orders which were

issued

issued by Alfonso; the vines and olives which grew along the banks of the Guadalquivir were rooted up; the hopes of the husbandman consumed; the moschs levelled to the ground; the villages abandoned to the flames; and the wretched inhabitants were awakened from security to slavery. The fortifications of Seville were respected by an army unprovided with battering machines; but the suburbs were insulted, and probably destroyed. Beyond that city Alfonso pursued his victorious career; surveyed at Xeres the fatal field which had witnessed the overthrow of the Visigoths, and the triumph of the Saracens; and from his camp in the neighbourhood of Gibraltar might behold the coast of Africa and the fortress of Ceuta. In his return at the head of his cavalry he encountered and overthrew the vanguard of the Moorish army; the main body trusted to the massy walls of Seville rather than to their valour; and without further interruption the march of the victors was continued through the desolated province of Estremadura to the friendly turrets of Talavera.

Yet on every side the banners of the Christians were not gilded with the same success; and as the aged king of Arragon pressed the siege of Fraga on the banks of the Cinga, he lost among the mountains his army and his life. His sceptre was broken by his death; the kingdoms of Arragon

ragon and Navarre, which had been united by his arms, were again separated; and while the former acknowledged the authority of his brother Ramiro, the latter submitted to the pretensions of his kinsman Garcias.

The son of Urraca could not hear without emotion the fate of a prince whom he had regarded as a father; and as a Christian king, he could not be indifferent to the defeat of Fraga and the triumph of the infidels. He entered Arragon at the head of a considerable army, and the apprehensions which Ramiro might have entertained at his approach, were dispelled by the assurance that he came as an ally to act against their common enemy, the Moslems. Their union probably deterred the Moors from pursuing their advantage; and Alfonso after a friendly interview with Ramiro returned to Leon.

It was in that city that the general voice and gratitude of the Christian princes of Spain hailed him with the title of *Emperor*; the pride of the successors of Constantine and Charlemagne might reject as an associate in the imperial dignity, a monarch whose influence was confined between the straits of Gibraltar and the Pyrenean mountains; but the pretensions of Alfonso were erected on the most solid foundations; and his new honours were the voluntary fruits of the esteem of his subjects and the admiration of his neighbours.

Yet

Yet jealousy is a passion more congenial to the bosoms of princes than gratitude; and the kings of Navarre and Portugal, who had been most zealous in conferring on Alfonso the title of emperor, were the first to confederate against him. Their league had originated in perfidy, and was dissolved with disgrace; they were successively compelled to sue for peace; and the terms were such as marked the moderation of the conqueror, desirous of preventing the effusion of Christian blood, and reserving his strength entire to act against the Mahometans.

With a formidable army Alfonso burst into the province of Andalusia, and extended his ravages over the open country; but his exultation was of short continuance; a detachment of his troops which had imprudently passed the Guadalquivir in search of plunder, was cut to pieces in his sight; after the loss of one of his principal generals and some thousands of his soldiers, he was compelled to retire from the walls of Coria; and though he reduced the strong fortress of Oraja, which had been constructed with the greatest skill on the frontiers of the kingdoms of Castille and Cordova, yet six months were consumed in the tedious enterprise. The acquisition was more than balanced by the loss of Mora, which awed the country between the Guadiana and the Tagus, and which was betrayed by the negligence or treachery of

the

the governor. But in the succeeding campaign, Alfonso took Coria, recovered Mora; and with the assistance of the naval squadrons of France, of Genoa, and of Pisa, invested the town of Almeria, on the coast of Granada. The former assailed the walls by land, the latter blocked up the harbour by sea. The resistance of the garrison was firm but ineffectual; Almeria submitted to the authority of Alfonso, and her treasures, the fruits of piratical adventure, were the reward of his allies. The dissensions of the Moors prevented them from interrupting the operations of the Christians; a new race of fanatics had arose amidst the sands of Africa; had precipitated themselves on Spain; and the dynasty of the Almovarides was lost in that of the Almohades.

The discord of the Moslems should have admonished the Christians of the advantages of union; yet the fondness of the father prevailed over the policy of the monarch; and in a national assembly the emperor recommended the division of his dominions; his advice was secretly condemned, and openly approved; his eldest son Sancho was declared his successor in both the Castilles, and his youngest, Ferdinand, in Leon and Asturia. Their hopes had no sooner been formally ratified by the states, than the emperor again took the field. His forces were swelled by those of Navarre, animated by the example of their

their king; and as the confederate host issued from the mountains of Sierra Morena, they beheld, and were charged by the rapid squadrons of the Moors; the shock was violent; but the Christians fought beneath the eyes of their respective monarchs; their ranks were restored by the skill of Alfonso; and their transient disgrace was effaced by a cruel slaughter of their enemies. Jaen was plundered, Seville insulted; and the country between the Guadalquivir and the Guadiana converted into a desert. But the triumphant entry of Alfonso into Leon was alloyed by the unwelcome intelligence of the indisposition of the king of Navarre, who soon after his return from the campaign expired at Pampeluna; and in his death the emperor deplored the double loss of an affectionate son-in-law, and an important ally.

The age of Alfonso, which did not amount to fifty years, and the experience of his past conduct, seemed to extend the prospect of the public felicity; a visit from Louis the seventh of France, who had married his daughter Constantia, did not divert the emperor from the toils of war. He traversed again the mountains of Sierra Morena, and pitched his camp under the walls of Andujar, which are washed by the Guadalquivir. The natural and artificial strength of that city had resisted the attacks of successive generals who had aspired to the possession of it; but it yielded to the

ardour

ardour or perseverance of Alfonso; and after a short visit to Toledo, the victor again took the field, with the pleasing expectation of completing the conquest of Andalusia; in a bloody encounter near Jaen he defeated the united force of the infidels; his last days were cheered by victory; but disease prevented him from improving it; the increasing ravages of a dysentery announced his speedy dissolution; and on his return towards Toledo, the emperor Alfonso expired in the obscure village of Fresneda.

The infidels exulted in the death A. D. 1157, of an enemy whose sword had so often 1158. proved fatal to their bravest warriors; the Christians lamented the loss of a prince whose genius had invariably conducted them to victory; the first were encouraged, the last terrified by the prospect of a feeble and divided administration. Yet on their respective thrones the virtues of Sancho and Ferdinand commanded applause and esteem; their fraternal affection was unimpaired by jealousy or ambition; and though in the first moments of a new reign the Moors recovered Andalusia, and planted again the standard of Mahomet on the towers of Andujar; yet no sooner had the king of Castille received the congratulations of his nobles and Christian neighbours, than he moved forward to conquest; in a long and bloody action on the frontiers of Andalusia he proved himself not unworthy of his illustrious father; the Moors fled before him; but the news of his victory was scarcely diffused before it was followed by that of his death; the surname of *the desired*, is expressive of his amiable qualities; and the suspicion that he fell a victim to his grief for the loss of Blanch, his much-loved consort, is an evidence of his feeling heart.

A. D. 1158.
1214.

The memory of his virtues, and the abilities of his faithful minister Don Guiterez de Castro, promoted the election of his son Alfonso, who when only three years old was acknowledged king of Castille. The administration of Guiterez was short and stormy; the envy of the nobles was excited by his appointment; and the family of Lara, not less remarkable for their wealth and descent than for their daring and turbulent spirit, were his declared enemies. They possessed themselves by fraud of the person of the young king; they asserted by force their pretensions to the regency; and a civil war would have been the immediate consequence of their ambition, had not the opportune death of Guiterez extinguished their rising discord.

On the decease of Guiterez, Don Manrique de Lara was formally recognized as the regent of Castille; and some vigour was displayed in the success with which he resisted the rival claims of the king of Leon, and the hostile incursions of the

the king of Arragon. But the family of Caftro were ftill the objects of his indefatigable hatred; and an attempt to deprive Ferdinand the brother of Guiterez of the government of the city of Toledo, was fatal to his own life; the angry paffions of the two factions urged them to battle; Manrique was killed, and his followers difperfed by the victor; yet Nugnez de Lara arofe to fupply with more aufpicious fortune the place of his brother. A new army was levied in the name of the king; the adherents to the houfe of Caftro were proclaimed rebels; Toledo obeyed the fummons of, and opened her gates to, her fovereign; and Ferdinand was compelled to feek an afylum among the enemies of his country and religion.

Under the name of Alfonfo, Nugnez de Lara governed for fome time with abfolute fway; he negociated and concluded a marriage between the king and Eleanora the daughter of Henry the fecond, who with England ruled over the extenfive province of Normandy. Yet the houfe of Caftro had rather been furprifed than vanquifhed; from Seville, Ferdinand their chief had repaired to the court of Leon, and was received with open arms by a monarch who had himfelf experienced the arrogance of Nugnez de Lara. The martial youth of Leon were permitted or encouraged to march beneath the ftandard of Ferdinand; his own retainers were ftill numerous; and the exile at the head of an army entered Castille, to solicit his pardon, and the punishment of his rival. To encounter his hereditary enemy, Nugnez advanced with a considerable body of forces hastily assembled; and their differences were terminated in a field of battle, which was adverse to the house of Lara; two counts of the name were slain in the conflict; and Nugnez himself, a prisoner, might have envied their fate; yet he was received with courtesy and dismissed with magnanimity; and Ferdinand aspired to the more noble revenge of subduing a second time by his generosity, the enemy whom he had first vanquished by his arms. Without violating the dignity of his sovereign, he led back his victorious followers to Leon; and in a marriage with the natural sister of his royal protector, who esteemed, and knew how to reward his merits, he renounced for ever his native country.

On the captivity of Nugnez de Lara, the reins of administration were assumed by Alfonso himself; but the unsteady hand with which he held them, was the affliction of his subjects and the exultation of his enemies; he provoked the resentment of his Christian neighbours, and engaged in a series of hostile and unsuccesful enterprises against the kings of Leon, of Arragon, and of Navarre. And when the formidable preparations of the Moors compelled him at last to solicit the friendship

friendship and succour of those monarchs, actuated by pride and jealousy, he rushed to the field to anticipate the diligence of his allies, and to erect alone the trophies his fond presumption had promised; near the town of Alarcon a broken monument still records the defeat of the Christians; the waters of the Xucar were purpled with the blood of twenty thousand Castilians. Unwilling to survive the effects of his own rashness, the king sought death amidst the thickest squadrons of the enemy; but his person was shielded by a brave and faithful nobility, who fought around him, and at length conveyed him from the scene of dismay and slaughter. In his retreat with the shattered remains of his army, he met the king of Leon advancing to his support; their interview was cold and reproachful; the son of Ferdinand, for Ferdinand himself was no more, upbraided the jealous temerity of Alfonso, and Alfonso accused with warmth the tardy prudence of his confederate; they parted with mutual disgust; and while Toledo was insulted and besieged by the infidels, the king of Castille was employed in ravaging the territories of a kinsman and Christian ally.

The magnanimity of Alfonso, for such also was the name of the son and successor of Ferdinand, was superior to the insult; he sacrificed his own resentment to the general interest of the Christian powers;

powers; and though he advanced at the head of an army, it was only to add weight to his offers of reconciliation. The murmurs of the Castilian nobility compelled their sovereign to subscribe an equal and honourable treaty; the bonds of political union were drawn more close by those of domestic alliance; in the cathedral of Valladolid the king of Leon received the hand of Berengara, the daughter of his cousin of Castille; and though the marriage was afterwards dissolved by the imperious voice of the Roman pontiff, yet the issue of it was declared legitimate; the title of Ferdinand the eldest, to the throne of Leon, was formally recognized; and in little more than thirty years his claims indissolubly united the dominions of his father and grand-father.

Whatever might be the secret aversion of the king of Castille to the new nuptials, he was forced to conceal or suspend his enmity; the power of the Moors had been nourished by the dissensions of the Christians, and to recover the kingdom of Toledo, the Moslems of Africa had obeyed with alacrity the summons of their brethren of Spain. Fourscore thousand cavalry were distinguished by the spirit of the horses and the dexterity of the riders; and the myriads of infantry which slowly followed their motions, are described as fatiguing the eye of the spectator; the innumerable host threatened to overwhelm all resistance; and their

common

common peril united the Christian princes from the mouth of the Tagus to the foot of the Pyrenees. But their confederate forces appeared unequal to the encounter; and the source of their danger pointed out to them the means of their defence.

Towards the conclusion of the eleventh century, the martial nations of Europe had been awakened by Peter the Hermit, to the recovery of the holy land. The impassioned eloquence of the fanatic had been seconded by the exhortations of the Roman pontiff; and in the council of Clermont, pope Urban the second urged the warriors of the west to march to the relief of their brethren in the east. At the voice of their pastor, the robber, the incendiary, the homicide, arose by thousands to redeem their souls, by repeating on the infidels the same deeds which they had exercised against their Christian brethren; and to use the words of the princess Anne Comnena, all Europe torn up from the foundation seemed ready to precipitate itself in one united body on Asia; four crusades had consumed in less than an hundred and twenty years, a million and an half of the enthusiasts of Europe, without exhausting the hopes of the survivors; and an engine, which in unskilful hands had been frequently abused, was sometimes employed to the most salutary purposes. Pope
Innocent

nocent the third liftened to the diftrefs of the Chriftian princes of Spain; his holy eloquence incited to arms the martial nobles of Gaul and Germany; and fixty thoufand warlike adventurers beneath their refpective chiefs traverfed the Pyrenees in queft of fpoil and glory; fome jealoufies between the kings of Portugal and Leon prevented them from joining them; but the armies of Caftille, of Arragon, and Navarre, were animated by the prefence of their monarchs; and the whole force was united under the walls of Toledo. Implacable againft the enemies of Chriftianity, and ftill more fo againft thofe who were rich and impotent, the pious warriors of Gaul and Germany were with difficulty diffuaded from plundering the Jews who dwelt in the fuburbs of Toledo; and the firft proof of their zeal had nearly been difplayed againft the fubjects of a prince to whofe fuccour they had been invited; they quitted with reluctance the tempting prey, and in their march overturned the walls of Melagon; thofe of Calatrava were defended by a brave and numerous garrifon which, though compelled to abandon the town, ftill difplayed the ftandard of Mahomet on the citadel. The con-confederate princes of Spain were unwilling to confume their ftrength in a tedious fiege; they propofed terms of capitulation; and a fafe retreat with their moft valuable effects was offered

to

to the garrison, and accepted. But the French and Germans had been taught that it was meritorious to shed the blood of infidels; they were not easily restrained from violating the treaty; and their murmurs accused the lenity of their allies, as a desertion of the Christian cause. The wealth of Calatrava might yet have appeased their discontent; but the king of Castille opposed with firmness their insolent clamours; and their ardour for an enterprise, which was neither recommended by blood nor spoil, gradually subsided. They complained of the heat of the climate; they proclaimed their intentions to return; and deaf to the remonstrances and solicitations of Alfonso, pointed back their disorderly steps towards the Pyrenees.

Arnauld, archbishop of Narbonne, and Tihbaud de Blacon, whose zeal for religion was more pure, or whose thirst for glory more strong, of the chiefs of Gaul and Germany remained alone beneath the banner of the cross; but the royal leaders, though their numbers were diminished by the desertion of their allies, still pressed forward to victory; they besieged and reduced the town of Alarcon; reviewed and reposed their followers at Salvatierra; and instead of attempting to force the passes which the Moors had occupied, under the direction of a shepherd they explored a new route across the mountains of Sierra Morena. As they descended into the plains beneath,

neath, they beheld the banks of the Gaudalquivir, between Jaen and Baeza, whitened with the innumerable tents of the infidels. Two days were allotted to recruit their strength which had been exhausted in the toilsome march; on the third they obeyed with alacrity the signal for action. Near Tolofo in firm order the Moors awaited their charge; the choicest bands of Africa and Granada were stationed in the centre; but some distrust of their own numbers and valour must have prevailed; and the iron chain that was stretched along their front, revealed their secret doubts or fears. The Miramolin, or Moorish monarch was distinguished from the host of his subjects by his splendid vest and majestic mien. In his left hand he held the koran, with his right he wielded a sabre. The first reminded the Moslems of the joys of paradise which had been promised by their prophet to those who bravely fell in battle; the last admonished his captains to dread less the swords of their enemies than the indignation of their sovereign. Nor did the Christian leader disregard the arts of superstition; the first place in danger and honour was claimed by the king of Castille; and as he spurred his horse to the encounter, the holy cross was exalted before him by the nervous arm of the archbishop of Toledo. In the mutual rage of the conflicting hosts, little room was allowed for the genius of the generals;

and

and each combatant depended rather on his vigour and the keenness of his own sabre, than on the address of his leader. Yet in a struggle of several hours, though the courage of the Christians was unbroken, their strength began to fail; they were incessantly assailed by fresh squadrons; and they panted on the verge of destruction, when they were arouzed by the generous despair of the king of Castille; on that day Alfonso redeemed the former errors of his reign; as he surveyed the field, he exclaimed a glorious death alone remained; and was with difficulty withheld from plunging singly amidst the Moorish ranks; his contempt of life was rewarded with victory; the Castilians were stimulated to a last effort by the example of their prince; they burst the iron chain, broke through the thick array of the infidels, and scattered in their career, dismay and death. The Miramolin fled from a field which he could no longer hope to restore; the slaughter of two hundred thousand Moors might fatigue the arms and blunt the swords of the Christians; but the reader must turn with disdain from the historians who assert that this advantage was purchased with the loss of only twenty-five of the victorious army; and who in their eager desire to establish the miraculous interposition of heaven, defraud of their just glory the champions of Christ who sealed their faith with their blood.

On

On the field of Tolofo the power of the Miramolin was for ever broken; yet the immediate conquests of the Christians were few and unimportant. They ravaged or reduced the open country as far as Baeza; but they in vain pressed the siege of Ubeda; and after refusing a liberal ransom, they were compelled by hunger to retire from the inauspicious walls. They led back to Toledo an army thinned by famine and disease; in that city they displayed in triumph, and rewarded their foreign auxiliaries with the spoils of victory; and after subscribing a treaty of future defence against the infidels, the French repassed the Pyrenees, and the kings of Arragon and Navarre returned to their own capitals.

The remembrance of his danger, seems to have awakened the dormant judgment of Alfonso; instead of yielding to the impulse of his passions, his conduct was ever afterwards regulated by just and sound policy; he cultivated the most perfect friendship with the king of Leon; he mediated between that monarch and the court of Portugal; and though his satisfaction was transiently clouded by a dearth which afflicted Castille, while he laboured to relieve the distress of his subjects, he beheld the strength of the Moors consumed by intestine dissensions. The Miramolin after his defeat repassed the seas to Africa; a crowd of petty chiefs disputed his sceptre, and dissevered

his

his dominions; and no sooner had the luxuriance of the enfuing harveft reftored plenty to their people, than the kings of Caftille and Leon marched againſt the infidels; the firſt in vain befieged Baeza; but the latter burſt open the gates of Alcantara; and as he paſſed over the ſtupendous bridge which for eleven hundred years had refifted the impreffion of time, he might juſtly admire the eternal monument of Roman architecture.

The prudence and moderation of Alfonfo in his latter years, had converted the contempt of his fubjects into efteem; but their vows for the continuance of his reign were rejected; and he had fcarce fhown himſelf worthy of the crown, before he was bereaved of it by death; he had fixed on the city of Placentia for an interview with his royal kinfman of Leon, to concert the operations of the enfuing campaign; but on his road he was feized with a malignant fever; his laſt hours were cheered by the fpiritual confolation of the archbifhop of Toledo, who had been his companion in victory, and was his comforter in death; and after naming his widow Eleanora for regent, he expired in the arms of that prelate.

Henry, the fon of Alfonfo, was but eleven years old when the ſtates of Caftille ratified the will of their late monarch, and acknowledged him as their fovereign. He was foon deprived

A. D. 1214.
1217.

deprived of the protection of his mother, whose health had been impaired by grief, and who was impatient to join her husband in the grave. The loss might have have been supplied by the experience of his sister Berengara, who had early been initiated to adversity in the persecution of the see of Rome, and who from her separation from the king of Leon, had deserved the love of the Castilians, by the active and affectionate performance of every social duty. Her natural pretensions were supported by the last testament of Alfonso, who had named her to succeed to the regency in case of the death of Eleanora. But her claims were opposed by the ambition of the brothers of the house of Lara, who, emerging from retirement, asserted the hereditary turbulence of their ancestors. In a national assembly their intrigues prevailed; and the reins of administration were committed to the hand of Don Alvaro de Lara; he might have trampled with impunity on the prostrate laity; but he presumed to invade the immunities of the clergy; their resentment was implacable; the churches resounded with the sacrilegious oppression of Alvaro; and the discontents of the people encouraged the party of Berengara to vindicate her right. Yet amidst the storms which agitated Castille, the address and boldness of Alvaro were conspicuous. By a negociation of marriage between Henry and the eldest daugh-

ter

ter of the king of Leon he diverted the latter from efpoufing the caufe of his former confort; in arms he menaced the chiefs who had confederated againſt his authority; and threatened with the dangers of a fiege the fifter of his fovereign, when his fchemes were broken by a melancholy and unexpected incident; as Henry purfued his amufements, a tile, that had been thrown in fport by one of his youthful companions, pitched upon his head, and was almoſt inſtantly fatal to his life, and to the ambitious hopes of Don Alvaro.

The title of his fifter Berengara was immediately recognized in an affembly of the ſtates; yet the houfe of Lara did not retire from power without a ſtruggle; but their refiſtance was overwhelmed by the tide of loyalty; the cities that had been moſt attached to their faction opened their gates to the queen; too proud to yield, they retired into exile; and Berengara after having held the fceptre of Caſtille for a few weeks, refigned it to Ferdinand, her fon by the king of Leon, and who had juſt entered on his fixteenth year. A. D. 1217, 1230.

Ferdinand, who from his virtues obtained afterwards the facred furname of Saint, afcended the throne amidſt the acclamations of his fubjects. His tranquil acceffion feemed fecured by the prudence and magnanimity of his mother, by the exile of the house of Lara, and by his natural claims to the protection of his father and neighbour the king of Leon. But the bosom that is inflamed with ambition, is seldom susceptible of the more tender passions; and such was the judgment of Alvaro de Lara when he chose the court of Leon as an asylum against the indignation of his prince. While Alfonso revolved his own aggrandisement, he forgot, or wished to forget, that Ferdinand was his son; and the coronation of the latter was interrupted by the unwelcome intelligence that his unnatural father and his rebellious subject were advancing towards Burgos at the head of a formadable army; the loyalty of the nobles of Castille was the security of Ferdinand; a numerous and gallant body of cavalry was hastily assembled; and Alfonso endured the mortification of abandoning with precipitation an enterprise which had been prompted by injustice; he acknowledged his error, solicited the friendship of his son; and scarce subscribed, before he again violated the terms of reconciliation. Yet his second attempt was equally fruitless with his first; and his penitence might not have been more permanent, but for the premature death of Alvaro de Lara; in an hostile incursion that chief had been taken prisoner by the valour, and released by the magnanimity of his sovereign; his haughty spirit was exasperated by disgrace,

and

and incapable of being subdued by gratitude; in the second invasion of Alfonso, at the head of a martial train of his adherents, he ravaged his native country and defied his king and conqueror. He obeyed with reluctance and indignation the signal of retreat; his heart was swelled by conflicting passions; and rage and despair delivered Alfonso from an injurious counsellor, and Ferdinand from an implacable enemy; yet the generosity of the king of Castille was conspicuous after death; and the funeral of Alvaro was celebrated with a magnificence worthy of his birth, by the liberality of a monarch whose life he had repeatedly sought, and whose peace he had incessantly invaded.

The pride of the Castilians was gratified by the marriage of their king with Beatrix, daughter to Philip, who, with his hereditary dukedom of Swabia, had been chosen to fill the imperial throne of Germany. From the couch of amorous enjoyment, Ferdinand was summoned by the cares of sovereignty; and he had scarce tasted the charms of Beatrix before he prepared to march against the infidels; his first campaign neither advanced his renown nor extended his dominions; and after beholding ten thousand of his followers perish by famine beneath the walls of Requena, he was compelled to raise the siege of that place. But the disgrace was soon effaced by success the most brilliant and decisive; the Moorish king of Valencia,

Valencia, and the chiefs of Baeza and part of Andalusia, consented to become his vassals; Baeza was surrendered into his hands; and for ten years, at the conclusion of as many campaigns, he led back his followers from the invasion of Valencia, of Murcia, and of Granada, laden with spoil and glory; at the expiration of that term he invested Jaen, which during the turbulent regency of Don Alvaro de Lara, had been recovered by the Moors. The fortifications were strong, the garrison bold and numerous; and Ferdinand yielded to the remonstrances of his generals; and abandoned, though with reluctance, the hopeless enterprise. He had scarce returned to Burgos before he received the intelligence that his father, the king of Leon, after a glorious victory at Merida over the infidels, had breathed his last in a pilgrimage to the shrine of St. James, of Compostella. The will of Alfonso displayed in the last moments the inconstant temper of that monarch, which his subjects had deplored throughout his reign; though Ferdinand had been recognized his heir in an assembly of the states, yet he bequeathed his dominions to his daughters, Sancha and Dulcia, the issue of his first marriage; to assert his right, Ferdinand advanced towards the frontiers of Leon; his train was swelled into an army by the Asturian and Gallician nobles who respected the sanctity of their former oaths, or

preferred

preferred the true interests of their country; all competition was extinguished by the moderation of the princesses Sancha and Dulcia; they renounced their claims; enjoyed in a private station, a princely income; and from the final union of the kingdoms of Castille and Leon under Ferdinand, we may date the future grandeur of Spain.

Chapter the Seventh.

Final union of Castille and Leon.—Rise and progress of chivalry.—Orders of St. Jago, Calatrava, and Alcantara.—Exploits of Ferdinand, surnamed the Saint.—He successively reduces the cities of Cordova and Seville.—He meditates the invasion of Africa. —His death.—Four hundred years after he is canonized at the request of the king and states of Spain.—Accession of Alfonso, surnamed the Wise. —He aspires to the imperial crown of Germany.— Distraction of his reign.—Revolt of his son Sancho. —Death of Alfonso.—He is succeded by Sancho the Brave.—Vigorous measures of that monarch.—He vanquishes his rebellious subjects.—Dies at Toledo. —The queen dowager is supplanted in the regency by Don Henry, uncle of the late king.—Stormy minority and reign of Ferdinand the fourth.—Pretensions of the house of de la Cerda.—Prudence of the queen dowager.—Persecution of the Knights Templars.—They are acquitted in Spain.—Hasty condemnation of two noblemen, by Ferdinand.— Particulars of the death of that monarch.—He is succeeded by his son Alfonso the eleventh.—Defeat of the Christians, and deaths of the regents Juan

and

and Pedro.—Alfonso assumes the reins of government.—He acts with vigour against his rebellious subjects and foreign enemies.—In conjunction with the king of Portugal, he defeats the Moors at Salsedo.—Takes Algezire.—Dies of the plague in the siege of Gibraltar.—Review of his character.

MORE than five hundred years A. D. 1230, had elapsed since the Christians had 1252. emerged from their craggy retreats in Asturia, and under the conduct of Pelagius ranged themselves in battle on the open plain. The success of their first enterprises was productive of confidence; and their rapid progress was accelerated by the divisions and decay of their common enemies, who were actuated by jealousy of each other, and were enervated by luxury. The descendants of the Arabian warriors who marched under the banners of Tarik and Musa, had degenerated from the simplicity, and had declined from the valour of their ancestors; their empire, which had been founded on fanaticism, had gradually receded in proportion as science and learning had advanced; and when Ferdinand, the third of the name who ruled over Leon, united that kingdom with Castille, the possessions of the Moors in Spain were limited to part of Andalusia, the kingdom of Granada, and the provinces of Murcia and Valentia.

Narrow as thefe territories might appear, they were not fuffered to cultivate them in tranquillity; that ardour and enthufiafm which had inflamed the firft Moflems, feemed to have paffed from their bofoms into thofe of their adverfaries; the fpirit of chivalry, which has been often confidered as a wild inftitution, the effect of caprice, and the fource of extravagance, diligently traced, muft be afcribed to the moft liberal and generous fentiments. Perpetual war, rapine, and anarchy, were congenial to the feudal ftate; and the limited power of the fovereign fuffered him not to protect from infult or injury, the weak and unarmed. The valour and generofity of private perfons afforded the moft effectual defence againft violence and oppreffion; fuch qualities might naturally have been expected from noble bofoms only, which had long entertained the moft lofty and delicate notions of honour; and the fons of peers who could produce four quarters or lines of anceftry without fpot or reproach, at firft might alone legally pretend to the diftinction of knighthood. But a fimple knight could impart according to his judgment the character which he received; and a warlike plebean was fometimes enriched and ennobled by the fword, and became the father of a new race. The ceremony was in

its

its origin fimple and profane; the candidate, after fome previous trial, was invefted with the fword and fpurs; and his cheek or fhoulder were touched with a flight blow, as an emblem of the laft affront which it was lawful for him to endure; but fuperftition was foon blended with the rites of chivalry; the fword of the novice was blefied by the minifters of religion; his folemn reception was preceded by fafts and vigils; and he was created a knight in the name of God, of St. George, and of St. Michael the archangel. He fwore to accomplifh the duties of his profeffion, to check the infolence of overgrown oppreffors, to refcue the helplefs from captivity, to protect or to avenge women, orphans, and ecclefiaftics, who could not bear arms in their own defence; to redrefs wrongs, and to remove grievances, were deemed acts of the higheft. prowefs and merit. Valour, humanity, courtefy, juftice, and honour, were the characteriftic qualities of chivalry. Each knight was attended to the field by his faithful fquire, a youth of equal birth and fimilar hopes; he was followed by his archers and men at arms; and four, or five, or fix foldiers, were computed on an average, as his martial train. He himfelf conftantly ferved on horfeback; his lance was his proper and peculiar weapon; and his fteed was of a large and heavy breed. When his long lance was fixed in the reft, he furioufly fpurred his

charge

charger against the foe, and transpierced or overturned in his career the naked bands and light squadrons of the Arabs. Religion, the prominent feature of the age, was conspicuous in the institution; and to recover the Holy Land from the dominion of the infidels, was the pious object of the majority of the knights of Europe. But those of Spain might exercise their valour within their native boundaries; and when Ferdinand ascended the throne, the associations of several of them had obtained the appellation of orders, and were distinguished by the saint they had chosen as their patron, or the spot they had pitched on for their residence.

The military order of St. Jago had been established in Spain towards the close of the twelfth century, under the auspices of Alfonso the ninth; it had been confirmed by the bull of pope Alexander the third; the object of it was to oppose the enemies of the Christian faith, and to restrain and punish those who disturbed the public peace; such an institution, while the open country was not only ravaged by the common enemy but was afflicted by the depredations of private banditti, could not fail of popularity and general encouragement. And in the ensuing century the wealth and importance of the order became so considerable, that according to one historian, the grand master of St. Jago was the person in Spain

of

of greateſt power and dignity next to the king. To the vows of poverty, and conjugal chaſtity, which were pronounced by the knights, was added that of implicit obedience to their grand maſter; they were capable of bringing into the field a thouſand men at arms; if theſe men were accompanied as was uſual in that age, they muſt, with their followers, have compoſed a formidable body of cavalry. Eighty commanderies, two hundred priories, and a variety of other benefices had, in little more than an hundred and fifty years been accumulated by the order; and it is not ſurpriſing that the command of ſo conſiderable a force, the diſtribution of ſo ample a revenue, and the diſpoſal of ſo many offices, ſhould have rendered the perſon who was intruſted with them ſcarce leſs formidable to his ſovereign than to the enemies of his faith. The orders of Calatrava and Alcantara, though neither ſo honourable nor opulent as that of St. Jago, were yet numerous and liberally endowed; and while they adhered to the purity of their firſt inſtitution, without becoming the tools to the ambition or reſentment of their grand-maſters, they muſt have given an energy to the operations of goverment which the feeble and divided Moſlems were incapable of refiſting.

The enterpriſing genius of Ferdinand ſuffered not the lance of chivalry to ruſt in inaction. An army under the command of his brother Alfonſo

penetrated

penetrated into the Moorish territories, and passed the Guadiana; they were surrounded by an host of infidels; and when they compared their own scanty numbers to the myriads of the enemy, their whole confidence must have been derived from their valour and piety; on these they relied in the hour of danger; and such was the unqualified hope they inspired, that had a retreat been practicable, they would have disdained the inglorious expedient. They were ranged in two lines; they advanced in close order to the charge; and the dexterity and courage that had been practised in tilts and tournaments, were effectually exerted to assert the glory of their country, and vindicate the purity of their faith. The bosom of the Moorish general was transpierced by the lance of a beardless youth who had been invested with the sacred honour of knighthood on the morning of the action; his followers were dismayed by his fate; and the bloody toils of the Christians were cheered by the firm belief that they fought beneath the conduct of their peculiar patron St. James. The vision which enthusiasm presented amidst the tumult of the battle, has been preserved by superstition; and the Spanish historians have gratefully commemorated the assistance they derived that day from the presence of their guardian saint.

To avail himself of the weakness of his enemies

mies and the ardour of his subjects, Ferdinand, accompanied by his gallant nobles, took the field, and encamped beneath the towers of Ubeda. The fortifications of that city were not long capable of resisting the weight of his machines; and with Ubeda, a considerable district of Andalusia, abounding in corn, in wine, and in oil, was added to the crown of Castille; yet the exultation of conquest was alloyed by domestic affliction; and while her royal consort pressed the siege of Ubeda, Beatrix had expired at Toro. In a period when the champion of God was equally that of the ladies, and when the emulation of the sons of chivalry was kindled by the approbation of chaste and high-born beauty, the tears of the men stained not the honour of the warrior; and on the loss of Beatrix, the generous nobles of Castille sympathised in the sorrows of their sovereign.

During an entire year Ferdinand suffered not his griefs to be invaded by the sound of the trumpet or the voice of glory; but at the expiration of that term he again assumed his arms; and the duties of the king prevailed over the affliction of the husband. The magnificence of the city of Cordova has been already described; and though with the waining strength of the Moors her meridian splendor must have gradually declined, yet still as the seat of Mahometan government, and the repository of Saracen wealth,

the

she excited the envy and avarice of the Christians. The discontents of some Moorish captives, whose fetters were rendered more heavy by the indifference of their countrymen, revealed the weakness of the garrison; a martial band were inflamed by the lustre of the achievement and the richness of the spoil; they marched under cover of a dark night, scaled the outward walls, and intrenched themselves in a quarter of the suburbs; the banner of Christ displayed from the ramparts summoned to their support don Alvaro de Perez, who had followed on their steps with a more considerable force; yet their united strength was inadequate to the completion of the enterprise; the interior part of the city was protected by solid works; and the swarms of the inhabitants which it contained, threatened to overwhelm the daring adventurers. The same messenger apprised Ferdinand of the success and the danger of his troops. He rushed to their succour, and was followed by the most valiant knights and nobles of his court. From the bridge of Alcala he commanded the opposite banks of the Guadalquivir; yet his situation was scarce less dangerous than the condition of those whom he had advanced to rescue; and had the Moorish monarch Aben-Hut pressed forwards at the head of the rapid and innumerable squadrons of Africa and Arabia, he must have crushed his adversary before the armies of Castille and

and Leon could have been affembled in his defence. But he was deceived and deterred by an infidious and exaggerated reprefentation of the numbers of the Chriftians; he was diftracted by the folicitations of the Moflem prince of Valencia, whofe capital was befieged by the king of Arragon; he marched to the protection of his ally; and on his route he fell a victim to domeftic treafon. His death extinguifhed the hopes of the inhabitants of Cordova; they beheld the camp of the befiegers fwelled by conftant reinforcements, every poft ftrongly occupied, and every fupply diligently intercepted; famine was not lefs terrible within the walls than the fword without; and they reluctantly yielded to the double danger. Thofe whofe ftubborn fpirits ftill refufed to bend to the Chriftian yoke, were permitted to retire with their effects; but the majority acquiefced under the dominion of their new mafters; the cathedral of Cordova was in folemn pomp purified from the profanation of the difciples of Mahomet; and in lefs than three centuries from the time that it had been erected, the Chriftian king of Caftille and Leon repofed in the palace of Abdalrahman the Great.

The unavailing forrows of Ferdinand for Beatrix had been abated by time and reafon; and the memory of that princefs was effaced by the charms of a new confort; Jane, daughter of the
count

count de Ponthieu, was chosen by Berengara to share the bed and throne of her son; the purity of her manners, and the sweetness of her disposition, vied with her graceful shape and the expression of her features. The nuptials were celebrated at Bourdeaux; and the operations of war were suspended by an year of festivity. The insolence of a factious and powerful subject, summoned Ferdinand from the arms of his bride, and no sooner had that monarch vanquished and pardoned Don Diego de Haro, than he took the field against the infidels; Jaen, that had so long resisted, submitted to his arms after a siege of eight months, and the kings of Murcia and Granada consented to become his vassals and tributaries. The wealth and importance of the rich and populous city of Seville inflamed his desires; seated in the midst of a spacious plain which is fertilized by the waters of the Guadalquivir, and which is diversified by vineyards and corn fields, the luxuriance of the country around, and the purity of the air, had recommended it successively to the natives and conquerors of Spain. It had been founded by the Phœnicians, had been extended and adorned by the Romans, and had been the residence of the Gothic kings before they removed their court to Toledo. After the defeat of Xeres it refused to acquiesce under the yoke of the victors; and the patience and courage

rage of the Moslems were tried in the siege and assault of Seville. In the revolutions which had rapidly succeeded the extinction of the house of Ommijah, it had become the seat of an independent government, and was still separated from the crown of Granada, when it tempted the ambition of Ferdinand. Two years were diligently employed in preparations for the arduous enterprise; and the want of a naval force, which must have rendered the design abortive, was removed by the persevering industry of the king of Castille and Leon. Thirteen large ships, and several of inferior size, were built, manned, and equipt under the direction of Raymond Boniface, whose skill in maritime affairs had preferred him to the confidence of his sovereign; and though the most considerable of the vessels in the present age would have been regarded with contempt, yet in that period of naval ignorance, their bulk excited the admiration of the Christians and the terror of the Moslems. The holy armament was not only sanctioned by the blessings of the clergy, but had been promoted by their liberality; and one-third of their tithes was readily granted to break the power of the enemies of their faith. The fleet cast anchor at the mouth of the Guadalquivir, blocked up the squadrons of the Moors, and intercepted all supplies from Africa, while the numerous army of Ferdinand ravaged the open country, and erected his engines againſt the towers of the devoted city. The king of Granada condeſcended to ſerve as his vaſſal; and the dexterity of the horſemen of Arabia was employed at the command of their ſovereign to ſubvert their own religion. The inhabitants of Seville beheld with indignation the banners of Chriſt and Mahomet blended in one camp, and united for their deſtruction. Yet though aſſailed by thoſe who ought to have ruſhed to their protection, their reſiſtance was long and glorious. The ſummer and autumn were conſumed in bloody but indeciſive attacks; and they might reaſonably have expected that the inclemency of the winter would have chilled the ardour and compelled the retreat of the beſiegers; but every obſtacle was vanquiſhed by the indefatigable care of Ferdinand, and the unwearied zeal of his ſubjects; a perpetual ſupply of proviſions was poured into his camp, which from its regularity aſſumed the appearance of a new and immenſe city; ſtretched over the plain, and covered the ruins of Italica, that has been celebrated for the birth of Trajan, of Hadrian, and Theodoſius the Great. The plenty which reigned through the hoſt of the beſiegers, inſulted the diſtreſs of the beſieged; yet their ſpirits were unbroken; and when on the return of ſpring Ferdinand again aſſailed their walls, he was encountered with a courage unimpaired by famine,

and

and unshaken by danger. Through a second summer and autumn the defence of Seville was protracted by the steady resolution of her inhabitants; but while her own numbers daily diminished, those of her adversaries increased; her magazines were exhausted; her hopes extinguished; and in the month of November a capitulation was subscribed, and the gates of the city were delivered to Ferdinand; yet the majority of the citizens chose to abandon their ancient habitations rather than live under a Christian master; and if three hundred thousand Moslems left the city to carry their arms and industry into countries that still reverenced and cultivated the Koran, the triumphal entry of the victor could have been witnessed only by his own forces; and some painful reflections must have arisen as he passed through the deserted streets to view the solitude his success had created.

The constitution of Ferdinand had not been proof against a reign of incessant care and toil; but his mind, superior to indisposition, still displayed its pristine vigour; in his last and most splendid campaign he ravaged or subdued the country from the walls of Seville to the mouth of the Guadalquivir; from the coast of Andalusia he surveyed the opposite shores of Africa; and he revolved the glorious design of planting again the banners of Christ on the towers of Ceuta, and of recovering the southern continent from the arms of the infidels. He solicited Henry the third of England to join in the splendid project; and the refusal of that monarch may rather be ascribed to the weakness of his disposition than to his policy. The disappointment of Ferdinand in the negociation did not deter him from pursuing the design; he urged the preparations with his wonted industry; a more formidable fleet than had yet issued from the Christian ports of Spain, was assembled; and Raymond, to whose skill and experience it was intrusted, not only insulted the coasts of Africa, but obtained a considerable advantage over the Moorish squadrons which had ventured to engage him; the king received the intelligence with undisguised exultation; but the strength of his body could no longer keep pace with the ardour of his mind; he laboured under the fatal weight of a dropsy; the arts of medicine had been fruitlessly exhausted to procure him relief; and as a Christian and an hero he prepared to meet his approaching end. His last words exhorted his son to govern with equity and moderation; and he expired in the sentiments of piety and resignation; his memory was long revered by a grateful people whose happiness he had invariably consulted. Above four hundred years afterwards, Clement the tenth yielded to the solicitations of the states and king of of Spain; the name of Ferdinand was inscribed by the Roman pontiff among the long list of saints; and the calendar, which had been so frequently disgraced by lazy monks and wild fanatics, received a lustre from the addition of a prince whose virtues had promoted the prosperity of his subjects, and had extended the influence of the Christian religion.

Yet it is probable Ferdinand expired not too soon for his glory, as the hostile coasts of Africa, on which the reputation of his successors has so often been wrecked, might have proved fatal to his fame. His sceptre descended to his son; and the *epithet* of Wise, which Alfonso the tenth had already attained, might inspire his subjects with the most pleasing expectations of his reign. But his hours had been wasted in unprofitable lucubrations; he was versed in every science but that of governing; and the royal grammarian and astronomer, who might have claimed the admiration of the academy, was exposed to the contempt and ridicule of the state. He engaged in and abandoned every enterprise with the same inconsiderate and disgraceful facility; his vain pretensions to the province of Guienne, provoked an open rupture with Henry the third of England; and though the harmony of the courts was restored by the mediation of the Roman pontiff, and by the marriage

A. D. 1252, 1284.

of Eleanora, the sister of Alfonso, with Edward the son of Henry, yet in peace the subjects of the former monarch groaned beneath all the consequences that they would have experienced from a wide and unsuccefsful war; new taxes were devised and imposed; the value of the coin was diminished; and every expedient was employed which could swell the royal coffers. The fervour of religious enthusiasm might support his people under their accumulated burdens; and they might fondly hope that the splendid capitals of Fez and Morocco, which had been erected by the disciples of Mahomet amidst the wilds of Africa, would be subverted by the Christian sword. But they heard with indignation that the African expedition was renounced, and that their blood was to be lavished in an ambitious competition for the imperial dignity. Alfonso was determined to assert the pretensions which he derived from his mother, the daughter to the duke of Swabia and emperor of Germany. His money, while it lasted, procured him friends and partisans; but it was soon drained by the avidity of the German princes; and after having consumed in the frantic project those treasures which might have expelled the Moors from the peninsula of Spain, his hopes were finally extinguished by the election of Rodolph of Hapsburgh.

While he wasted his hours and wealth in the vain

vain purfuit, his throne was affailed by the intrigues of open and fecret enemies; the ftrength and fpirits of the Moors had been reftored by peace; and the hopes of the factious had been inflamed by the unfteady hand with which the reins of government were held. Againft the former Alfonfo took the field in perfon, and the fuccefs which attended his arms may rather be afcribed to the ftrict difcipline which had been eftablifhed by his father, than to his own military talents. The infidels were defeated; Xeres was furrendered; the cities of Bajar, of Sidonia, Rota, St. Lucar, and Arcos, were evacuated on the approach of the Chriftians; the kingdom of Murcia funk into an obedient province; and new colonies to fecure her fidelity were eftablifhed from Caftille and Arragon. The refources of Granada were yet formidable; but her monarch dreaded to provoke the conteft; and confented to purchafe a difgraceful peace by the humiliating ceremony of homage.

Whatever fatisfaction Alfonfo might derive from foreign war, was clouded by domeftic commotion; a powerful confederacy had been filently cemented againft his authority; the illuftrious houfes of Lara, of Haro, of Caftro, and Mendoza, affembled their numerous vaffals and retainers; and their rebellion derived an increafe of dignity and confequence from the acceffion of prince Philip,

Philip, the brother of the king. Yet they were unwilling to submit their pretensions to the arbitration of the states; they were incapable of withstanding their sovereign in his own dominions; and they withdrew with their followers into the territories of the king of Granada. Near three years their secret intrigues and open incursions embarrassed the counsels and afflicted the frontiers of Castille; and when at length, weary of exile, they consented to accept a pardon, they dictated the terms of reconciliation; and the language of clemency could not disguise the weakness of their prince.

Their unnatural counsels had urged the king of Granada to re-assert his independence; he invoked the assistance of the king of Morocco; and that monarch, who had not been indifferent to the preparations of the Christians for the invasion of Africa, readily listened to his solicitations. He cast anchor in the bay of Gibraltar; was admitted by his ally into the fortresses of Tarif and Algezire; and at the head of seventeen thousand of the choicest horsemen of Africa ravaged the country between the Guadalquivir and the Guadalato. Within the walls of Eciza, Nugnez de Lara might have derided his impotent attacks; but he was desirous of effacing by some splendid achievement the remembrance of his former revolt; and he rushed forth at the head of his martial garrison

to

to encounter the invaders; he was oppressed by their superior numbers; an honourable death was all that was allowed him; and his head was transmitted by the king of Morocco as the trophy of his victory to his ally of Granada; with the same temerity and the same fortune, the archbishop of Toledo, near the walls of Martos, in Andalusia, had charged the forces of Granada; his valour could not atone for his imprudence; he perished in the bloody conflict; and the appearance of Don Lopez de Haro, at the head of a vigorous reinforcement, preserved alone the Christian army from total destruction. He recovered the cross from the hands of the infidels; but the strength and spirits of the Christians had been broken in the beginning of the day; and the signal of retreat that was reluctantly given by the general, was obeyed with disgraceful alacrity by the soldiers.

The intelligence of the defeat and distress of the Christian army, had quickened the steps of Ferdinand, the eldest son of Alfonso; but as he rushed forward at the head of the chivalry of Castille, his course was arrested by a mortal fever, the effect of his incessant toil and anxiety. His death opened to his brother Sancho the career of glory and ambition; he assumed the command of the united forces of the Christians; assembled a strong fleet; alarmed the king of Morocco for

the

the safety of his own dominions; and compelled the king of Granada to retire from the walls of Jaen, which he had invested. The popular applause which accompanied his actions inflamed his hopes of royalty; and in his pretensions to the crown, he overlooked or despised the feeble children of his deceased brother, whose age allowed them not to assert their claim by arms. The infants de la Cerda sought with their mother Beatrix, an asylum in the court of Arragon; and by the voice of the states-general, and the consent of the king, Sancho was called to the certain succession of the crowns of Castille and Leon.

The daring spirit of Sancho rendered him the idol of the army, and his unbounded profusion endeared him to the multitude. In a second and successful war against the Moors of Granada, he established and extended his renown; and in his impatience to ascend the throne, he hesitated not to violate the double duties of a son and a subject. The exigencies of the state or the improvidence of the sovereign, had reduced Alfonso to recruit his exhausted coffers by the most dangerous expedients; and the proposal of raising the denomination of the coin, though ratified by the states-general, was justly considered by the people as a measure the most pernicious, and as a breach of the public faith. Their indignation was favourable

able to the defigns of Sancho; he fummoned his adherents to Valladolid, painted in glowing colours the weaknefs of Alfonfo, and the diftrefs of the kingdom; and in an affembly which ufurped the title of the ftates-general, though with affected diffidence he declined the name, he confented to receive the authority of king, and to govern under the diftinction of regent.

At Badajoz the unfortunate Alfonfo was firft acquainted with the refolution of the council of Valladolid, and of the almoft univerfal defection of his fubjects. The moft confiderable cities of Caftille and Leon had already opened their gates to his rebellious fon; and the title of Sancho to the regency, was formally acknowledged by the kings of France, of Portugal, and of Arragon, who courted his alliance. Palencia alone was confirmed in her loyalty by the magnanimity of Don Alvaro de Lara; and Badajoz by her fteady zeal repaid the confidence of her prince who had committed his fafety to her walls. Prudence might have recommended to Alfonfo to have refigned a fceptre which he could not retain without involving his country in the calamities of a civil war; and his retreat might have been afcribed to a generous reluctance to turn his fword againft his fon and his fubjects. But every prudent reflection and public confideration were overwhelmed by the paffions of the man; Alfonfo yielded to

the

the resentment of a king and a father; his ambaſſadors preſented themſelves in the court of Morocco, and a Mahometan prince was prevailed upon by policy and compaſſion to arm in ſupport of a Chriſtian monarch. The Miramolin croſſed again the ſtraits; and the town of Zara on the confines of Granada was the ſcene of interview between the two princes; the king of Morocco yielded to his illuſtrious ſuppliant the place of honour; and even the Chriſtians were compelled to acknowledge, in the enemy of their faith, the magnanimity of his ſpirit. " I treat you " thus," ſaid he to Alfonſo, " becauſe you are " unfortunate; and enter into alliance with you " merely to avenge the common cauſe of all " kings and all fathers." Yet a confederacy founded on the pureſt motives, was far from being attended with the ſucceſs it merited. The adherents of Alfonſo with the forces of Morocco and Granada in vain united in the ſiege of Cordova; the patience of the Miramolin was exhauſted in the tedious enterpriſe; he reimbarked for Africa; and his alliance ſerved only to render Alfonſo more obnoxious in the eyes of his Chriſtian ſubjects.

But the advantages which Alfonſo had fondly hoped from the arms of the Miramolin, he derived from the pity of the Roman pontiff; the ſucceſſors of St. Peter, after an inſenſible progreſs during

during several ages of darkness and ignorance, had erected their head above all the princes of Europe, and interposed their decrees in the quarrels of the greatest monarchs. The tremendous sentence of an *interdict*, dissolved the bond of domestic and political alliance, and transformed the assassin into the saint or martyr. The thunders of the Vatican were already brandished against Sancho, when he resolved to avert the bolt by submission. He deputed a nobleman who enjoyed his confidence to negociate a reconciliation with his father; in the anguish of his heart Alfonso had renounced his rebellious son as a stranger to his crown and blood; but he was not proof to the language of repentance; and the pardon of his ungrateful offspring was accelerated by the intelligence that he languished under a dangerous indisposition at Salamanca; the last breath of Alfonso revoked the curse he had denounced; but the will that he had dictated in the hour of resentment still subsisted, and bequeathed to his younger son Juan, the cities of Seville and Badajoz, with the districts under their immediate jurisdiction.

The health of Sancho was scarce restored when he received the news of his father's death; from his former conduct, we may justly doubt how far he sincerely lamented an event which established his authority over the realms

A. D. 1284, 1295.

realms of Caſtille and Leon. In the cathedral of Toledo he received the crown from the hands of the archbiſhop of that city; among the crowd who poured forth their congratulations on his royal fortunes, the homage of his brother Don Juan was probably the moſt reluctant; but the ſpirit of Sancho was known and dreaded; he regarded the will of the deceaſed king, which would have diſſevered Seville and Badajoz from the monarchy, as equally injurious to himſelf and the ſtate; and though in his addreſs to the national aſſembly he ſpoke with veneration of the virtues of his father, yet he declared his reſolution to preſerve the kingdom entire againſt every pretender.

The ſurname of *Brave*, had been early acquired by Sancho; and he was impatient to ſignalize his courage againſt the enemies of his country and his faith. His naval ſquadrons were joined by thoſe of Genoa; the fleet of the Moors was defeated, and the coaſt of Africa inſulted. The Miramolin had formed and preſſed the ſiege of Xeres; while he daily expected the ſurrender of that city, he was aſtoniſhed by the appearance of an hundred ſail of Chriſtian veſſels in the ſtraits of Gibraltar, and by the return of his ſcouts who had already deſcried the banners of the Chriſtian army; he abandoned the ſiege with precipitation; and retired within the territories of the king of Granada;

Granada; his retreat was conducted without order, and effected with difficulty; and Sancho was defrauded of the glory he had anticipated from the total destruction of the infidel host, by the disobedience and intrigues of a powerful and factious subject, and an ambitious and envious brother.

The wealth and influence of the illustrious house of Haro had more than once excited the jealousy, and supported them against the resentment of their sovereigns; they had been frequently suspected; they had sometimes been trusted; and during the commencement of the reign of Sancho, he had lavished, with an impolitic prodigality, every office and honour on Don Lopez de Haro, With the title of count, he united the important trusts of high-treasurer, and prime-minister; the troops and government of the province of Andalusia were committed to his brother Diego; and he was raised to an alliance with royalty by the marriage of his daughter Maria with Don Juan, the king's brother. But distrust soon succeeded to favour; and the arrogant disposition and overgrown power of Don Lopez inspired Sancho with the most serious alarms. The latter had lately recalled from exile, and admitted into his confidence, Don Alvaro de Lara, the hereditary enemy of the house of Haro; the pride of the minister was wounded by the promotion of the ancient rival

rival of his family; and he might forefee in the elevation of that noble, his own downfall. But inftead of endeavouring to conciliate his prince by fubmiffion, he afpired to defend his power by arms; he found a ready confederate in his fon-in-law, who ftill in fecret cherifhed the claims which he derived from his father's will, and readily embraced the firft opportunity to affert them by force; on the confines of Portugal, Don Juan affembled his adherents; and in Caftille the numerous vaffals of the houfe of Haro obeyed the fummons of their chief. Yet the confpirators after having prefumed to draw the fword, were weak enough to fheath it; they confented to an interview with the fovereign they had infulted; and in a conference at Alfaro, in return to the demand of the king, that Lopez fhould evacuate the fortreffes he had feized or corrupted, that haughty fubject anfwered by the expreffive menace of applying his hand to the hilt of his fword. His infolence was the fignal of his death; an hundred nobles jealous of the dignity of their prince ftarted from the feats, and their weapons were inftantly plunged into the bofom of the daring traitor. Don Juan was the witnefs of the fate of his accomplice; but Sancho amidft his refentment refpected the blood of his brother; he yielded to the folicitations of his mother; and the ambitious prince, inftead of being raifed to a throne, found himfelf immured in a prifon.

The

The spirits of the house of Haro were rather exasperated than intimidated by the death of their chief. The brother and son of Lopez retired within the limits of Arragon, and prevailed on that monarch to espouse the title of the infants de la Cerda, the grand-children of Alfonso the tenth, by his eldest son. The greatest part of the province of Andalusia was influenced by Diego to declare in their favour; and the forces of Arragon were swelled by their numerous partisans to an host of an hundred thousand men. The courage of Sancho rose with his danger; and the inferior number of his troops was more than compensated by his own vigour and activity; he suffered not long an enemy to brave him in his dominions; and the king of Arragon trembled in the presence of an hero who had been familiar with victory. His retreat was hastened by the intelligence of domestic commotion; and his steps were closely followed by Sancho, who retorted the invasion of Castille, by ravaging Arragon to the banks of the Ebro.

Badajoz had imprudently declared for the infants de la Cerda; and the obstinacy of her citizens was confirmed by the dread of the inexorable severity of Sancho. But they were incapable of withstanding the fury of the assailants, who were inflamed by the hope of spoil, and animated by the presence of their king. A capitulation was

VOL. I. U tardily

tardily subscribed, and immediately violated; and though the massacre of the inhabitants of Badajoz may be ascribed to the intemperate rage of the soldiers, yet it reflects no small dishonour on the memory of the prince who permitted it.

If Sancho was stern and implacable in victory, he was bold and diligent in war. From chastising his rebellious subjects, he again turned his arms against his foreign and natural enemies. A new fleet had issued from the ports of Africa; but it was encountered and defeated by the combined squadrons of Castille and Genoa; and the strong fortress of Tarif, which on an eminence at a small distance from Gibraltar, awed the adjacent country, and invited the invasion of the hordes of Africa, was, after a long siege, wrested from the infidels by Sancho.

The advantages which his subjects might have derived from the martial virtues of the king of Castille, were diminished by their own turbulence and levity. Four years of imprisonment had not subdued the ambitious spirit of Don Juan; and he was less sensible of his life that had been spared, than of the captivity he had endured. He was scarce restored to freedom before he entered into new intrigues; and the croud of adventurers who listened to his solicitations, enabled him soon to appear openly in arms. To chastise their temerity, Sancho rushed forwards at the head of of his faithful nobles; his approach diffolved their confederacy; and the leaders who had been vanquifhed by the terror of his name, were pardoned by his magnanimity. From the juftice of a brother whom he had fo repeatedly offended, Don Juan fought an afylum in the court of Lifbon; he was followed by the ambaffadors of Sancho; and, banifhed by the policy or averfion of the king of Portugal, he croffed the feas and implored the protection of the king of Morocco. He was intrufted with the command of a confiderable armament; landed his followers on the coaft of Andalufia; and in the fiege of Tarif he ftimulated the ardour of the infidels by the promifed plunder of a Chriftian fortrefs. He was repulfed by the valour and vigilance of the governor Alonfo de Guzman, whofe fteady mind in the difcharge of his duty was indifferent to every other confideration. His infant fon had fallen into the hands of Juan; and was by the command of that prince expofed under the walls of Tarif, with the painful admonition, that the furrender of the fort could alone ranfom the life of the child. "If," replied Guzman, as he threw indignantly his fword to the inhuman ruffian, " if you who were born a prince, and educated " a Chriftian, dare commit fo foul a crime, " know that I not only prefer the lofs of my " fon to that of my honour, but dare furnifh

"you with a weapon for the murder you medi-
"tate." The Moors and Christians in silent admiration at his heroic spirit awaited the event. But the heart of Juan was incapable of approving the virtue he had never felt; and in the presence of the father he plunged his dagger into the bosom of the unfortunate victim.

Without shaking the fortitude of Guzman, Juan beheld himself the object of general detestation; the avenger of his people's injuries was at hand; and the banners of Sancho were no sooner descried, than the precipitate retreat of the inhuman assassin proved, that a timid and cruel spirit are in general nearly allied. After the failure of an enterprise, for the success of which he had confidently answered, he ventured not to present himself to the king of Morocco; and in the court of Granada, though he eluded the vengeance of his brother, he could not escape the contempt and abhorrence of mankind.

In action, the daring valour of Sancho had been often applauded; and his conduct towards the faithful and unhappy Guzman, attested that he was not insensible to the softer emotions of the heart. In a letter that expressed his grateful sense of his loyalty, he conferred on him the name of the *Good*; and he lamented, while he invited him to his court, that his own health suffered him not to hasten to Tarif, and to console him in person.

Amidst

Amidſt the bloody and difguſting annals of violence and flaughter which the hiſtorian is compelled to trace, he dwells with pleaſure on the gentler traits which diſtinguiſh the character of the man from that of the king; and in the hour of death, Sancho himſelf muſt have derived more ſatisfaction from his generous ſympathy for the afflicted Guzman, than from the trophies he had erected over his rebellious ſubjects and infidel enemies.

That hour already rapidly approached; during eleven years that Sancho had reigned, foreign war or domeſtic commotion had ſcarce ever permitted him to lay aſide his armour; and his conſtitution ſunk at length under inceſſant toil and care. He acknowledged the ſymptoms of inevitable death; and his laſt concern was to provide for the tranquil ſucceſſion of his ſon Ferdinand, whoſe feeble age was expoſed to the factions which had long agitated the kingdom. In the preſence of the moſt illuſtrious prelates and nobles of Caſtille, he bequeathed with the diſtinction of regent, the reins of adminiſtration, and the education of the royal infant, to his conſort Maria, whoſe virtues well entitled her to the ſacred truſt; and at Toledo, the air of which had been vainly preſcribed as the laſt hope of recovery, he expired in the forty-fifth year of his age.

A. D. 1295, 1312.

A turbulent nobility who had often revolted againſt, and always reluctantly ſubmitted to, the rule of a warlike and vigorous monarch, were not likely to acquieſce under the authority of a child ſcarce ten years old, and the government of an inexperienced woman. Yet in the ſtation that ſhe occupied, the prudence of Maria muſt have been confeſſed, and her magnanimity applauded. The pretenſions of Don Juan were revived; he even afpired to wreſt the ſceptre from his nephew; and though the Moors might deteſt his baſeneſs, their intereſt prompted them to ſupport his claims. The reſtitution of his honours and eſtates, which had been attainted under the laſt reign, reclaimed him to his allegiance; the hoſtile preparations of the king of Portugal were arreſted by the ceſſion of ſome conſiderable frontier towns; and the powerful houſes of Haro and Lara, who had fuſpended their hereditary enmity to unite againſt the authority of their ſovereign, were reconciled by the redreſs of thoſe grievances which they had alleged as the objects of their revolt. Yet if, to maintain the public tranquillity, Maria ſacrificed the dominions, and circumſcribed the privileges of her ſon, ſhe was not more tenacious of her own rights; and rather than kindle a civil war, ſhe reſigned to a new pretender the title and power of regent, which ſhe derived not only from the

the will of her deceafed hufband, but from the fuffrages of the ftates-general.

Henry was the third fon of Ferdinand, furnamed the faint, by his firft queen, Beatrix. In his early youth he had been addicted to, and confided in, the fcience of judicial aftrology; and the allufive prediction, that Alfonfo the tenth was to be dethroned by a near relation, had pointed his fword againft his brother. By a hafty and difgraceful flight from an adverfe field of battle, he eluded the punifhment of his revolt; and the afylum which had been denied him in the court of Arragon, he found in that of Tunis. In that ftation he ftill maintained a correfpondence with the malecontents of Caftille, and fomented the factions which diftracted the reign of Alfonfo; weary of a life of inaction, he embarked at Tunis for the fhores of Italy, and engaged in the enterprife of his kinfman Conradin, the laft heir of the imperial houfe of Swabia. That unhappy youth in his endeavour to wreft Sicily from Charles of Anjou, became the prifoner of the ufurper; and his execution on a public fcaffold extinguifhed the pretenfions of his family. Henry, in the rafh adventure, had participated in the misfortunes of his chief; and after the death of Conradin, he found himfelf plunged into a dark dungeon, and involved in the excommunication of the Roman pontiff, which had been pronounced against those who assailed a throne founded on the decrees of the successors of St. Peter. By the most abject submissions Henry disarmed the resentment of the holy see, and by the intercession of the pope was restored to freedom. After an absence of twenty-seven years he returned to Spain, and found his nephew Sancho seated on the throne of Castille; he was received with the generosity that was due to an unfortunate kinsman, whose former misconduct had been severely atoned by his subsequent sufferings, and he repaid the benevolence of that monarch with the blackest ingratitude. The turbulence of the times was favourable to his ambitious hopes; his guilt had been forgotten, and his vices concealed in exile; and the Castilians remembered only that he was the son of that Ferdinand whose virtues were the object of their adoration. His claim to the regency was supported by the clamours of the multitude, and the general suffrages of the nobility; the prudence of Maria taught her to avoid a competition which might have been fatal to the interests of her son; she abandoned the title and authority she had been invested with; and only reserved to herself the care of the person and education of the infant king.

Henry found but little satisfaction in the possession of a dignity for which he had violated the most sacred obligations. The clouds of civil and foreign

foreign commotion gathered on every fide, and the throne of Ferdinand was fhaken to its very foundation by the fury of the tempeft. A fecret and formidable league had been concerted by the kings of France, of Arragon, and of Portugal, in fupport of Don Alfonfo de la Cerda, the grandfon of Alfonfo the tenth, by his eldeft fon Ferdinand; the fpecious claims of that prince were efpoufed by the king of Granada who, amidft the diffenfions of the Chriftians, hoped to extend his own boundaries; the reftlefs fpirit of Don Juan prompted him to embark in the confederacy, and the kingdom of Leon and Gallicia were to be the reward of his perfidy; the houfe of Lara was difgufted by the preference that had been given to that of Haro; and every hour fwelled the number of the malecontents, and diminifhed the ftrength of the royal party.

The defigns of the confederates were firft announced to the queen dowager and the regent by the fuccefs of their arms; and the court of Burgos heard with aftonifhment the intelligence, that Leon and Gallicia had acknowledged the authority of Don Juan, and that Alfonfo de la Cerda had been proclaimed king of Caftille by the armies of Portugal and Arragon. Had the latter followed the impulfe of his own ardour, and at the head of the allied hoft preffed forwards to the capital, he might have furprifed or crufhed the

feeble

feeble son of Sancho, unprepared for flight or refiftance. But he was perfuaded on his march to attempt the reduction of the town of Majorga; and the ruinous ftate of the fortifications encouraged the hope that it could not long withftand the attacks of the befiegers; every deficiency was however fupplied by the active zeal of the garrifon, faithful in the caufe of their prince; the affailants were repeatedly repulfed; their fpirits drooped; their ranks were thinned, and their vigour was exhaufted by an epidemic difeafe; the troops of Arragon were the firft to abandon the tedious enterprife; and Alfonfo himfelf was the companion of their retreat; his inglorious example was reluctantly followed by the other allies; and from the tranfient poffeffion of Leon and Gallicia, and from the fond vifion of entering in triumph the city of Burgos, Don Juan was reduced to wage a feeble and indecifive war on the banks of the Duero.

On the oppofite frontiers, the fquadrons of Granada had ravaged the fertile province of Andalufia; and to check their progrefs, the regent himfelf took the field at the head of thofe troops that could be fpared from the protection of Burgos. But in the hour of difficulty and danger, Henry was inftructed how unequal was his genius to the ftation he had obtruded himfelf on. He was defeated in battle; and the prefumption

with

with which he had marched to the encounter, was succeeded by the most abject despair; by a treaty of peace that he subscribed, he consented to deliver the strong fortress of Tarif to the Moors. But the honour of the crown of Castille, which had been sullied by the weakness of a man, was vindicated by the firmness of a woman. Amidst the distress of her country, the virtues of Maria shone forth with superior lustre; she exclaimed against the ignominious conditions which had been signed by the trembling hand of Henry; her spirit was applauded and seconded by the states; and in a national assembly it was determined to prefer the chance of war to an inglorious and doubtful peace.

Yet had the allies on the side of Portugal acted with vigour and unanimity, even the prudence and fortitude of Maria must have been oppressed in the unequal struggle. It was proposed in the camp of the confederates, instead of wasting their strength in the reduction of the frontier towns, to penetrate into the heart of Castille, and invest the king and his mother in Valladolid; the flower of the Castilian nobility were distant and engaged in the defence of Andalusia, and the enterprise appeared not more glorious than easy; but it was frustrated by the returning loyalty of Don Juan de Lara, who declared his resolution not to act immmediately against the person of his king;

his

his scruples embarrassed his associates; and the languor with which they prosecuted the war, sufficiently evinced that they only waited the favourable moment to conclude a peace.

On that event, amidst the din of arms, the mind of Maria had been intent; the character of Henry stood forth in its true colours; he was haughty, fickle, and turbulent; cruel and avaricious; abject in adversity, and insolent in prosperity; and the queen dowager rose in proportion as the regent sunk in the opinion of the public. Beneath her auspices a negociation was opened with the court of Lisbon, and a double marriage was concluded between Ferdinand and his sister, and the daughter and son of the king of Portugal. The nuptials of the daughter of Don Juan de Lara with the regent himself, restored that powerful family to their obedience; and though the king of Granada insulted or ravaged the open country, he was repulsed with loss from the walls of Jaen; and was obliged to retire within his own dominions without achieving any permanent or important conquest.

After recruiting an army which had been broken with toil and disease, James, king of Arragon, had taken the field with the fairest prospect of success. His first operations were equal to his most sanguine expectations. He over-ran the province of Murcia; and Alicant, whose situation

on

on the shores of the Mediterranean still attracts the eye of commercial adventure, consented to receive a garrison, and to acknowledge the authority of the king of Arragon. That monarch encountered a more obstinate resistance in the siege of Lorca; had not the counsels of the queen-dowager been secretly embarrassed by the envy of the regent, he must either have abandoned the enterprise with disgrace, or staked his fortune in a field of battle. But Henry marched with reluctance to promote the glory of Maria; his intrigues retarded the steps of his companions; and before the banners of Castille were displayed on the banks of the Guadalantin, Lorca had surrendered. The fame which the queen-dowager had been defrauded of by the mean jealousy of the regent, she derived from her own fruitful genius. She fomented in Arragon the spirit of discontent; and the rising disaffection recalled James to guard his own throne; on his retreat he offered to evacuate all his conquests in Murcia, with the single exception of Alicant; but the proposal was rejected as unworthy the dignity of the crown of Castille; and his ambassadors might be astonished at the magnanimity of the queen-dowager in the reply, that his restoring all the places he had seized, could alone prove the foundation of an honourable and permanent peace.

Had

Had the counsels of Maria neither been embarrassed by intrigue nor revolt, she probably would soon have compelled the king of Arragon to have subscribed the conditions she had dictated. She called into action the power of the nation; and the train of gallant nobility that accompanied her to Valladolid, and in the assembly of the states supported her interests, impressed with fear the prince Don Juan, who abandoned his vain hope of reigning over Leon and Galicia, and renewed his homage and oath of fidelity to his sovereign. The timid Juan was terrified into obedience, the venal Henry was bribed into compliance; his death soon after delivered Maria from a formidable rival and a faithless associate; and the moment seemed arrived when undisturbed by factious competition, she might vindicate the glory of her country, and train the inexperienced youth of her son to prove the terror of his enemies and the delight of his subjects.

But the fond illusion, if Maria indulged it, was soon dissipated; some differences which threatened the tranquillity of Castille on the side of Navarre, had summoned her to Victoria; and she returned exulting in the success of her negociations abroad, to endure the mortification of finding her power undermined at home. The ear of Ferdinand had been poisoned by the artful representations of the prince Don Juan, and the house of Lara; they

maliciously

maliciously contrasted his own situation with that of his mother; and he was taught to dread as an enemy, the only person whom he could rely on as a friend. He declared his resolution to assume the reins of government. In celebrating his marriage with Constantia, the daughter of the king of Portugal, he displayed the pomp, and asserted the authority of a sovereign; and the multitude, ever prone to change, and intoxicated with the desire of a new administration, applauded his presumption; the city of Valladolid alone remained firm to the party of the queen-dowager, whose judgment they had so long experienced; the inhabitants shut their gates against the troops of Ferdinand; and it was only to the remonstrances of Maria herself that they yielded, and consented to receive a royal garrison; but their indignation survived their submission; they forbade their deputies to appear in the assembly of the states; and refused to sanction by their presence the measures which they could not approve.

Maria would have been unworthy of the reputation she had acquired, had she attempted by force to constrain the inclinations of her son; and she would have been insensible to the feelings of a mother, had she remained a silent spectator of his imprudence; she expostulated, but she expostulated in vain; and against her advice, the king of Castille agreed to accept the king of

Portugal

Portugal as umpire between himself and the king of Arragon. The decision of the royal arbitrator was such as the queen-dowager had foreseen and foretold; the Segura, which intersects the province of Murcia, was fixed on as the boundary of the dominions of Ferdinand and James; and with the important city of Alicant, the country to the north of that river was dismembered from the crown.

The pretensions of the infants de la Cerda might yet interrupt the repose of Ferdinand; and to extinguish the embers of civil discord, that monarch consented to resign to the eldest, Alfonso, the cities of Moncon and Tormes, with several towns, the revenues of which afforded him an ample maintenance; to the youngest, Ferdinand, he promised an income equal to that which had been allotted for a prince of Spain; and the brothers, after receiving hostages for their security, appeared at court, and submitted to the ungrateful ceremony of homage.

It would have been extraordinary indeed had not the weakness and concessions of the king of Castille multiplied the number of the factious and ambitious. The hereditary enmity of the houses of Haro and Lara was again suspended, that they might brave with impunity their sovereign; and though the former was reconciled by the grant of the important province of Biscay for his life, the

latter

latter still maintained a dangerous independence in arms, and allured the prince Don Juan to his party. Yet Don Juan had scarcely betrayed the cause of his royal kinsman, before he himself was deserted by the family of Lara, who solicited, and readily obtained as the reward of their perfidy, the pardon and favour of Ferdinand.

The uninteresting annals of domestic discord and treachery are transiently varied by a feeble but foreign war; through the mediation of the queen mother a new reconciliation was effected between Don Juan and the king; and Ferdinand embraced the moment of tranquillity to march against the natural enemies of his country and religion. He surprised the fortress of Gibraltar, the importance of which was then but slightly known; yet he failed in his attempt on Algezire; and the ill success of that siege, and the fresh intrigues of the prince Don Juan, induced him to listen to the overtures of the king of Granada, and in consideration of a considerable sum of money to subscribe a peace with the Moors.

The majesty of Ferdinand had been often insulted by the turbulence, and his confidence frequently abused by the professions of the prince Don Juan; yet in the revenge that he meditated, he should not have forgotten his own character. And when instead of the sword of a sovereign he condescended to employ the dagger of an assassin, he revealed the weakness of his government, and forfeited what yet remained of the esteem of his subjects. The nuptial feast of his sister with the duke of Brittany, was to have been polluted with the blood of a kinsman; but the design had not been so secretly concerted as entirely to escape the suspicion of the destined victim; on the first alarm Don Juan withdrew abruptly from court; proclaimed the cause of his flight; and derived some share of popularity from the general abhorrence of the treachery of Ferdinand.

From the moment the king had assumed the reins of administration, the counsels of Maria had been disregarded; and it was not until he was alarmed by the preparations of Don Juan, that he condescended again to solicit the mediation of his mother; the virtues of the queen dowager had secured the respect of all parties; on her assurances of safety Don Juan returned again to court, and the public harmony was re-established.

It was not only the court of Spain that was disgraced by perfidy and cruelty; the persecution of the knights templars excited the attention of all Europe. During the first fervour of the crusades, that order, by uniting the popular qualities of devotion and valour, had rapidly advanced in credit and authority; their services in the recovery and defence of the Holy Land, had been repaid by the piety of the Christian inhabitants of Europe;

Europe; but in France especially their acquisitions had extended through every province, and enabled them to support a royal magnificence. The abuse of their riches had in time relaxed those virtues which first preferred them to esteem; and instead of braving the dangers of martial pilgrimage, they chose to enjoy their opulent revenues in ease and luxury. Of illustrious birth, and according to the custom of the age without any tincture of letters, they scorned the ignoble occupations of a monastic life, and passed their time in the fashionable amusements of hunting, gallantry, and the pleasures of the table. But though this conduct had diminished the respect they had once possessed, yet the immediate cause of their destruction in France proceeded from the rapacious and vindictive spirit of Philip the Fair. They were accused of every species of sensual vice that degrades human nature, and every act of impiety which could prove offensive to religion. But their accusers were two of their brethren condemned by the order to perpetual imprisonment for their profligacy, and who obtained their forfeited lives from the secrets they affected to reveal. The doubtful evidence was readily received by the tyrant; and above an hundred unhappy gentlemen on the rack were tortured to confess the justice of the charge; several supported their agonies with unabated

constancy;

conſtancy; but the majority yielded to the excruciating anguiſh, and ſigned the declaration of their own criminality. Yet they were no ſooner releaſed from the engines of torture than they retracted the confeſſions which had been extorted from them. But the avarice and reſentment of their perſecutor was deaf to every remonſtrance; their eſtates were confiſcated; and without the form of trial fifty were condemned to, and ſuffered death with manly fortitude; the grand-maſter, with the three great officers, were in the preſence of their royal oppreſſor conſumed by a ſlow fire; and aſſerted with their laſt breath the purity of their conduct. Their firmneſs commanded the belief of the people; but the barbarous injuſtice of Philip was ſanctioned by the ſentence of his creature pope Clement the fifth, who then reſided in France; and who, without examining a witneſs, or making an enquiry into the truth of facts, by the plenitude of his apoſtolic power aboliſhed the whole order.

A greater degree of moderation and equity prevailed through the councils of Spain; the charges againſt the order were heard; but they were heard with impartiality; and the knights were acquitted by the unanimous voice of their judges. Yet though in their deciſion the latter diſregarded private views and public clamour, they could but vindicate the reputation of the accuſed;

accused; the decree of the Roman see was irresistible; the order was dissolved; the knights were distributed into several convents, and their possessions were by the command of the pope transferred to the order of St. John of Jerusalem, whose poverty had preserved unsullied the purity of their professions, and who still distinguished themselves by their martial enterprises against the disciples of Mahomet; yet the states-general of Spain eluded in part the holy judgment; they represented their own situation; and they were permitted to retain the spoils of the templars to support themselves against their infidel neighbours.

The rejoicings which the birth of a son and heir to the crown might occasion, did not interrupt the preparations for renewing the war against the Moors; a considerable army marched under the conduct of Don Pedro, the brother of the king, and invested the town of Alcandeta on the frontiers of Andalusia. From the adjacent situation of Martos, Ferdinand himself observed the operations of the siege; two brothers of the house of Carvajal had been apprehended as guilty of the murder of a nobleman at Palencia; they were brought before the royal tribunal; and the indignation of the king suffered them not to vindicate their innocence; they were commanded instantly to be hurled from a rock; and the intemperate

temperate sentence was executed without delay.
On the verge of eternity, they summoned their
inexorable judge within a month to appear before
his God; and the death of Ferdinand on the
thirtieth day, was regarded in a superstitious age
as the effect of their solemn citation.

It is the wish of a lively French writer, that
the story was either true, or generally believed;
and that the example might instruct all princes
who think they have a right to follow their own
imperious wills at the expence of their fellow
creatures, to dread the retribution of a superior
power; but though the execution of the brothers
of Carvajal, and their last words, are confirmed
by a variety of historians, yet we may gather
from the candid pages of Mariana, that the
health of Ferdinand had long been shaken, that
he was just recovered from a severe indisposition, and that his indulgence in the pleasures of
the table, well warrant the short space that
was fixed by the culprits as the term of his
life, whose hasty sally of resentment would have
been buried in oblivion, had it not been preferred
to notice by the event.

A. D. 1312, 1350. The civil commotions which had agitated the kingdom during the minority and reign of Ferdinand, were revived with increase of fury on his death; the invidious office of regent was declined by the prudence of Maria, and

and the pretenfions of Don Juan, and of Pedro, the brother of the late monarch, were fupported by their refpective partifans with clamour and violence; yet though the widow of Sancho refufed to fuftain again the weight and odium of government, fhe neglected not to watch over the infancy and fafety of Alfonfo the eleventh. Her voice extinguifhed or fufpended the enmity of the rival factions; the authority was divided between, and the title of regent was equally imparted to both the princes Juan and Pedro; but the ftates-general that ratified the agreement were not unmindful of the future welfare of their king, and to Maria was affigned the duty of protecting his perfon and forming his mind.

The promife of fpoil had again allured the Moors of Africa to pafs the ftraits of Gibraltar; and the regents determined by the vigour of their meafures to anticipate the defigns of their enemies. In his march Don Pedro reduced the ftrong fortrefs of Tifcar; and under the walls of Alcandeta he joined the forces of his affociate Don Juan. The confederate hoft fwept the open country, and pitched their tents within fight of the towers of Granada; and while the Moorifh monarch affembled the ftrength of his nation, the Chriftian leaders exulted in the hopes of an eafy conqueft; but no fooner were the fquadrons of Granada united with thofe of Africa, than Ifmael rufhed rushed to the defence of his capital. On the day that was to decide the fate of Granada, though her sovereign encouraged his warriors by his presence, yet the chief command in the hour of battle was entrusted to the experience of Osmyn. The right of the Christians was led by Don Juan; and in the front of the left was displayed the banner of Don Pedro. Their rival exertions long resisted the superior numbers of the Moors; and if we may rely on the credit of Mariana, they sunk at length without a wound, and expired exhausted by the slaughter of their enemies. But we may safely venture to reject the partial narrative, which might gratify the vanity of the chivalry of Castille, but cannot command the belief of posterity; and the regents were undoubtedly involved in the general carnage of the Christians. A wretched remnant escaped under cover of the night to relate the fate of their brethren. The calamities of war were retaliated on the vanquished; from the walls of Granada the victorious torrent rolled on to those of Jaen; and from the stream of the Oro to the northern banks of the Guadalquivir, the fertile fields of Andalusia were converted into a desert.

The progress of the infidels might still have been checked by the unanimity of the Christians; but the death of the regents opened a new scene of dissension; and the reigns of administration were

were disputed by four powerful competitors, Don Philip, the uncle of the king; Don Juan Emanuel, who had married the daughter of the king of Arragon, and commanded on the frontiers of Murcia; Don Juan, son to the regent of the same name, and who from the loss of an eye in his infancy was distinguished by the epithet of the *Deformed*; and Don Alfonso de la Cerda, who, thrust aside from the throne, without the title aspired to the authority of king; each was supported by numerous vassals and adherents, and each was indifferent to the means by which he could attain the object of his ambition. In vain did Maria exert her influence and address to controul their presumption, or conciliate their regard; in vain did the Roman pontiff interpose to repress their discord; the constitution of the former was unequal to the struggle, and incessant anxiety extinguished the expiring taper of life; while the latter was instructed that the thunders of the Vatican were more efficacious in kindling than suppressing the flames of civil commotion. Regardless of his censures, the rivals exerted every engine of fraud and force; and Alfonso de la Cerda, and Juan the Deformed, sooner than suffer the natural claims of Don Philip to prevail, abandoned their own, and declared in favour of the party of Don Juan Emanuel.

During thirteen years from the death of Ferdinand,

dinand, the kingdoms of Caſtille and Leon had experienced all the calamities which flow from faction and anarchy. But in the lapſe of that term the underſtanding of Alfonſo had rapidly advanced and far ſurpaſſed his age; in his fifteenth year he proclaimed his reſolution to break the ſhackles he had been held in, and to claim the rights of a king. The diſtracted ſtate of the nation was favourable to his intentions; in a general aſſembly at Valladolid his authority was recognized; the hopes of the competitors expired or were concealed in the preſence of their lawful prince; and Alfonſo the eleventh beheld a tranſient calm ſucceed the tempeſts which had afflicted his minority.

Yet the proſpect was ſoon again overcaſt; the diſcontent of Don Juan Emanuel was no longer concealed; he withdrew from court; to attach Don Juan the Deformed effectually to his intereſts, he propoſed to beſtow on him the hand of his daughter Conſtantia; and the formidable alliance muſt have overſhadowed the luſtre of the crown. The character of Alfonſo will not ſuffer from the artifice which he deſcended to at this critical moment; he affected himſelf to be ſenſible of the charms of Conſtantia, and of the merits of her father; he intimated that policy as well as inclination prompted his union with the daughter of ſo powerful a ſubject; the ſtratagem was attended
with

with the effect he expected; and on the first rumour of the paffion of the king, Emanuel flew to Burgos to renew his oath of fidelity and allegiance.

While the nobles of Caftille preferred in arms their own claims, or fupported thofe of their chiefs, every fpecies of diforder had multiplied throughout the kingdom; large bodies of banditti violated the public peace, and in contempt of the laws levied their contributions not only on individuals but towns and cities. To reftore the tone and vigour of the law was the firft object of the royal attention; with a fmall band of difciplined troops Alfonfo flew from province to province; explored their retreats in the depths of the forefts and mountains; and though the immediate execution of the offenders has been conftrued into cruelty, yet it muft be remembered, that the juftice of a king admits not of the compaffion which adorns a fubject; and that lenity to the guilty, is too frequently an injury to the good.

From the feverity of their monarch, the needy and defperate found a refuge with Don Juan the Deformed; and the numbers of daring adventurers inured to blood and rapine who flocked to the ftandard of that prince, enabled him to brave the vengeance of his king. His negociations were extended to the courts of Arragon and Portugal, and he urged Don Alfonfo de la Cerda to refume resume his pretensions to the crown. His intrigues eluded not the vigilence of his sovereign; and Alfonso, after having in vain endeavoured to reclaim him to his duty by the most liberal offers, determined to deliver himself from his factious and enterprising spirit by a decisive though dishonourable blow. In the execution of the design, his address rather than his integrity must be commended; he proposed to give him in marriage his sister Eleanora; and the presumption of Don Juan induced him to accept the invitation of his king, and to present himself at Toro; he came attended with a train which resembled rather the army of a powerful sovereign than the establishment of a private person. But his confidence in his strength was fatal to his life; as he passed through the royal apartments, he was assailed by a chosen and determined band; two gentlemen who accompanied him, and attempted to draw their swords in his defence, shared his fate, and were extended lifeless on the ground; the hall of audience was thrown open, and Alfonso from his throne avowed the orders he had issued; he represented Don Juan as a traitor too great for the laws, and declared that his blood alone could have prevented an immediate and dangerous civil war. The clamours of the multitude were hushed by the imperious voice of their sovereign; the adherents of the unhappy victim were happy to conceal

conceal their attachment in silence; but the bonds of society were loosened by the fatal expedient; and when a monarch can have recourse to the practice of an assassin, the most virtuous of his subjects have reason to tremble equally with the most guilty.

 The first to dread his fate, and to attempt to avenge it, was Don Juan Emanuel, whose sword had been drawn successfully against the Moors, but who on the intelligence of the death of Don Juan the Deformed, signed a private peace with the king of Granada, and trusting to the strength of his castle of Chinchilla, and to the number of his vassals, erected the standard of revolt. His rebellion dissolved the hopes of his daughter Constantia; and that lady, who had already borne the title of queen, beheld herself a prisoner in a city which she had fondly regarded as the capital of her future power and splendour. The haughty spirit of Emanuel was exasperated to fury by the insult; he obtained from his father-in-law the king of Arragon, a promise of support; with the forces that he could hastily assemble he laid waste the frontiers of Castille; and his resentment to the sovereign was proclaimed in his barbarous warfare against his people.

 But the spirit of Alfonso was not to be braved with impunity; in open war or secret confederacy his valour and vigilance extorted the admiration

ration of his enemies; by land or by sea, on horseback or on foot, in every encounter his genius and courage shone conspicuous. The piratical squadrons of the Moors had issued from the ports of Africa; but they were attacked and defeated by the fleets of Castille; the cities of Zamora and Toro had revolted; they were quickly reduced and severely punished; Don Alvaro Nugnez Osorio, who had enjoyed the entire confidence of his master, was the first to desert him in his distress; the ungrateful favourite was stabbed by the command of the king in the midst of his retainers. A new king of Arragon had succeeded to the father-in-law of Emanuel; and was readily persuaded to desert the cause of that chief; a negociation was entered into with the court of Lisbon, and the marriage of Alfonso with the daughter of the king of Portugal secured to the former a powerful and faithful ally.

Yet the bosom of Alfonso was less susceptible of private revenge than of public glory; he still offered to Emanuel the free pardon of his guilt, and the restoration of his estates and honours; and urged him, instead of weakening by his obstinacy, to strengthen by his union the common cause, and to march in conjunction with him against the infidels. The refusal of the haughty rebel could not check the ardour of Alfonso; Spain resounded with his preparations; and the

court

court of Granada was aftonifhed and difmayed by the rumour of the fleets and armies he had affembled; the prudence of Mahomet, the fucceffor of Ifmael in the throne of Granada, inftructed him to prevent by fubmiffion a conteft which threatened the total fubverfion of the Moorifh power. His ambaffadors were difpatched to Seville; and the humiliating conditions they fubfcribed, fufficiently reveal the terror with which they were impreffed; the king of Granada confented to hold his fceptre as the vaffal of the crown of Caftille; and to acknowledge the fupremacy of his lord by the annual tribute of twelve thoufand pieces of gold.

The terms which had been extorted by fear, were violated with the return of confidence. It was from Africa alone that Mahomet could hope for fuccour; he croffed the ftraits; reprefented in the court of Morocco the increafing power of Caftille, and was heard with attention; feven thoufand horfemen were granted to his immediate diftrefs; a more confiderable detachment followed under the conduct of Abu Malic, the fon of the king of Morocco; the tranfports which conveyed them eluded the vigilance of the Chriftian fleet; the king of Granada renewed his alliance with Don Emanuel; and the fiege of Gibraltar was inftantly formed by the Moflem hoft.

The

The allegiance of the houſe of Lara had been corrupted by the intrigues of Don Emanuel; and at the moment that Alfonſo beheld his dominions expoſed to foreign invaſion, he found his reſources diſtracted by civil commotion. At the head of the troops which yet were faithful to their ſovereign, he pointed his ſteps towards Gibraltar. In his march he was ſolicited to an interview with the diſaffected lords; he accepted their invitation; and ſuperior to fear, entered without attendants the caſtle of Becerril, which was garriſoned by their followers; they were awed by his magnanimity; and at the feaſt that he ſhared without reſerve, they engaged on the payment of a ſum of money to return to their duty; the engagement was fulfilled on the ſide of Alfonſo, but baſely broken by Emanuel, who employed the gold he had received in fomenting new cabals, and making new levies againſt his ſovereign.

The ſpeed with which Alfonſo had advanced to the relief of Gibraltar, only expoſed him to a freſh mortification; he was arrived within ſight of that fortreſs, when he was informed the governor had meanly betrayed his truſt, and ſurrendered it to the infidels. He aſpired to recover it; but while he yet preſſed the ſiege with the faireſt proſpect of ſucceſs, he was recalled to the centre of his dominions by the cries of his ſubjects. The contagion of revolt had reached the

the house of Haro, and Don Alonzo, the chief of that family, with Don Emanuel, and Don Juan de Lara, had started to arms at an appointed signal, and marked their different routes through Castille with slaughter and devastation.

We may easily believe it was with reluctance and indignation that an high-spirited prince like Alfonso, signed a treaty with the Moors, which left Gibraltar in their possession, and released the king of Granada from the humiliating condition of tribute. But the danger was pressing; and while his kingdom was rent by intestine discord, he could not hope to triumph over his foreign enemies. He had no sooner subscribed the peace, than he marched with diligence to the protection of his capital. As he advanced, the confederates retired; but they were not able to elude the vengeance of an injured monarch. The precipitate flight of Don Juan de Lara preserved indeed his life; but his estates were laid waste or confiscated; and his fortresses in the mountainous province of Biscay were attacked and reduced.

A severer doom awaited Don Alonzo de Haro; he was surprised in his castle, led in chains before his king, and sternly reproached with his guilt and ingratitude; the resentment of his sovereign suffered him not long to languish in doubt, and the second day after he was made prisoner, he was beheaded on a public scaffold.

The factious nobles of Castille heard with terror that the chief of the powerful house of Haro had perished by the hand of the common executioner. Neither the most illustrious extraction nor extensive connexions could secure them from the wrath of majesty; and in the fate of Don Alonzo, Don Juan de Lara trembled for his own. He dispatched a trusty messenger to learn if yet the road to mercy was open; but though the king assured him of his personal safety, he still refused to see him; he was more indulgent to Don Emanuel; and on his reconciliation with that nobleman, he released his daughter Constantia, and consented to, and facilitated her marriage with, his brother-in-law the prince of Portugal.

After so long a period of turbulence, Alfonso might have hoped to have tasted some moments of repose; but his life was destined to incessant toil; and he had scarce sheathed the sword of civil war, before a new enemy arose on the side of Navarre. The king of Castille endeavoured to prevent open hostilities by every offer of accommodation which the dignity of his crown would admit of; but when compelled to take the field, his preparations were carried on with vigour and alacrity. The chivalry of Castille, at the command of their sovereign, consented to march beneath the conduct of Martin Fernandez, an officer whose obscure descent they despised, but whose

whose worth they revered. In a field of battle the appointment of Fernandez was approved; the troops of Navarre were broken or slaughtered; and the peace that was re-established between the two kingdoms was dictated by Alfonso.

The exultation of the king of Castille at his victory, was allayed by the information that the intrigues of Don Juan de Lara, and Don Emanuel, were still continued. Exasperated by their frequent perfidy, he appealed against them to the assembly of the states; they were declared traitors by the unanimous voice of the representatives of the nation, who granted at the same time a liberal subsidy to prosecute the war to their entire distruction.

The king of Castille suffered not the weapon to rust which the states-general had trusted to his hand. With a numerous army he invested in the walls of Lerma, Don Juan de Lara. The obstinacy of the garrison, and the strength of the fortifications, protracted the siege; and Don Emanuel marched to the relief of his associate; the king advanced to meet him at the head of a select detachment; the rebels were defeated, and their chief escaped with difficulty from the pursuit of Alfonso; the victorious king continued the siege of Lerma with unwearied diligence; the towers of that city were already shaken by his engines; and Don Juan, baffled in every attempt to fly, anticipated the consequences of unsuccessful rebellion. A last, but slender hope was reposed on the mercy of his sovereign; and even the stubborn temper of Don Juan was not proof against the clemency he had so ill deserved; his life had indeed been promised on his submission; but he was received by Alfonso with a generosity which reflects the brightest lustre on the character of that prince; he was restored to his estates and honours, invested with the high dignity of standard bearer of Castille, and during the remainder of his life approved himself a dutiful and grateful servant.

The example of Don Juan de Lara influenced the conduct of Don Emanuel; whose return to his allegiance extinguished the war which his intrigues had kindled between Castille and Portugal; a general pacification between the Christian princes of Spain succeeded; and Alfonso at length found himself at leisure to attend to the progress of the Moors of Africa and Granada.

At Seville the royal standard was displayed; and the factions which had so long pursued each other with kindred rage, confessed a generous emulation as they marched against the common foe. They penetrated without seeing an enemy to the walls of Ronda; that fortification, erected on a craggy rock, derided their menaces; the exhausted country no longer supplied them the means

means of fubfiftence; and they again pointed their fteps towards the frontiers of Caftille; but the fignal of retreat was fcarcely given before a cloud of duft revealed the approach of the fquadrons of Granada and Africa. The Moors were animated by the prefence of Abu Malic, the fon and heir to the crown of Morocco; and Alfonfo with impatience awaited in open field the charge of an adverfary who had wrefted from him the ftrong fortrefs of Gibraltar. In the tumult of the day Alfonfo, with Don Juan de Lara, and Don Emanuel, were diftinguifhed above the crowd of combatants. The Moors, incapable of withftanding their rival ardour, fled to an adjacent mountain; under a fhower of ftones and miffile weapons the fteep afcent was climbed by the impetuous Chriftians; and fo defperate was the refiftance of the vanquifhed, and fo inexorable the victors, that not a fingle Moor efcaped the promifcuous flaughter.

Whatever tears the king of Morocco might fhed over his unfortunate fon, were foon dried by the hope of vengeance. His voice arouzed the the tribes of Africa from their lethargy; the propagation of the koran and the promife of fpoil affembled the rapacious difciples of Mahomet; two hundred tranfports were convoyed by thirty gallies; a favourable wind enabled them to elude the Chriftian fleet; they were joined by the forces of Granada; and the hoſt which inveſted Tarif has been computed at two hundred thouſand men.

The danger of that fortreſs was quickly conveyed to Alfonſo; but the ſtrength of Caſtille was unequal to the conteſt; and to his queen was intruſted the important commiſſion of awakening the court of Liſbon to the common defence of Chriſtianity; the king of Portugal was not deaf to the ſolicitations of his daughter; and policy quickened his ſteps at the head of his martial nobility; he was received in Seville with every honour by his ſon-in-law; but the diſtreſs of Tarif allowed not the monarchs to waſte the hours in feaſts and tournaments; forty thouſand infantry and twenty thouſand cavalry, confident in their faith and valour, marched beneath their banners. A thouſand horſe and four thouſand foot cut their way through the lines of the beſiegers, and reaſſured the fainting ſpirits of the garriſon of Tarif; and on the enſuing morning the ſignal for general action was diſplayed. On the plains of Salſado the king of Caſtille charged the ſquadrons of Morocco, and the king of Portugal advanced againſt thoſe of Granada; the encounter was long and bloody; and it was not until the conflict had been maintained ſeveral hours with various ſucceſs, that victory declared for the Chriſtians. One hundred thouſand Moors fell in the battle, or were ſlaughtered in the purſuit;

the

the king of Morocco fled with precipitation to Algezire, and inftantly reimbarked for Africa; while the king of Granada with the fhattered remnant of his forces, retired within his own territories, and trembled for the fafety of his capital.

On the field Alfonfo offered to recompenfe the zeal of his ally with the wealthy fpoil and captives of their joint valour. But the generous fpirit of the king of Portugal rejected the rich prize; fome arms rather curious than valuable were all he could be prevailed on to accept; and after having interchanged mutual vows of amity with his fon-in-law, he led back his troops into his own dominions. His difinterefted conduct funk deep in the mind of Alfonfo; the private life of the king of Caftille had been lefs pure than his public; intereft rather than paffion had prompted his marriage with the princefs Maria of Portugal; but his heart had been long captivated by the wit and charms of Donna Leonora de Guzman, the widow of Don Juan de Velafco. To her his hours were facrificed, and his affections devoted; and thofe who were permitted to approach and gaze on her beauty, forgot the guilt of his attachment in the admiration of his choice. But Alfonfo could not be infenfible to the ardour with which Maria had ferved him in the hour of diftrefs; he was penetrated by the generofity of her father the king of Portugal; gratitude fupplied the place of love, and religion confirmed his refolution ever after to renounce the licentious pleafures which he had fhared with Leonora, and to confine himfelf to the arms of the lawful partner of his throne and bed.

With his victorious army Alfonfo fwept the frontiers of Granada, reduced by famine Alcala, and by force Molin; the fortifications of Algezire demanded more weighty preparations; the fquadrons of Portugal and Arragon were readily perfuaded to act in concert with that of Caftille; twelve gallies were hired of the Genoefe, whofe naval fkill about the middle of the fourteenth century was celebrated throughout Europe; thefe blocked up the harbour, and intercepted all fupplies from Africa, while Alfonfo regularly invefted Algezire by land with an army which might fafely defy the feeble attempts of the king of Granada. The eyes of Europe were turned on the enterprife; the walls were ftrong, the garrifon numerous; and the thunder of the artillery, the firft that had been ufed in Spain, was heard with aftonifhment by the befiegers; but the tremendous effect which was produced by the firft difcharge, was foon effaced; and the troops of Alfonfo dreaded lefs the deftructive fire of the cannon, than the gradual approach of famine. Six months had tried the patience of the auxiliaries, and exhaufted the magazines of the affailants; hunger already began to be felt through the camp; and

to

to fupply the demands of his allies, and relieve the diftrefs of his own troops, the king ordered his plate to be coined into current money at a higher rate than the common ftandard. The difgraceful and dangerous expedient was averted by the zeal of the moft confiderable cities of Spain; every province freely contributed its proportion in corn, in wine, or in fpecie; fome pecuniary affiftance was derived from the holy liberality of the pope; and the ardour of the warriors of Spain was rekindled, and their emulation inflamed by the martial nobles of France and England, who haftened to fhare the glory and hazard of the enterprife.

Yet it was not until the fecond year, when every offer for raifing the fiege had been rejected, and the walls of Algezire tottered beneath the inceffant ftrokes of the engines of the befiegers, that the garrifon, diminifhed by famine and the fword, fubmitted to propofe terms of capitulation. The foldiers and citizens were permitted to retire without moleftation; the Chriftian ftandard was again difplayed on the towers of Algezire; and a truce for ten years was fubfcribed between the king of Caftille, and the monarchs of Granada and Morocco.

The valour and activity of Alfonfo had been approved in war, and in peace his courtefy and generofity were admired. Several of the daughters

ters of the king of Morocco had, on his defeat at Salfado, become the captives of the king of Caftille; they had been treated by the latter prince with the refpect due to their birth; and no fooner was peace reftored than they were difmiffed with magnificent prefents to their father's court; amidft the annals of a fanguinary age, the mind is rarely relieved from the bloody narrative by the contemplation of the more amiable qualities of humanity and politenefs; and fome praife is due to Alfonfo, who, amidft religious and political enmity, was ftill careful to cherifh the generous fentiments of chivalry.

Yet one paffion ever rages in the bofoms of kings; and if the courtefy of Alfonfo commands our applaufe, his ambition cannot be defended from our reproach; four years of peace had fcarcely fkinned over the wounds of war, and the inhabitants of Caftille ftill groaned beneath the double fcourge of peftilence and famine, when the royal ftandard was difplayed; and their monarch fummoned his martial nobles again to the field. The Moorifh banners that ftreamed from the towers of Gibraltar infulted his pride; and he recollected with indignation that during his reign that important fortrefs had paffed from the hands of the Chriftians to thofe of the infidels; without a previous declaration of war he fuddenly fummoned the garrifon to furrender; and urged in perfon the

fiege

siege with his usual ardour. But the seeds of disease lurked in the veins of his soldiers, and the plague soon broke out in his camp; the remonstrances of his officers could not prevail on him to abandon the enterprise, or withdraw from the scene of infection; he was the victim of his perseverance; his blood was tainted; and he expired in the moment that the distress of the besieged afforded him the strongest assurances of success.

Such was the fate of Alfonso the eleventh, who of the princes that succeeded Ferdinand the Saint, is most entitled to our admiration; the turbulence of the times he reigned in was his glory; the factions which had overshadowed the power of the throne were broken by his vigour; and the foreign enemies of the state who had availed themselves of the hour of civil dissension, were chastised by his valour; the execution of the chief of the house of Haro awed the haughty spirits of his nobles; and though the means by which he delivered himself from the incessant enmity of Don Juan the Deformed cannot be justified, yet the confidence that he reposed in Don Emanuel, and the clemency that he extended to Don Juan de Lara, cannot be too warmly applauded. The love of martial fame was his predominant passion as a king; and to that his life was at length sacrificed, when it would have been most serviceable to his subjects. As a man,

man, his attachment to the fair seems to have been his sole failing; one son, of the name of Peter, and who had attained his sixteenth year, was his only issue by his consort Maria; but Donna Leonora had proved more fruitful in his embraces; and her second son, Henry of Transtamare, was destined to avenge the fate of his mother, and after a long and bloody contest, to ascend, by the destruction of his brother, the throne of Castille.

Chapter

HISTORY OF SPAIN.

Chapter the Eighth.

Accession of Peter, surnamed the Cruel.—*His perfidy and barbarity.—He is dethroned by his half-brother Henry, count of Transtamare.—He is restored by Edward, the Black Prince.—Is a second time defeated by Henry, and put to death.—Reign of Henry the second.—Is succeeded by his son John.—Pretensions of John to the crown of Portugal.—His defeat at Aljubarrota.—Makes peace with Portugal and England.—Felicity of his general administration.—Account of his death.—His infant son Henry the third is acknowledged king.—Dissensions of the nobility.—Henry assumes the government at thirteen.—His vigorous conduct.—Meditates the expulsion of the Moors from Spain.—His death.—Integrity of his brother Ferdinand.—John the second is proclaimed.—Wise administration of Ferdinand.—He is chosen king of Portugal.—Competition for the regency of Castille.—Long and disastrous reign of John.—Revolt of his son, the prince of Asturias.—Execution of his favourite, Alvaro de Luna.—He dies, and is succeeded by his son Henry the fourth, surnamed the* Impotent.—*His marriage with the princess of Portugal.—She is delivered*

vered of a daughter.—*The nobility refuse to acknowledge the child as the king's.—Formidable confederacy against Henry.—He is solemnly deposed at Avila;—and his brother Alfonso proclaimed.—Death of Alfonso.—Treaty between Henry and his nobles.—The king acknowledges his sister Isabella, his successor, in prejudice to the princess Joanna.—Marriage of Isabella with Ferdinand the king of Sicily, and son of the king of Arragon.—Death of Henry.—Ferdinand and Isabella are proclaimed.—The king of Portugal claims the crown in right of Joanna.—He is defeated at Toro.—Death of the king of Arragon.—Ferdinand unites the crowns of Castille and Arragon.*

A. D. 1350. 1369. WHEN Peter, whose sanguinary manners affixed to him the surname of Cruel, was acknowledged king of Castille, the memory of his father had prejudiced in his favour the minds of his subjects. The haughty spirits of the nobility had been awed, the power of the Moors had been broken; though the siege of Gibraltar was abandoned, the national honour was preserved; it was to disease that the assailants yielded; they retired slowly and in order; and their enemies were content to observe, without attemping to molest their retreat.

But

But the fair prospects of tranquillity and prosperity were soon clouded by the passions of Peter himself, and those of his mother; as the consort of Alfonso, the patience and moderation of Maria had been the theme of general praise; as his widow, her vindictive spirit was the source of destruction to her son; she gave a loose to female resentment; and her rival Donna Leonora de Guzman was the unfortunate victim that she claimed.

Though from the battle of Salsado, Alfonso had renounced all amorous commerce with the beautiful Leonora, yet he had not been inattentive to her future safety or interest. He had assigned the town of Medina Sidonia for her retreat; had strengthened it with new fortifications; and had provided it with a numerous and faithful garrison, commanded by the gallant Alonzo Cardonel. Four sons, the fruits of her illicit interviews with the king, had attained to manhood; and if the imbecility of Sancho allowed her not to repose her confidence on the eldest, she must have observed with pleasure that the enterprising temper of the second, Henry, count of Transtamare, was supported by the fraternal affection of his brothers Ferdinand and Tello.

By her own feelings it is probable that Donna Leonora judged of the intentions of the queen dowager;

dowager; and on the first intelligence of the death of Alfonso, she sought refuge within the walls of Medina Sidonia; to that city gratitude or ambition induced several of the most illustrious Castilians to repair; and though in the contest with the power of the crown, Leonora and her adherents would probably have been overwhelmed, yet their resistance would not have been inglorious, and in their deaths they might at least have enjoyed the satisfaction of revenge.

While Peter contemplated with contempt the virtues of his father, he was impatient to emulate his crimes. The same arts which had been exerted to achieve the destruction of Don Juan the Deformed, were practised to accomplish the ruin of Leonora. By the most solemn professions of safety and regard, she was prevailed upon to quit the fortifications of Medina Sidonia; but she had scarce entered Seville before she found herself a prisoner. Her son, the count of Transtamare, who by his marriage with the daughter of Don Emanuel had excited the jealousy of the king, by a timely flight to Portugal escaped the orders that had been issued to arrest him; but his brothers, Ferdinand and Tello, were still received with marks of esteem; and while Peter declared himself incapable of protecting Leonora from the just vengeance of his mother, he was liberal in his protestations of future regard and kindness to her children.

At

*At Talavera, the palace of the queen dowager was polluted with the execution of her unhappy rival. But the refentment of Maria was not perpetuated to the offspring of the hated Leonora; and her counfels joined with thofe of the king of Portugal in urging a reconciliation with the count of Tranftamare; Peter confented with reluctance, and probably with little fincerity; and Henry could but ill confide in the profeffions of a court that was ftained with the blood of his mother.

The firft fanguinary exertion of the royal power might be afcribed to the influence of the queen mother; but it was not long before Peter afferted the independent prerogative of guilt. Rapacious and bloody, he confidered the treafures and lives of his fubjects as intended for his fole ufe; and the pertinacity with which they defended the former, was often punifhed by the profcription of the latter. Yet while the great were fatisfied, the clamours of the multitude were difregarded; and it was not until a fatal paffion armed the tyrant againft his own family, that the public indignation was fupported and guided by the moft illuftrious nobles of Caftille.

The birth of Donna Maria Padilla was rather decent than fplendid; and her anceftors, in a life of obfcure virtue, had either declined, or been excluded from the honours of the ftate. But nature had imparted every qualification to atone for the deficiency of rank and fortune; her form was small but elegant; her features delicate and expressive; and her countenance was animated by a mind and spirit formed to excite admiration and command respect. Her situation of companion to the wife of Don Juan de Albuquerque, the king's favourite, had exposed her to the sight of Peter; and the eyes of that monarch sufficiently revealed the emotions that her charms had occasioned. It is seldom that a favourite is slow in discerning the inclinations of his master; and Don Juan de Albuquerque exulted in a connexion which he flattered himself would secure his own authority over his sovereign. An interview was contrived at Sahagan; and that passion which the beauty of Donna Padilla had inspired, was confirmed by her wit; yet she refused easily to yield to the ardour of her royal lover; a private marriage reconciled the scruples of the lady; and it was as her husband that Peter ascended her bed.

At the moment that the king was rioting in the embraces of Donna Padilla, his mother had been engaged in negociating an alliance for him with Blanch, the sister of the queen of France. The proposal had been accepted by the court of Paris; it was ratified by Peter; his authority imposed silence on Donna Padilla; and he had scarce bestowed his hand on the latter, before he publicly celebrated with royal magnificence his nuptials with Blanch.

If

If Peter condefcended to facrifice for a moment to policy, he foon returned to pour out his vows on the altar of love. The influence which Donna Padilla had acquired over him, in a fuperftitious age was confidered as the effect of magic; but we need not have recourfe to fupernatural caufes to account for the dominion of wit and beauty over a youthful and ardent mind. And it is probable that the afcendancy of the fair was eftablifhed by a prudent filence at the tranfient infidelities of her royal admirer. Her relations were advanced to the higheft pofts of honour and truft; the grand-mafterfhips of St. James and Calatrava were transferred by violence to her brothers; and Don Juan de Albuquerque found their rifing power overfhadow his own. He concealed not entirely his difcontent; his murmurs had reached the ear of his king; the dark and daring fpirit of Peter was unreftrained by the remembrance of former regard, or the dread of immediate infamy. At an interview which he propofed for their reconciliation, he planned the murder of Don Juan and his principal adherents; but his intentions were fufpected or his defign betrayed, and Don Juan fought a refuge from his cruelty in the court of Lifbon.

Above fear or fhame, from the moment that the king of Caftille was abandoned by his former favourite, his reign prefents an headlong career of oppression, rapacity, and sanguinary caprice. The unfortunate Blanch was by his orders immured in a prison; an obsequious council of bishops pronounced a venal sentence of divorce; and Peter, at the foot of the altar, received in solemn pomp the hand of Donna Joanna, the widow of Don Diego de Haro, and the sister of Don Ferdinand de Castro. The reign of Joanna was not longer than that of Blanch; in a few months she was repudiated with contempt; and was doomed to deplore in solitude the unhappy effect of her charms, which had exposed her to the desires of the licentious tyrant.

The pride of the house of Castro was wounded by the ignominious treatment of Donna Joanna; Henry, count of Transtamare, with his brothers Frederic and Tello, could not trust to the professions of a prince whose hands were stained with the blood of their mother; Don Juan de Albuquerque panted to revenge himself on the family of Padilla; and the queen mother deplored the injuries of Blanch, who had entered Spain under her auspices. A secret confederacy was formed; all former enmities were buried in oblivion; and the sons of Leonora, and her persecutress Maria, were embarked in the same enterprise.

From Burgos, Blanch had been removed a prisoner to Toledo; even the tyrant could not refuse, or did not distrust her request to offer up her

her devotions in the cathedral of that city; she entered the holy walls, availed herself of their privileged sanctity, and declared her resolution never to quit them. The inhabitants of Toledo were inflamed by her misfortunes, and their own piety; they arose by thousands, and expelled the royal guards; the news of their revolt was quickly conveyed to the count of Transtamare; he presented himself with his associates at the gates, and was received amidst the acclamations of the multitude.

Toro, on the banks of the Duero, followed the example of Toledo; and the power of the party became so formidable, as compelled Peter to descend to the language of negociation; an in'erview was appointed at Toro; and while the public hours of the king were apparently occupied in listening to the grievances of the confederates, his private moments were employed in dissolving the league by an artful application to the passions or interests of each individual. Several of the most considerable lords professed their inclinations to return to their duty; with greater constancy Don Juan de Albuquerque adhered to the cause he had espoused; his sudden death was attributed to poison; and in the moment of dismay the king escaped from Toro to the walls of Segovia.

In that city the royal standard was erected,

and a numerous army was assembled; and though Peter was repulsed by the prudence and valour of the count of Transtamare in an attempt on Toro, he moved with a fairer prospect of success towards Toledo. In his march he proclaimed his intention of recalling Blanch to his bed and throne; he was outstripped by the zeal and alacrity of Henry, who had already entered Toledo, and exhorted the citizens to a vigorous resistance; but compassion to Blanch had first excited them to arms; they either feared the resentment or believed the professions of the king, and determined to open their gates; yet before their surrender, Henry had the address to effect his escape, and with the royal treasure gained the friendly walls of Talavera, which were devoted to the will of the queen mother.

The inhabitants of Toledo had soon reason to repent of their credulity; every condition was violated by the tyrant; twenty-two of the principal citizens were executed in his presence; and the unhappy Blanch was committed a close prisoner to the tower of Siguenca.

The siege of Toro was again formed; the walls were shaken; and the illustrious chiefs of the confederacy escaped from its tottering towers to behold themselves invested in the fortress of the Alcazal. Maria became an humble but fruitless suppliant to her inexorable son for the promise mife of life to herfelf and her adherents. She was compelled to truſt to his mercy; and though he refrained from parricide, the agony of death muſt have been flight in comparifon to her emotions on witneſſing the execution of her moſt faithful friends. The confort of Henry was among his captives; but the fears or policy of Peter prevailed above his thirſt of blood and revenge; and the freedom of her huſband was the fafety of Joanna.

On the furrender of Toro, the count of Tranſtamare had quitted Caſtille, croſſed the Pyrenees, and fheltered himfelf in the court of France; from this retreat he was fummoned by the intelligence of a rupture between the crowns of Caſtille and Arragon; he offered his wrongs and his fword to the king of Arragon; waged a fuccefsful war on the frontiers againſt the tyrant; recovered by the pious fraud of a domeſtic his confort Joanna; and when peace was re-eſtabliſhed between the rival kingdoms, regained his former afylum at Paris.

Could Peter have moderated his own paſſions, he might have difregarded the enterprifes of his fugitive brother; but no virtue appears to have found place within his bofom, and his reign was one continued feries of cruelty, of perfidy, and oppreſſion. After the reduction of Toro, his brothers, Frederick and Tello, had confented to live

live in peace under his authority; the former was assassinated in the hall of audience in Seville, the latter on board a small bark was saved by a storm from the pursuit of the sanguinary tyrant. Don Juan of Arragon was the kinsman, and had acted as the minister of Peter; he presumed to claim the reward of his services; and he was stabbed as he preferred his request. The guilt of his aunt Leonora was her pity for Blanch, and the cup of poison which she swallowed was prepared by the command of Peter. Wealth, virtue, or noble birth were equally fatal to their possessors; the finances of Castille had been intrusted to a Jew of the name of Levi; the heresy of the royal treasurer might have been overlooked, but his riches could not be pardoned; the warrant for his death was signed; he expired on the rack; the tyrant boasted of the wealth he extorted by his murder; and only lamented that his torments had shortened his life before he had time to reveal the whole of his treasure.

The unfortunate Blanch herself, without friends or resources, might have hoped in prison to have been considered no longer as an object of jealousy. But the injustice of the tyrant was reproached by the existence of the consort he had injured; she was removed to the fortress of Xeres; and the governor was informed that her death was the most acceptable service he could ren-

render to his sovereign. He turned with disdain from the proposal; but every description of ruffians had been cherished and multiplied under the reign of Peter; a ready minister of his barbarous will was soon found; and the potion that was administered to Blanch for the restoration of her health, was too fatal in its effects to leave a doubt of the hand that prescribed it.

Yet indifferent as Peter appeared to the sufferings of his family and his subjects, he was not totally divested of the feelings of a man; he could inflict death, but he could not protract life; and the premature loss of Donna Padilla transiently avenged the miseries of his people; Castille was far from participating in the sorrows of her sovereign; and fear alone restrained in public that exultation which was inwardly indulged on the fate of the mistress. Yet the grief of the tyrant was transient; affliction had not softened his heart, and every moment presented some new instance of perfidy and cruelty.

Mohammed Barbarossa had usurped the crown of Granada; while the prince whom he had driven from the throne trembled within the fortifications of Ronda for his safety. The domestic enemies of Peter were crushed, and he was impatient to avail himself of the dissensions of the Moors. The lust of spoil supplied the thirst of military fame; and he listened to the insidious

intel-

intelligence that the wealthy and important city of Cadiz was defended by a feeble and negligent garrison. To surprise, it he detached the grandmaster of Calatrava, and Don Henriquez, with one thousand horse and two thousand foot. They arrived within sight of Cadiz without perceiving an enemy; from that city a small body of cavalry issued as if to reconnoitre their march; it was rapidly followed by more numerous detachments; and before the Christians could discern their danger, they were surrounded and overwhelmed; the majority of the soldiers perished by the sword; and the grand-master of Calatrava, Don Henriquez, and the principal officers, were led captives to Granada.

Mohammed Barbarossa felt the fears of an usurper; he knew the king of Castille was impetuous and resentful; and that his own subjects were fickle or disaffected. He was unwilling to commit to the chance of war the throne he had obtained by fraud; and to propitiate Peter, he dismissed his captives with magnificent presents, and expressions of friendship and respect. When he found this act of generosity had not disarmed the wrath of his haughty adversary, he even determined to acknowledge himself the vassal of the crown of Castille; and he was invited to Seville to ratify the conditions of peace by the ceremony of homage. It is uncertain whether

Peter,

Peter, in the commencement of the negociation, meditated the dark crime he perpetrated, or whether he was ſtimulated by the gold and jewels that his royal gueſt and his train imprudently diſplayed; but while Barbaroſſa ſhared with confidence the banquet, he was ſeized, with the Mooriſh nobles who had accompanied him, was mounted on an aſs, expoſed to the deriſion of the populace of Seville, and received his mortal wound from the hand of Peter himſelf; his head was tranſmitted to Ronda; and aſſured the prince whom he had dethroned, that he might re-enter in ſecurity the capital from which he had been ſo lately expelled.

Whenever revenge and avarice ſlumbered, the memory of Donna Padilla obtruded itſelf on the mind of Peter; the beauty he had ſo paſſionately adored, was no more; but their mutual children were ſtill the object of his care. One ſon and three daughters had been the fruits of their embraces; and it was the earneſt wiſh of Peter that the ſceptre of Caſtille might, after his death, deſcend to the infant Alfonſo. In an aſſembly of the ſtates which was held at Seville, he declared his previous marriage with Donna Padilla; three witneſſes were produced who ſwore they were preſent at the ceremony; whatever might be the doubts of the aſſembly, they were cautious to ſuppreſs them; the legal pretenſions of Alfonso were recognized; and in cafe of his death, his three fifters, according to the rights of primogeniture, were called to the fucceffion of the crown.

It was immediately after this council that Peter haftened to Soria to confer with an ally worthy of his confidence. The furname of *Bad* or *Wicked*, had been beftowed on Charles king of Navarre, and his character and conduct juftified the appellation. He was defcended from the males of the blood royal of France; his mother was daughter of Lewis Hutin; and he had himfelf efpoufed a daughter of king John, who was taken prifoner by the Englifh on the difaftrous field of Poictiers. With regard to his perfonal qualities, he was courteous, affable, engaging, eloquent; full of infinuation and addrefs; inexhauftible in his refources, and enterprifing in action. But thefe fplendid accomplifhments were attended with fuch defects as rendered them pernicious to his country, and even fatal to himfelf. He was volatile, faithlefs, revengeful, and malicious; reftrained by no principle or duty; infatiable in his pretenfions; and whether fuccefsful or unfortunate in one enterprife, he immediately undertook another, in which he was never deterred from employing the moft criminal and difhonourable expedients.

Yet practifed in and enamoured as Charles was of guilt, he confeffed a mafter in the prefence of
Peter;

Peter; the difcourfe of the latter was abrupt and paffionate; and his expreffions feemed only half to reveal what his thoughts revolved. He dwelt with pleafure on the perfidious and inhuman murder of the king of Granada; he expatiated with violence on his hatred to the king of Arragon; and he demanded of Charles to enter into an offenfive league againft that monarch; the fate of Barbaroffa was before the eyes of the king of Navarre; he confented with alacrity to whatever was propofed; and with the fame facility violated every condition the moment that he had gained the fhelter of his own dominions.

Though Peter foon perceived that he had been deceived by the king of Navarre, yet he commenced and carried on the war againft Arragon with vigour. The death of the infant Alfonfo, though it clouded his views, did not fufpend the ardour of his preparations. The domeftic lofs he had fuftained was fupplied by the birth of a fon by another miftrefs; and his negociations were extended to the courts of Granada and Portugal; but the meafure of his crimes was almoft full; a general abhorrence of him had prevailed; the fovereigns of Arragon and Navarre were combined againft him; the count of Tranftamare openly afpired to the throne; and the policy and refentment of the court of France combined in fupporting his pretenfions.

The

The moft fertile provinces of France had been defolated by the arms of the Englifh; and after a long war, Charles the fifth had been reduced to fubfcribe a peace which ceded to the king of England the extenfive countries of Guienne, Poictou, Saintonge, Perigort, the Limoufin, &c. But his treaty with Edward did not immediately reftore the tranquillity of his kingdom; large bands of martial adventurers who had followed the Englifh ftandard refufed to lay down their arms, and perfevered in a life of military rapine. They regarded with contempt the cenfures of the church; and they even rejected the authority of the king of England, who, enraged at their infolence, offered to crofs the feas to chaftife them. But Charles was not defirous of the prefence of fo formidable an ally; he was content with cooly declining the propofal; and adding, that he himfelf had conceived a project which would deliver him from thofe dangerous inmates.

It was at this critical moment that Henry, count of Tranftamare, renewed his folicitations to the court of France, already inflamed againft Peter on account of the murder of Blanch de Bourbon; and Charles determined to employ the daring bands of the companions to the deftruction of the tyrant. He imparted the defign to Bertrand du Guefclin, a gentleman of Brittany; and one of the moft accomplifhed characters of the

the age. The abilities of du Guefclin were the means of fecuring thefe adventurers. He remonftrated to the leaders, by many of whom he was already beloved as the former affociate of their toils and dangers, on the ignominy of their lives, and the difhonourable fubfiftence which they drew from plunder and rapine. To the plea of neceffity, he oppofed an honourable expedition which promifed equal advantages with their prefent licentious incurfions; the chiefs of the companions, fo high was their confidence in his honour, confented to follow his ftandard, though ignorant of the enterprife he meditated; and the fingle ftipulation they required was, that they fhould not be led againft the prince of Wales, who in the name of his father governed the provinces of France which had been ceded by the late treaty. The filent acquiefcence, if not the open concurrence of Edward was obtained; and Charles contributed what little he could fpare from his flender revenues, to haften and complete the preparations.

Du Guefclin joined the martial band at Chalons on the Soane; and probably defcended that river and the Rhone to Avignon, the refidence of a Roman pontiff. From Innocent the fixth he demanded, fword in hand, an abfolution for his foldiers, and the fum of two hundred thoufand livres. The firft coft nothing, and was inftantly granted; but the

the second request was received with hesitation. When complied with, the pious successor of St. Peter extorted the money from the inhabitants of Avignon; but the generous du Guesclin refused to trample on the oppressed; "It is not my pur-
"pose," cried the humane warrior, "to injure
"those innocent people; the pope and his car-
"dinals themselves can well spare me the sum
"I require, from their own hands. This money
"I insist must be restored to the owners; and
"should they be defrauded of it, I shall myself
"return from the other side the Pyrenees, and
"oblige you to make them restitution." The pope submitted to the peremptory language of du Guesclin; and the success of his first negociation was rivalled by that of his arms.

It was with terror that Peter received the intelligence of the rapid approach of Henry at the head of troops long celebrated for their valour, and accompanied by a general whose military skill was deemed second to none. Yet his throne was apparently defended by a gallant nobility and a numerous army; but he justly distrusted the loyalty of both; and though he was strongly solicited to remain at Burgos, and rely on their fidelity for the defence of his capital, he embraced the less glorious, but more secure expedient of a precipitate retreat to Seville; and thence, after possessing himself of the treasures he had amassed

in

in that city he continued his flight to the frontiers of Portugal.

The count of Tranftamare was received in Caftille with the tranfport which might naturally be expected from a people who had long groaned under the yoke of a relentlefs tyrant, and were eager to teftify their gratitude to their deliverer. Burgos open her gates; and the nobles who had fo lately been lavifh in their proteftations to Peter, haftened to acknowledge the authority of his victorious brother; the crown was placed on his head with holy pomp by the archbifhop of Toledo; the example of the capital determined the provinces; the adherents of the tyrant were only anxious for their perfonal fafety; and the martial followers of Henry might complain that no opportunity was allowed them to difplay their valour.

Yet if they were defrauded of the glory they had anticipated by the flight of Peter, they were amply recompenfed for the march they had undertaken by the generofity of Henry. The royal treafures which that prince found in Burgos he immediately divided among the companions; nor were the fuperior merits of du Guefclin neglected; and the rich lordfhip of Molina, befides a confiderable fum of money, was allotted as the reward of his fervices.

While the victors divided the riches he had extorted

extorted from his oppressed subjects, the fugitive Peter revolved the means by which he could hope to regain his throne; from Portugal he had ventured to present himself in Gallicia; but the approach of Henry, and the unfavourable disposition of the inhabitants, induced him to retire; with what he had preserved of his wealth he embarked at Corunna; though closely pursued he gained Bayonne; and entered a suppliant the court of the prince of Wales.

Edward, who from the colour of his armour was surnamed the Black Prince, and who ruled over Aquitaine with the power and pomp of a sovereign, was not more distinguished for his high courage and military talents, than for his generosity, humanity, and affability; he had early encouraged the enterprise against Peter; but the appearance of that monarch seems to have changed his sentiments. Whether he was moved by the generosity of supporting a distressed prince, and thought, as is but too usual among sovereigns, that the rights of the people were a matter of much less consideration; or dreaded the acquisition of so powerful a confederate to France as the new king of Castille; or what is most probable, inflamed by the thirst of fame, and impatient of rest and ease, was desirous of an opportunity for exerting those abilities in war by which he had already acquired so much renown,

he

he promised his assistance to the royal suppliant; and having obtained the consent of his father, he levied a great army, and set out on the enterprise; he was accompanied by his younger brother John of Gaunt, lately created duke of Lancaster; and Chandos, who bore among the English the same character as du Guesclin among the French, commanded under him.

Each of the rivals was desirous of engaging in his interest the king of Navarre; and Charles, with his usual perfidy, negociated with and deceived both. He signed a treaty with Henry, by which in return for Logrono, and sixty thousand pistoles, he engaged to oppose the march of the confederates; and in a few days after on the promise of the strong and important town of Victoria on the frontiers of Navarre, he entered into an alliance with Peter, and assured him of a free passage through his dominions for himself and his auxiliaries. To preserve appearances with Henry, he suffered himself to be surprised by a knight of the name of Mauny, and conveyed a prisoner to the castle of Cherburgh in Normandy, while Peter and the prince of Wales pursued their course through Navarre without molestation.

The first blow which Edward gave to Henry, was the recalling of the companions from his service; and such was their reverence for the prince of Wales, that the majority immediately inlisted

A a 2 under

under his banners. Henry however, beloved by his new subjects, and supported by the king of Arragon and others of his neighbours, was able to meet the enemy with an army of one hundred thousand men; forces three times more numerous than those which were commanded by Edward. Du Guesclin advised him to delay any decisive action, and his counsel was supported by the most experienced officers; and to content himself with harassing and cutting off the provisions of his antagonist, who in the open field had hitherto always proved victorious; but Henry confided too much in his superior numbers; he was sensible that his reputation must suffer in a defensive war; and he probably dreaded lest the intrigues of his brother might be extended to his camp. The plain which surrounds Najara afforded an ample theatre to the rival armies; the forces of Henry were permitted to pass a river in their front; but they were scarce formed on the opposite bank when they were charged by their enemies; their resistance was far from obstinate; and in less than an hour the immense host was totally dispersed. On the side of the English, only four knights and forty private men perished; but of the Castilians thousands fell by the sword, or were overwhelmed in the river; du Guesclin was taken prisoner; and Henry himself, with a few of his officers of rank escaped with difficulty the pursuit of the victors.

The

The vanquished prince reposed a few days in the territories of Arragon, but he distrusted the faith of that monarch, and sought a more secure asylum within the limits of France, while his victorious competitor was received into Burgos, and once more beheld Castille subject to his fury. Even on the field of battle he was with difficulty restrained by the generous Edward from satiating his revenge by the massacre of his captives; and his entrance into his capital would have been stained with the blood of his principal nobility, had they not been saved from his malignant rage by the same powerful mediation; yet the satisfaction which the prince of Wales experienced from the success of this perilous enterprise, was soon alloyed by the ingratitude and treachery of the tyrant he had restored; Peter refused the recompense he had promised to the English forces; and Edward, after a fruitless expostulation, returned to Guienne with his army diminished, and his own constitution fatally impaired by the heat of the climate.

His retreat released Peter from the awe which his presence had imposed. A severe inquisition was made into the guilt of his subjects; and the most distant connection with the party of Henry was attended by confiscation or death. His ferocious temper had been heightened by his former exile, and his present prosperity; and he considered and treated

treated his people as vanquished rebels. Even the more helpless sex was included in his thirst of blood; and several of the most illustrious ladies of Castille were the victims to his cruelty.

While Peter abused his prosperity, the fugitive Henry endeavoured to awaken the compassion of the princes of Europe in his cause. He was received at Avignon with respect by the Roman pontiff, Urban the fifth, who affected to believe the marriage of his mother Leonora de Guzman with Alfonso the eleventh, pronounced him free from the stain of illegitimacy, and dismissed him with his benediction, and the more acceptable present of a considerable sum of money; the count of Foix suffered him to levy forces within his territories; but his chief reliance was on the king of France. Charles was not deterred by the late reverse of fortune which his ally had experienced, from hoping a more auspicious event. The barbarities of Peter had increased his confidence in the cause of Henry; he furnished the latter with whatever pecuniary aid he could spare; he paid the ransom of du Guesclin; and the name of that chief was itself an host. Henry again passed the Pyrenees, and he had scarce unfurled his standard within the limits of Castille, before the detestation of Peter swelled his martial train to a numerous army; he formed the siege of Toledo; and only abandoned the

the enterprife to meet his brother in the plains of Montial.

The city of Cordova had been driven by the rapacity and cruelty of the tyrant into revolt; in conjunction with his ally the king of Granada, Peter invefted the walls, and urged his attacks with vigour; but the fainting fpirits of the citizens were rekindled by the reproaches of their wives, who avowed their refolution to perifh in the flames, fooner than fubmit to the royal favage; their defpair prevailed; and the affailants were compelled to retire from a city they had already entered; the retreat of Peter was quickened by the intelligence that Henry had paffed the Pyrenees and menaced Toledo. His confidence was infpired by a review of the forces of Caftille and Granada, which ftill profeffed their loyalty or fidelity; his impetuous mind ill-brooked delay; he rufhed forwards to chaftife the rafh intruder; at a fmall diftance from Toledo he defcried the enfigns of his rival, and in the plains of Montial he pitched his laft camp.

The pretenfions of the competitors admitted not of compromife, and their claims were referred to the decifion of the fword; in the tumult of battle Peter difplayed a courage not unworthy of his anceftors; but his foldiers fought coldly in his caufe; and the troops of Granada felt themfelves but little interefted in the quarrel;

they fled; and their example was soon followed by the Castilians; the horse of Peter bore him from the carnage; and the fortifications of Montial checked the immediate pursuit of the victors.

Impatient to establish his throne by the death of his brother, Henry from the field of battle advanced to, and invested the castle of Montial; strong lines lines of circumvallation were drawn around it; and every hour increased the difficulty of escape, and diminished the means of resistance. Peter beheld with terror the approach of that death which he had so often wantonly inflicted; he endeavoured to corrupt the fidelity of Bertrand du Guesclin; and he offered an immense sum to pass in the night through the quarter where the latter commanded. He was allured to an interview; but in the tent of du Guesclin instead of a confederate he found a rival; the negociation had been communicated to Henry, who stood ready to receive his destined victim; some moments of ungrateful respite were allowed to reproach; but the remembrance of Leonora shortened the suspense of Peter; and the dagger of Henry was buried in his bosom.

A. D. 1369, 1379. The reign and fall of a tyrant has too long occupied our attention; the claims of his posterity were feebly supported by the duke of Lancaster, the son of Edward of England, who had married the eldest daughter of Peter;

Peter; Toledo opened her gates to Henry; and his authority was fanctioned by the unanimous suffrages of the states-general. But the turbulence of the times suffered him not to enjoy his crown in peace; and during the ten years that he reigned, he was succeffively attacked by the forces of England and Granada, of Portugal, Arragon, and Navarre; in defending his dominions he displayed the fame addrefs and valour as he had fhewn in acquiring them; by negociation or force he evaded or repelled the attempts of his enemies; and Caftille looked forwards to the moment of general tranquillity, when the profpect was clouded by the premature fate of Henry; his death in the forty-fixth year of his age was afcribed to poifon; the public fufpicion fell on the king of Granada, who in the formidable preparations of Henry, was fuppofed to dread the total fubverfion of the Moorifh power in Spain; and the venom was reported to have been conveyed in a pair of bufkins which had been fent by that monarch as a prefent to the king of Caftille; the account ferves only to expofe the ignorance of the age; and the indifpofition which brought Henry to the grave, may more probably be attributed to inceffant toil and anxiety.

His throne was immediately filled by his fon John, a prince not unworthy of his illuftrious father. In a war which he main- A. D. 1379, 1390.

maintained in defence of his dignity with England and Portugal, he displayed the same prudence and spirit. The death of his confort Leonora had left him a widower in the flower of his age; and as the first condition of peace he readily confented to receive the hand of Beatrix, the daughter of Ferdinand of Portugal. The treaty was favourable to John; and it was stipulated that his children by Beatrix should succeed to the throne of Portugal on the death of Ferdinand. That event was not far distant; and two years after John had celebrated his second nuptials, he was informed that his father-in law was no more. He afferted the claim of his infant son Henry; but the Portuguefe dreaded his afcendancy; their pride was wounded by the fear that their country might fink into a province of Caftille; and to the pretensions of that prince, they oppofed thofe of a namefake and kinfman. John, to diftinguifh whom from his coufin we fhall annex the title, of Portugal, was the half brother of the late king, and fon of Peter, by his celebrated miftrefs Agnes de Caftro. The ftain of his birth was effaced by his fplendid qualities; and the affections of the Portuguefe accompanied him to the field. Yet the commencement of his reign was overcaft with clouds; the forces of Caftille penetrated to the mouth of the Tagus, and invefted the ancient city of Lifbon, which boafts its fabulous foundation

from

from Ulyffes; a peftilential diftemper which broke out in the camp of the befiegers, compelled them to retire; but with the return of fpring they were in arms again; and the banners of Caftille were once more difplayed on the banks of the Tagus. The Portuguefe army confifted not of above twelve thoufand men; but its pofition at Aljubarotta was naturally advantageous, and ftrongly fortified; the troops which marched under the king of Caftille were computed at thirty thoufand; and their numbers infpired their royal leader with fatal confidence. His ardour rejected the falutary counfels of the French ambaffador, whofe experience was the refult of forty years fpent in war; and without waiting to refrefh his followers, he fpurred his horfe to the charge. His imprudence was feverely punifhed; the Caftilians were entangled in a morafs which protected the front of the Portuguefe; feveral thoufands, with many of their principal officers, perifhed; and the king could not reproach the precipitate flight of the furvivors, fince he himfelf never ventured to ftop until he repofed within the fortifications of Santaren, at the diftance of thirty miles from the field of battle.

The defeat of Aljubarotta extinguifhed the hopes of the king of Caftille, and revived the fpirits of his enemies; an hoftile league was negociated and concluded between Portugal and England;

land; and the Duke of Lancaster was easily persuaded to arm in support of the claim which he derived from his marriage with the eldest daughter of Peter the Cruel. He landed at Padron in Gallicia, with an army less remarkable for its numbers than its valour and discipline; was received into Compostella; and solemnly proclaimed king of Castille. His rival dreaded to encounter that impetuous courage which had so lately proved fatal to France; his mind was still impressed with the defeat of Aljubarotta; and he contented himself with adopting a less glorious, though more certain plan of defence; he laid waste the greatest part of Gallicia; and as the English advanced, they beheld on every side a dreary and desolate country; their strength was impaired by famine; and transported from the temperate island of Britain, they languished in the sultry climate of Spain. Yet John was far from relying on the distress of his adversary; he was impatient to secure his own, and his subjects' tranquillity; and while the duke of Lancaster revolved the difficulties that surrounded him, he was surprised by the appearance of commissioners from the king of Castille; his ardent wish had been to raise his daughter to that throne; and he listened with pleasure to the offer of six hundred thousand pieces of gold to reimburse the expences he had incurred, and the proposal of a marriage
between

between his daughter Catalina, and Henry the eldeſt ſon of John. The treaty with Portugal was an immediate obſtacle; the war and negociation was continued through a ſecond year; but on the expiration of that term a peace was formally ſubſcribed; the infant Henry, though only in his tenth year, was contracted to the princeſs Catalina, who had entered her fourteenth; and the title of Prince of Auſturias, which on this occaſion was imparted to Henry, has ever ſince become the diſtinction of the eldeſt ſon of Spain.

The ſubjects of the king of Portugal had ſtarted to arms to maintain their independence; but it was with reluctance they followed the ſtandard of their monarch in the invaſion of Caſtille; after the treaty between the duke of Lancaſter and John, their averſion to the continuance of hoſtilities increaſed; the war was confined to a few deſultory enterpriſes; and the mutual weakneſs of the rival nations recommended the doubtful expedient of a truce. The interval of public repoſe was improved by John; and however his people might have doubted his talents in war, they were loud in their applauſe of his virtues in peace; their happineſs ſeemed the only object of his attention; and the ſevere frugality who he practiſed himſelf, was the ſource of his liberality to his ſubjects; the taxes were diminiſhed; commerce revived and agriculture flouriſhed; but
their

their exultation was transient; and in the vigour of his age the Castilians were condemned to deplore the loss of their father and their king. The vicissitudes of public or private life had induced several of the Christians of Spain to seek a retreat or subsistence in Africa; in exile they still maintained the purity of their religion, and panted after their native soil. The king of Castille was not insensible to their solicitations; his weighty mediation was used with the emperor of Morocco, and they were permitted to return; John advanced to meet them at Alcala on the road to Andalusia; trained in all the evolutions of the manage amongst a nation of horsemen, he admired the dexterity with which they guided their coursers. As he spurred his own in imitation, the feet of the horse plunged into an hole; he fell upon his master, and crushed him to death.

A. D. 1390, 1404. Thus died in the thirty-third year of his age, and at the critical juncture when his prudence and experience were most necessary, John king of Castille; his son Henry the third, on whom the crown devolved, was but eleven years old, and the surname of *Sickly*, was expressive of his delicate constitution. A council of regency was formed to administer the kingdom; and the members of it were Frederic duke of Beneventa, the natural son of Henry the second, and the uncle of the late king; Peter, count of Tranftamare; Alonzo of Arragon, marquis of Villera; the archbifhops of Toledo and Compoftella; the grand mafters of St. James and Calatrava; and fixteen deputies from the principal cities of Caftille. In the firft moments they feemed willing to facrifice their private views to the public good; but the fpirit of patriotifm was not proof againft the fuggeftions of intereft; and it was not long before their jarring pretenfions threatened the moft fatal confequences.

The duke of Beneventa was haughty, artful, and ambitious; the archbifhop of Toledo was fincere, credulous, and bigotted; the judgment of the latter was feduced by the addrefs of the former; and his approbation ferved to fanction the defigns of his intriguing affociate. The duke of Beneventa had pretended to the hand of Leonora, a princefs of the blood royal, and the richeft heirefs of Spain; fuch a match would have exalted him in power and influence too near the crown; and to difappoint his views, Leonora was betrothed to Ferdinand, the king's brother. The baffled lover immediately conceived a new project; he demanded in marriage the natural daughter of the king of Portugal; and to diffuade him from the alliance, the regency were obliged to make him a prefent of the fame fum as he was to have received in dowry with that princefs.

The domeftic diffenfions of the nobles of Caftille

tille encouraged the infolence of her neighbours; the language of the king of Portugal was arrogant and hoftile; and an irruption of the Moors of Granada revealed their confidence in the inteftine difcord of the Chriftians; yet Henry had not been an inattentive fpectator of the intrigues which convulfed his kingdom; a vigorous mind animated a feeble frame; and though he had not yet completed his thirteenth year, he determined to aſſume the reins of government; he was encouraged in this refolution by an embaſſy from Charles the fixth, king of France, who aſſured him of his fupport fhould his nobility prefume to oppofe his authority. At Madrid the ftates-general were convened; and the firm tone of an inexperienced youth commanded their acquiefcence; the council of regency was diſſolved; and the entire privilege of king was refigned into the hands of Henry.

The firft meafure of the youthful monarch was more grateful to the nation at large, than to his own family. The prudent conduct of his father was his example in the appropriation of the public wealth; but the period of his minority had been abufed; and an interefted regency had allotted large penfions to every perfon who was allied to the throne. Thefe lavifh grants Henry inftantly reclaimed; but he foftened the rigour of the ftep, by the promife that when the affairs

of

of Castille would admit the expedient, he should be ready to afford any support to the dignity of the royal family. It is seldom that individuals can be prevailed upon to relinquish their own for the public advantage; and the relations of the king were the first to oppose his administration; the disaffection even gained the females of his blood; and his court was deserted by the princes and princesses of the blood; at the same time the duke of Beneventé, the marquis of Villena, and the count of Transtamare assembled their partizans, and retired to their castles.

Before their designs could be matured, or they could confederate in their rebellion, Henry, confiding in the integrity of his own intentions, and the fidelity of his people in general, was in arms. Jealous of his reputation, he suffered not the archbishop of Toledo to accompany him, left his conduct might be ascribed to the counsels of that prelate. His vigour recalled the rebels to a sense of their danger; and the marquis of Villena was the first to implore and experience his clemency; the haughty genuis of the duke of Beneventé was awed by his resolution; he solicited peace, and obtained it; but the transaction proclaimed the magnanimous spirit of the king; and he dismissed the duke of Beneventé to a fortress of his own, that he might there revolve the treaty he proposed to sign, and be excluded from any pretence afterwards, that his consent had been extorted. The interval of suspense was dangerous to a mind that fluctuated between hope and fear; the duke hoped still to deceive his sovereign; and though he renewed his intrigues with the count of Transtamare, he hesitated not to present himself before the king at Burgos; but his steps had been closely watched; his correspondence detected; and as he entered the court he was arrested, and sent prisoner to the castle of Almadovar.

The count of Transtamare was the last of the confederates to return to his allegiance; deserted by his associates, he stood exposed to the wrath of his sovereign; but vengeance was too base a passion to find admission within the bosom of Henry; and no sooner did the count of Transtamare prostrate himself at the feet of his king, than his pardon was sealed; yet when the honour of Castille required her monarch to arm, the vigour of his preparations anticipated the designs of his enemies. In the hour of peace and confidence, the Portuguese had surprised the strong town of Badajoz, which commands the banks of the Guadiana. But they were not suffered long to exult in their perfidy; a formidable army was rapidly collected and moved beneath the conduct of Henry himself; the fertile fields along the banks of the Tagus were laid waste; the naval squadrons which had issued from the port of Lisbon were

defeated,

defeated, and in part deftroyed; the pride of the king of Portugal was humbled; he fued for peace; and the reftitution of Badajoz was the preliminary of a truce for ten years.

The fleet that had been fuccefsfully employed againft Portugal, on the fufpenfion of hoftilities with that country was deftined by Henry to act againft the rovers of Barbary. Thefe had over-fpread the narrow feas between the coafts of Spain and Africa; no laws nor treaties could reftrain their thirft of fpoil; their cruelty equalled their rapacity; and not only the wealth of the merchant became their prey, but the wretched crew who fell into their hands were often maffacred with circumftances of wanton barbarity. Their haunts were explored by the fquadrons of Caftille; their veffels burnt; and the town of Tetuan, the repofitory of their plunder, befieged; its walls were not long capable of refifting the ardour of the affailants; the lives of its inhabitants atoned for the injuries of the Caftilians; and the victors were glutted with the treafures that had been accumulated during years of piratical adventure.

Burfting from the narrow limits of Zagatai, the renown of Timour had extended from the eaft to the weft. He had fubdued or over-run Perfia, Tartary, and India; in the plains of Anjora he had trampled under foot the ftrength of the Ottomans, and cast into chains the haughty sultan Bajazet; it was while his mind was elated with his recent victory, that he was saluted by the ambassadors of Henry; the Mogul emperor was not insensible to courtesy; a Tartarian envoy presented himself at Burgos; two Hungarian ladies who had been found among the captives of the vanquished sultan, were deemed by Tamerlane the most acceptable present that he could offer to the king of Castille; and to express the satisfaction of Henry, a second embassy undertook the laborious pilgrimage to the camp of Tamerlane.

The correspondence between Henry and Tamerlane, whose dominions lay so distant, and whose faiths were so discordant, must have been rather prompted by vanity than policy; and at the time that the king of Castille vied in acts of courtesy with the most zealous of the Believers, he meditated the expulsion of the disciples of Mahomet from Spain. He beheld with indignation the fertile fields which were watered by the Guadalquivir in the hands of the Moors; he embraced the opportunity which the predatory incursions of the king of Granada offered; and the vigour with which his preparations were carried on, inflamed the hopes of his subjects and struck terror into his enemies.

But the prospects of victory which the Castilians had fondly indulged, were soon darkened.

An

An affembly of the ftates had been fummoned to Toledo; but the indifpofition of Henry fuffered him not to be prefent; and to his brother Ferdinand was affigned the care of opening to the deputies the glorious profpects which their fovereign revolved. A ftrict and honourable economy had replenifhed the public coffers; a martial nobility reftrained from domeftic feuds languifhed to exercife their valour againft the common enemy; the propofal for war was received with loud applaufe; the expedition was fanctioned by the holy approbation of the clergy; the whole force of Caftille would have been poured upon the aftonifhed infidels; nor is it probable that the Moors of Granada, unfupported by the powers of Africa, could have withftood the fury of the torrent; but while the ftates deliberated on the moft efficacious means of fupply, the plan was entirely diffolved; and Henry, whofe wifdom had concerted it, and whofe experience alone could have executed it, had breathed his laft at Toro. His only fon was a feeble infant of fourteen months old; and the Caftilians already anticipated the evils with which the kingdom during a minority had been fo frequently afflicted.

It was the obfervation of Henry, and it ought to be treafured in the mind of every prince, "that " he feared the curfes of his people more than " the weapons of his enemies." Yet however careful he was to guard against the former by a reign of moderation, when the dignity of the crown demanded, he knew how to punish as well as to reward; he studiously repressed the pride of the nobility, whose influence when he ascended the throne overshadowed the power of the sovereign; and in a sedition of the city of Seville, he admonished the multitude to dread the anger of their monarch; one thousand of the citizens atoned for their guilt with their lives; yet the instances of severity which he adopted were rare; more ready to pardon than to chastise, he was regarded rather as the father than the king; and his memory was embalmed by the tears of his people; his virtues were supposed to have hastened his fate; and the confessions of some Jews were eagerly received, who accused the king of Granada of having undermined by poison the life of a prince whom he dreaded to encounter in the field. Yet Henry's constitution had been always delicate; his disorder was tedious; and the effect of slow poison has been doubted if not refuted by a more enlightened age.

A. D. 1404, 1450. When the death of Henry was announced, a silent astonishment prevailed through the assembly of the states; it was broken by a voice that proposed, instead of admitting the succession of a feeble infant, that a prince of mature wisdom should be chosen to fill the

the throne of Castille; the name of Ferdinand the brother of the late king was pronounced; but that prince considered himself as the natural guardian of the rights of his nephew; at the proposal he started with horror and indignation from his seat; he commanded the standard of Castille to be unfurled, and John the second to be proclaimed. His resolution fixed the wavering minds of the assembly; every murmur was suppressed; and the oath of allegiance was unanimously taken to the son of Henry.

The integrity of Ferdinand did not leave the states long in doubt on whom to repose the trust of the regency. With that prince was joined the name of the queen mother; but while the latter watched over the health and education of her son, the cares of government were confided to the former. The fleets and armies which had been assembled by Henry only waited the signal for action; and though the death of that monarch had dissolved the splendid project of conquest, yet the defence of Castille demanded the most vigorous measures. The king of Granada, to anticipate the designs of his adversaries, had passed the frontiers of his dominions and invested Alcandata in the mountains of Sierra Morena, with an host of eighty thousand men; but a veteran garrison derided the unskilful attacks of the besiegers; the exhausted country no longer afforded

forded them subsistence; the disgraceful expedient of a retreat was adopted; and the rear of the infidels was closely pressed, and repeatedly broken by the charge of the Christian cavalry.

The piratical squadrons of Tunis and Tremecen had sallied from their ports; they were encountered and defeated by the fleet of Castille; but the measures of Ferdinand were rather calculated to protect than extend the dominions of his nephew; the disorders to which a minority is exposed continually recurred to his mind; and he was willing to provide against domestic dissension by extinguishing the flames of foreign war. It might have been difficult to have adjusted the discordant claims of Castille and Granada in a permanent peace; but the Moors were disgusted with the rival pretensions of two brothers, and the ill success of their enterprises; two powerful factions distracted their own government; and a truce allowed each party to resume his claims at a proper opportunity; the expedient was approved by the court of Castille; it was first signed for eight months; and though transiently interupted by the reduction of Antequera, a strong town about twelve leagues from Granada, which surrendered to Don Ferdinand, was frequently afterwards prolonged.

To his integrity Ferdinand had sacrificed one crown, and his moderation was soon rewarded

with

with another; Martin, king of Arragon, had expired without children; and a variety of pretenders aspired to ascend the vacant throne. The pretensions of Ferdinand were drawn from his descent from the great aunt of the late monarch; they were strengthened by his own reputation, by the influence of the Roman pontiff Benedict the thirteenth, and by the treasures and forces of Castille; yet his competitors yielded not without a struggle; and it was not until he had reduced the strong fortress of Balaguer on the northern banks of the Segro, and which was defended by his rival count Urgal, that Ferdinand entered in triumph and celebrated his coronation within his capital of Saragossa.

His reign was short; and even the little time that was allowed him to taste of royalty was alloyed by domestic conspiracy and discontent; the count of Urgal, who had been pardoned by his magnanimity, renewed his intrigues, and even attempted his life by poison; and the states of Catalonia, jealous of their privileges, refused to contribute to support the claim of his younger son to Sicily. His thoughts were still turned to Castille and the prosperity of his nephew; he concluded a marriage between his eldest son Alfonso, and Maria the sister of the king of Castille; but as he advanced to Burgos to confer with the queen dowager, he was attacked on the road with a mortal distemper,

per, and was succeeded by Alfonso, who even surpassed in renown his father, and wrested from the house of Anjou the kingdom of Naples.

The death of Ferdinand was followed soon by that of the queen dowager; and though John had only entered his thirteenth year, it was deemed expedient by the most powerful of the Castilian nobility, to extinguish a dangerous competition for the regency, by resigning into his hands the reins of government. But his weakness and inexperience tempted the ambition of the kindred princes of Arragon; and John and Henry, the brothers of Alfonso, contended for dominion over their royal cousin. In the career for power the daring spirit of the latter outstripped the former; and Henry, seconded by the constable of Castille, and the bishop of Segovia, possessed himself of the person of the king at Tordesillas. Whatever indignation that monarch might feel on beholding himself the captive of his faithless kinsman, he was careful to suppress every emotion of resentment. He consented to a double marriage; he received as the partner of his bed and throne Maria, the sister of Henry; and bestowed the hand of his own sister Catherine, on his treacherous relation; but while Henry exulted in his new alliances, and in the hour of confidence relaxed from his usual vigilance, his dream of grandeur was interrupted by the flight of the king.

During

During more than thirty years that elapsed from the escape of John to his death, his subjects were afflicted with every calamity which can arise form civil war; yet amidst the tempest which incessantly shook his throne, he displayed no inconsiderable share of firmness; he arrested his brother-in-law Henry, who had presumed to present himself at court at the moment that he was labouring to excite new commotions; and though he released him in compliance with the mediation of his brother the king of Arragon, and of his second brother John, who in right of his wife has ascended the throne of Navarre, yet neither fear nor gratitude were sufficient to restrain the turbulent Henry. A new war soon broke out, in which the forces of Castille and Arragon engaged with various success; during a short suspension of hostilities, the gloom which involves the reign of John was transiently gilded by a decisive victory over the Moors of Granada; but it was not until the affairs of Italy occupied the attention of the kings of Arragon and Navarre, that Castille was suffered to repose for some time from their hostile enterprises.

Even that period was far from tranquil; Don Alvaro de Luna, with the office of high constable, possessed and perhaps abused the favour and confidence of his sovereign; his insolence or their envy stimulated the nobles of Castille to arms;

arms; they were the victims of their own temerity; and their defeat promised to establish the power of John when it was suddenly shaken by those who appeared most interested to maintain it.

Though the spirits of the malecontents were broken, their numbers were still far from despicable; and Henry of Arragon had even in their name surprised the city of Toledo, when that event was obscured by a new incident still more astonishing; the queen and the prince of Asturias openly declared on the side of the rebels; the former was influenced by her hatred of Don Alvaro de Luna; the latter by his impatience to seize a sceptre which, when it devolved on him, he was incapable of retaining. John was unable to resist the torrent of disaffection; he subscribed the dismissal of his favourite; consented to change his ministers; and while his rebellious nobles obtruded themselves into every office of trust or emolument, was suffered to retain the name and state without the authority of a king.

From this dependent situation he was rescued by a second revolution not less rapid nor unexpected than the former. The banishment of Don Alvaro de Luna had reconciled Maria to her consort; and the prince of Asturias, while he exclaimed against his father's abandoning himself to the counsels of the constable, was himself a slave to the address of Don Juan Pacheco. The latter was

was perfuaded by the bifhop of Avila to exert his influence to reftore the royal authority; his remonftrances tranfiently awakened the prince to a fenfe of the infamy which attended his confederacy againft his father; a new league was filently formed; the royal ftandard was difplayed; and the king, eluding the vigilance of his guards, efcaped from the caftle of Portillo, and placed himfelf at the head of the forces which had been affembled by his fon.

The rebels had advanced too far to recede; the king of Navarre, whom neither the difafters of his Italian expedition could intimidate, nor the general caufe of kings could influence, appeared in arms on the fide of the confpirators; their camp was pitched on the banks of the Adaja, in the neighbourhood of Olmedo; and it was there they awaited the charge of the royal army. The indignation of John impelled him to inftant action; and the impetuous courage of the prince of Afturias ill brooked delay. Yet the refiftance of the confederates was long and bloody; and though compelled to abandon the field, the king of Navarre, and his brother Henry, merited the praife of fkill and valour; a wound in the hand was attended by a mortification and proved fatal to the latter; but the former, under cover of the darknefs eluded the purfuit of the victors, and gained the frontiers of Aragon.

In

In the moment of distress John had consented to banish from his councils the constable Don Alvaro de Luna; but with the return of prosperity his attachment to that nobleman revived; and he was not only recalled to court but invested with the dignity of grand-master of the order of St. James; at the same time the death of Maria left the king of Castille a widower, and he was prevailed upon by his favourite to bestow his hand on the princess Isabella of Portugal. The return of Don Alvaro, and the second marriage of his father, were equally disagreeable to the prince of Asturias; his actions were rather the effects of caprice than principle; and the transient remorse he had lately felt on having violated his duty as a son and a subject, was overwhelmed by the lust of empire. He abruptly retired from court, and flew to arms; but the forces he had collected were far from numerous before he was surprised in the plains between Aravalo and Madrigal, by the appearance of John, who with a select detachment had hastened to chastise his disobediance. The troops on each side were nearly equal; and if the king could not wish to survive the loss of his dignity, the prince could not hope to escape the punishment of his double guilt; yet both were alike impatient for the encounter; with different emotions their followers awaited the signal to charge; on which ever side they turned

turned their eyes, they beheld near relations or
bosom friends; and the exultation of victory must
have been alloyed by the destruction of those who
were most dear to them; while they gazed with
horror on the adverse ranks, the interval of suspense was dexterously seized and improved by
the prelates and clergy who had accompanied the
king and the prince; their holy mediation proved successful; the sword for a moment was
sheathed; but the oath of filial affection and future obedience which passed the lips of the prince
of Asturias, never found admission to his heart.

The king of Navarre still continued his hostilities; a rapacious host of Gascons was allured by
his promises to traverse the Pyrenees, and to consume the plenty of Castille; the Moors of Granada insulted and ravaged the frontiers of Andalusia, while the prince of Austurias was an indolent spectator of their destructive progress; and
in the fond hope that the public distress might
induce John to abdicate the royal dignity, exulted in every event that contributed to diminish
the reputation of his father.

Yet there were moments when interest or caprice induced Henry to assume the appearance of
filial duty, and to act in conjunction with his
royal parent; and it was one of these that proved
at length fatal to Don Alvaro de Luna. In the
possession of the important offices of high constable

ble of Castille and grand master of St. James, the power of the favourite seemed secure even against the frown of his master; a faithful company of guards was raised in his name, and commanded by his natural son Don Pedro; and while these protected his person from immediate danger, his liberality seemed daily to swell the number of his adherents; yet in his ascent to greatness, every step had only served to render his situation more perilous; envy had been the constant companion of his fortune; those he had promoted considered him as the obstacle to their future aggrandisement; and those he had neglected, if they concealed their murmurs, only concealed them to accomplish with greater ease his ruin. In the field he had braved the heir of the crown, and in the court his magnificence had obscured the possessor of it; and Henry was neither destitute of resentment, nor John totally devoid of observation; from the moment that jealousy entered the bosom of the latter, the destruction of Alvaro was determined; and it was only the means of achieving it with least danger, that occupied the thoughts of the king of Castille.

In the prosecution of the design some degree of artifice was requisite; and new marks of confidence were heaped by John on the devoted victim; he accepted of Alvaro's invitation to Tordesillas; and the sumptuous manner in which he

was

was entertained, served to confirm his resolution. His counsels however had not been taken so secretly but some rumours of them had transpired; and when the court proposed to return to Burgos, the suspicions of Alvaro were revealed by demanding of the king a solemn assurance for his safety; the alacrity with which it was granted, ought to have increased the fears of the minister; and long practised in reading the human heart, he should have known, that to doubt the faith of his sovereign, was to convert him into an implacable enemy.

He had scarcely entered the capital before he found the report of his disgrace became more general: the queen herself, who owed her marriage to his intrigues, had been disgusted by his arrogance; and Don Alfonso de Vivaro, who already possessed the place of high treasurer, and aspired to that of minister, under the mask of friendship was indefatigable in his efforts to undermine him; his artifices were penetrated by the eye of Alvaro, and the desire of vengeance surpassed that of safety; he summoned to his palace his adherents, and Vivaro presented himself amongst the number; the seat of council was a lofty tower which overlooked the city; and no sooner had Vivaro ascended than he was thrown headlong from the summit, and dashed to pieces on the stones beneath.

It is probable that Alvaro nourished a secret hope that the fate of his rival might be imputed by his sovereign to accident; but he should have recollected, that it is not easy to lull the jealousy of a monarch when once it is awakened; the king was impatient to chastise his presumption; the queen was zealous to avenge the death of her favourite; and a crowd of hollow courtiers were loud in their indignation against a minister for whose smiles they had so lately contended. To the multitude, the minion of the prince is ever odious; and Alvaro had too frequently heard the execrations of the populace, to rely on their assistance. His palace was surrounded by the royal guards; and though his own spirit might have preferred immediate destruction to submission, he declined by a fruitless defence to involve his friends in his ruin. He obtained a promise from the king, that nothing should be attempted against his life and honour; but the word *unjustly*, was insidiously inserted; the engagement was evaded; and Alvaro was conducted a prisoner to his own castle of Portillo.

A commission was immediately granted to proceed against him; and had he been innocent, he could have expected but little justice from judges who had been chosen by his prosecutors. Yet though he was free from the stain of treason, he could not vindicate himself from the murder of Vivaro. He

He was declared guilty, and sentenced to suffer death by the hands of the common executioner. He heard the decree without changing colour; and in the laſt and moſt trying moment of his life he aſſerted the courage of a Caſtilian noble, and diſappointed by his fearleſs behaviour the malice of his enemies. No entreaties for mercy, no expreſſions unworthy of the rank he had filled, eſcaped him; in the market-place of Valladolid he aſcended with a firm ſtep the ſcaffold; and confeſſed in his approaching fate the juſt puniſhment of his ſins; he obſerved near him the maſter of the horſe to the prince of Aſturias. " Bereza," ſaid he, " tell " your maſter from me, that he will do well not " to follow his father's example in thus reward- " ing his old and faithful ſervants." As he ſurveyed the pole on which his head was to be fixed; " no death, added he, can be ſhameful, which is " ſupported with courage and intrepidity; nor " ought to be conſidered as untimely, when a " man has been for many years at the head of " affairs, and conducted all things with dignity " and reputation." With decent compoſure he preſented his throat to the executioner, and received with intrepidity the fatal ſtroke; for ſeveral days his headleſs body was expoſed to the public view; his treaſures had been confiſcated by his rapacious ſovereign; and it was to common charity that his remains were indebted for a burial.

burial. Yet the hatred or compassion of the populace are ever in extremes; the faults of Alvaro were forgotten in the magnanimity with which he suffered; and an awful admonition was impressed on the surrounding crowd, while they revolved the bloody relics of a man who had equalled the greatest princes in wealth and power, left to depend for their funeral rites on the alms of those who had so lately trembled at his name.

John lived not long enough to repent his ingratitude to a minister who, however he had oppressed the people, had defended amidst the storms of civil dissension the authority of the crown. As the king of Castille rapidly pressed his journey towards Medina del Campo, to confer with his sister the queen of Arragon, he was attacked by a burning fever; his constitution resisted the immediate fury of the disease; but he reached Valladolid in a state of weakness; his disorder returned; and after a long and turbulent reign, he expired in the sentiments of piety and resignation in the forty-seventh year of his age.

A. D. 1450, 1474. The vacant throne was immediately filled by his son Henry, who without the virtues possessed the failings of his father. He was equally destitute of the talents of a king, and the vigour of a man; and the cause of his divorce from his consort Blanch, the daughter of the king of Navarre, was perpetuated in his surname

name of *Impotent*. His underſtanding was frigid as his body; Don Juan de Pacheco ruled with the ſame abſolute dominion over the preſent monarch as Don Alvaro de Luna had exerciſed over the late; and ſcarce had Henry received the homage of his nobility, before he diſguſted them by conferring on his favourite the title of marquis of Villena, and encouraging him to hope for the office of grand-maſter of St. James. The commons were exaſperated by the extravagance, the nobles by the inſolence of this new minion of fortune; and the miniſter was not more odious than the king was contemptible; the jealouſy of the latter was extended even to the feeble years of Alfonſo and Iſabella, the children of Henry by his ſecond marriage; and inſenſible to the diſgrace which had accompanied his ſeparation from Blanch, he ſolicited the hand of Joanna of Portugal. The ambition of that princeſs prompted her to become the partner of his throne; yet Joanna in the marriage bed reſigned not the claims of nature; and five years after her nuptials were celebrated, her pregnancy was announced; a daughter was born, who was baptiſed after her mother; was acknowledged heireſs to the crown of Caſtille; and the validity of whoſe title was recognized by Alfonſo and Iſabella. Yet every precaution ſerved only to increaſe the public ſuſpicion; the impotency of Henry was ſtill the favourite theme; nor in the fifteenth century, such had been the progress of depravity, was Spain deficient in examples where the chastity of the wife had been sacrificed by the husband from motives of revenge or policy.

Amidst the general discontent one event darted a ray of lustre through the gloom of administration; and Gibraltar, which had been wrested from the Christians under the reign of Alfonso the eleventh, was recovered from the infidels in that of Henry. The latter had with his usual precipitation engaged in a war with the court of Granada; and the inability with which he conducted it must have exposed him to considerable loss, had not the kingdom of Granada been distracted at that instant with civil commotion; the throne was disputed by two rival princes; and the garrison of Gibraltar had rushed to the field to partake the conflict. It was at this critical moment that a Moor of the name of Zurro was desirous of renouncing the visions of Mahomet for the pure doctrines of Christ; he felt the zeal of a new proselyte; and was ardent to signalize his conversion by some act of service to those whose tenets he had determined to espouse; in an age when the lines of civil duty were obscured by superstition, it was not difficult to persuade him that perfidy to those whose faith he had abjured was meritorious. He betrayed the weak-

weakness of Gibraltar. A considerable force marched silently from the neighbouring fortress of Tarif; and before the inhabitants could shut the gates part of the assailants had already entered the town, and displayed the Christian standard from the ramparts; the count of Arcos was among the foremost of the daring adventurers; but it was to the duke of Medina Sidonia that the citizens of Gibraltar surrendered; and so elated was Henry with the important acquisition, that in addition to his former titles he assumed that of king of Gibraltar.

It was not alone in Granada that the genius of discord seemed to have established her sway; and the tempest of civil war agitated also the kingdom of Arragon. Hardy, daring, and independent, the character of the Catalans has been always the same; and when the sceptre of Arragon was held by John the second, the inhabitants of Catalonia were impelled by hatred to the consort of their sovereign to erect the standard of revolt. Henry was rather willing than able to avail himself of their rebellion; and he suffered himself to be proclaimed at Barcelona their king. But the assistance he afforded was tardy and inadequate; his favourite the marquis of Villena was averse to the war; and in the prosecution of it, it was deemed prudent to consult Lewis the eleventh, who, as king of France was to be feared as an enemy or courted as an ally.

An interview was appointed between the two kings at Mauleon on the confines of the kingdom of Navarre; and on their meeting their different difpofitions were evinced by their contrafted appearance. Henry, vain, magnificent, and haughty, was attended by a fplendid train; Lewis, mean in his perfon, clad in coarfe cloth, fhort and unbecoming, was flenderly accompanied; but the wealth the former had expended in his fumptuous preparations, the latter employed to bribe the minifters of Caftille; the marquis of Villena promifed to fecond the views of the king of France; and with mutual proteftations of friendfhip, Henry and Lewis parted; the former difgufted with the fordidnefs of the latter; the latter full of contempt for the underftanding of the former.

The marquis of Villena hefitated not at the expence of his fidelity to his fovereign, to fulfil the conditions he had entered into with Lewis; and in compliance with the inclinations of that monarch, he foon perfuaded Henry to abandon the Catalans to the refentment of their prince; yet the king of Caftille had fcarce figned the treaty before he was awakened to a fenfe of his ignominy; and the exile of the marquis from court was the immediate confequence of his difgraceful counfels.

Accuf-

Accuftomed to baſk in the fmiles, the marquis of Villena ill-brooked the frowns of his fovereign. One moment effaced from his memory the favours that had been heaped upon him in the patronage of twenty years; and he was fcarce baniſhed from court before he became the favourite of the nobility, who before had confidered him as the object of their envy. A powerful confederacy was formed between the high admiral of Caftille; the counts of Placentia, Beneventé, and Offuna; the archbiſhops of Toledo and Compoftella; and the grand-mafters of Calatrava and Alcantara; to thefe the marquis of Villena joined himfelf; and hoped by his fword not only to regain his wanted afcendancy over the counfels of his fovereign, but to extort from him the high office of grand-mafter of St. James, the peculiar object of his ambition, and which the prudence of the king had hitherto withheld. In cafe Henry refufed to gratify the wiſhes of the confpirators, it was determined to declare him unworthy of the crown, and to place it on the head of his brother Alfonfo, from whofe youth they might expect a more ready compliance.

It was while the king of Caftille was engaged in vifiting Gibraltar that he was firft informed of the dangerous combination that had been cemented againſt him; he returned immediately to Madrid; and in the tranfport of his indignation

tion at the ingratitude of the marquis of Villena, he invested his rival the count of Ladesma with the office of grand-master of St. James; but the intelligence that the king of Arragon had acceded to the league, inclined him to more moderate measures; he consented to an interview with the principal conspirators; promised to redress their grievances; and as a pledge of reconciliation, declared his willingness to bestow the grand-mastership of St. James on the marquis of Villena. In the execution of the treaty the consent of the count of Ladesma was necessary; and the possession of the office could not reflect so much lustre on the character of that nobleman, as did the alacrity with which he resigned it. "I am happy," said he, "as he surrendered the ensigns of the "appointment, in rendering service to him to "whom I owe all I possess; and of proving to "his subjects that he has at least raised one man "of merit and fidelity;" the reproof was heard and felt by all; a faint blush overspread the countenance of the marquis of Villena; and though hardened in the commerce of courts, and elated by his triumph over his sovereign, he must for a moment have envied the feelings of his rival.

It is seldom those concessions which are extorted from the crown, are faithfully executed; the nobles of Castille who yet retained their allegiance,

ance, reproached the weakness of Henry; and that prince, ever influenced by the laſt counſel, determined to aſſert his dignity in arms. He collected a numerous body of forces; and the confederates heard of his preparations without being diſmayed; they publiſhed a manifeſto in which they upbraided him with having endeavoured to defraud his brother Alfonſo of the ſucceſſion, and to impoſe in Joanna a ſuppoſititious child on the nation. They claimed as one of the privileges of their order the right of trying and paſſing ſentence on their ſovereign. That the exerciſe of this power might be as public and ſolemn as the pretenſion to it was bold, they ſummoned all their party to meet at Avila. A ſpacious theatre was erected in a plain, without the walls of the town; an image repreſenting the king was ſeated on a throne, clad in royal robes, with a crown on its head, a ſceptre in its hand, and the ſword of juſtice by its ſide. The accuſation againſt the king was read, and the ſentence of depoſition was pronounced in preſence of a numerous aſſembly. At the cloſe of the firſt article of the charge, the archbiſhop of Toledo advanced, and tore the crown from the head of the image; at the cloſe of the ſecond, the count of Placentia ſnatched the ſword of juſtice from its ſide; at the cloſe of the third, the count of Benaventé wreſted the ſceptre from its hand; and at

the

the close of the last, Don Diego Lopez de Stuniga tumbled it headlong from the throne; and at the same instant Don Alfonso, Henry's brother, was proclaimed king of Castille and Leon in his place.

At the head of a numerous and loyal army Henry might have despised the farce which had been acted at Avila; but he was again vanquished by the arts of the marquis of Villena. By the professions of that nobleman he was prevailed upon to dismiss his forces, and to expect the voluntary submission of the confederates; but he was soon awakened from the delusion; Simancas was reduced; Toledo declared for Alfonso; and Henry beheld the spirit of revolt rapidly extending through his dominions. He hastily assembled what troops were still faithful to their oath of allegiance, and advanced to the relief of Medina del Campo, which was besieged by Alfonso. In the plains which stretch around that city he beheld the army of the confederates; and both parties prepared with alacrity for action. The forces of Henry consisted of eight hundred lances, seven hundred light horse, and two thousand infantry; those of Alfonso were nearly equal. Though the understanding of Henry was despised, yet his personal courage had never been doubted; but on this occasion he displayed not the same ardour as had characterized him when prince of Asturias; and the inglorious counsels

of

of his courtiers perfuaded him to retire from the conflict. His youthful competitor fuftained a nobler part; his banner was unfurled in the front of the line; and the archbifhop of Toledo, whofe facred habit was laid afide for a crimfon fcarf embroidered with white croffes, charged with Alfonfo. The fhock was violent; and the engagement which was began about noon continued till fatigue and darknefs parted the combatants. Fve hundred Caftilians were extended lifelefs on the field; but the lofs was mutual; the victory undecided; and both armies dreaded to renew the engagement; and withdrew to their refpective camps.

The town of Segovia on the banks of the Arayada was foon after furprifed by the confederates; but the caftle in which were depofited the royal treafures ftill held out for the king; and Henry received an ample compenfation for the lofs of that town in the acquifition of the important city of Toledo. The inhabitants of Toledo had been among the firft to declare for Alfonfo; and they had lately repulfed the king from their walls; but by one of thofe fudden tranfitions which fo frequently occur in civil diffenfions, they determined to return to their allegiance; they expelled the garrifon of the confederates; and proclaimed their joy on the entrance of Henry in tumultuous acclamations.

The

The rebels, who already laboured under no inconsiderable diftrefs from the cenfures of the fee of Rome, could not but be highly mortified at this inftance of defertion; fome vigorous effort was neceffary to reftore the credit of their arms; but before they rifked their hopes in a battle, they apparently determined to provide for the fafety of their youthful leader. With a ftrong efcort Alfonfo prepared to retire to Avila; but he was not allowed to reach that place; the fecond night of his journey he retired to reft in perfect health, and was found dead, without any marks of violence, in a few hours after.

The fudden and myfterious fate of a young prince whofe fpirit and abilities were not unequal to the ftation he afpired to, could not fail to excite fufpicion. Yet the reputation of Henry has efcaped free from ftain; nor has he ever been charged with promoting a death which promifed him the greateft advantages. The confederates were not confidered as equally guiltlefs; they were fuppofed to have dreaded the rifing genuis of Alfonfo; and by poifon to have blafted the profpect of a reign which would have controuled their factious turbulence. In the natural weaknefs of her fex, Ifabella offered a fairer inftrument to their ambition; yet the prudence of that princefs difappointed their views; and to their proffer of the crown, they heard with aftonifhment her anfwer;

answer; "that it was not theirs to bestow; but "was held by Henry according to the laws of "God and man." Yet she concealed not her pretensions to the succession; and the revolted lords deprived of a chief, were happy to embrace any opening for negociation; the king consented to a conference; waved the claims of Joanna; acknowledged Isabella as the heirefs to his dominions; and in the immediate, enjoyed the pleasing hope of future tranquillity.

The peace that was established between the king and his nobles, confirmed the marquis of Villena in the post of grand-master of St. James; yet after the black ingratitude he had been guilty of he could scarcely hope to regain his ascendancy over the mind of his master. But the feeble understanding of Henry required a favourite on whom he could repose the cares of government, and he returned to his former confidence. The marriage of Isabella was the first object of the new counsels; and among a variety of pretenders, Ferdinand, who with the title of king of Sicily joined as the son of the king of Arragon and Navarre the succession of those thrones, was considered as the most eligible; yet he was scarcely preferred, before the marquis of Villena plunged into new intrigues to evade the marriage; his schemes were traversed by the archbishop of Toledo, who on this occasion seemed actuated by a

just

just sense of his country's interest. He carried the princess privately to Valladolid, invited the king of Sicily, and pronounced himself the nuptial benediction; yet in his zeal he neglected not to provide for the supremacy of the Catholic church, the present quiet of Henry, and the future independence of Castille.

Ten articles were presented by the archbishop, and subscribed by the king of Sicily before he received the hand of Isabella. By the first, Ferdinand engaged to acknowledge the pope as head of the church, and to maintain all ecclesiastical immunities; by the second, to behave with respect to his brother-in-law Henry, and to conform himself in all things to the accommodation that was made when he acknowledged the princess for his successor. In the third, he stipulated to administer justice impartially, and not to infringe in any respect the laws, usages, prerogatives, or privileges of any of the cities, towns, places, or persons in his dominions, agreeable to the oath taken by the kings of Castille, at their accession. By the fourth, he was not to alienate any town or fortress without the consent of the princess. By the fifth, all orders were to be signed jointly by Ferdinand and Isabella; and no person to be admitted into the council, government, or offices of state, that was not a native of Castille. By the Sixth, all dignities ecclesiastical and civil were to

be

be disposed of by the princess. By the seventh, Ferdinand was to grant a general amnesty with respect to all things which had happened in former civil wars; and was never to set up any claim or pretensions to those lands and estates which his father had possessed in Castille, and which had been given away by the crown, and were in the hands of several of the nobility. By the eighth, that the archbishops of Toledo and Seville, and the grand-master of St. James should ever enjoy their respective ranks in the monarchy, as also all other lords and knights who have steadily adhered to the princess's party, and have contributed to secure to her the succession of the crown. By the ninth, That Ferdinand should reside in the dominions of Castille, and should make war against the Moors as soon as it was in his power; but otherwise should not take up arms without the consent of his consort; in case however that any civil war should break out in Castille, he engaged to furnish as long as it lasted a thousand lances from Arragon to remain during that space in the pay of the crown. And by the tenth, that over and above the sum of one thousand florins of gold, the princess shall have and enjoy the towns of Borga, Magalon, Elcha, and Carvallen in the kingdoms of Arragon and Valencia, and Syracuse and Catanea in the kingdom of Sicily.

Such were the conditions dictated by the archbishop

bishop of Toledo, and accepted by Ferdinand; yet though ultimately beneficial, they procured not immediate peace to Castille; if Henry considered Joanna as his daughter, his feelings must have been wounded by the preference which he had been obliged to give to his sister; and if conscious of his own impotency, his pride must have been violated by a compromise that implied a tacit confession of the imposture; the marquis of Villena, ever restless and intriguing, stimulated him to break the treaty which he himself had imposed; the queen, bold and vindictive, urged him to assert the right of a child who at least called him father; Henry was not capable of long resisting their counsels and importunities; he published a manifesto in which he recalled his former concessions, vindicated and confirmed by oath his belief that Joanna was his daughter, and declared her the heiress to his crown; it was opposed by a proclamation from Ferdinand and Isabella, which warned the people of Castille not to be deluded by the representations of Henry, or the artifices of his favourites; each party aspired to maintain their claim by argument, but it was by the sword alone that it could be finally decided.

Two negociations of marriage for Joanna had been entered into by the marquis of Villena, and both had proved abortive; the first was with the duke of Berri of the blood royal of France; but
Lewis

Lewis the eleventh, intent on his own aggrandifement, and unwilling to increafe the power of his brother, liftened with coldnefs to the propofal; the fecond was with Henry of Arragon, the fon of that Henry who had feized the perfon of John the fecond, and for ten years embarraffed Caftille by his pretenfions to the adminiftration; the fon was not more fuccefsful than the father; his haughty manners offended the Caftilian nobility; and his thirft for power excited the jealoufy of the marquis of Villena; the latter abandoned his interefts; and refted his laft hopes of a powerful alliance for Joanna on the king of Portugal; that monarch liftened with pleafure to the propofal, and received the favourite with every mark of refpect at Lifbon; but on his return, while the marquis of Villena exulted in the fuccefs of his negociations, he was attacked by a mortal difeafe, and expired lefs lamented by the people whom he had oppreffed, than by the fovereign whofe confidence he had abufed.

Henry himfelf furvived his favourite only to impart to his fon the fame proofs of regard as he had lavifhly beftowed on the father; a flow fever had for fome time preyed upon his fpirits; and the approach of death was acknowledged by his phyficians; he heard the fentence with greater fortitude than might have been expected from a review of his life; and his laft breath declared the princess Joanna his daughter and successor; but he could not hope that his will which had been continually opposed when he was alive, should be respected when he was dead; the majority of his subjects declared in favour of Ferdinand and Isabella; they were admitted into Segovia; were put into possession of the royal treasures; and were jointly proclaimed the sovereigns of Castille and Leon.

A. D. 1474, 1478. The decease of Henry did not extinguish the ambitious hopes of Alfonso king of Portugal; at the head of a formidable army he entered Castille, espoused the princess Joanna, and was supported in his claim to the throne by the young marquis of Villena. But at a small distance from Toro his pretensions were decided on a field of battle; after a long struggle the Portuguese were compelled to yield to the superior valour of the Castilians, or the skill of Ferdinand; yet their retreat was conducted with order; and they gained their own frontiers without being pursued by the victors. But in the event of the day they confessed their adverse fortune; the marquis of Villena submitted, and reconciled himself to Ferdinand; the less powerful malecontents followed his example; and Castille breathed at length from the calamities of civil war.

Ferdiand, had scarce established his authority over

over Castille, before his attention was recalled to Arragon; his aged father John still held the sceptre, but he held it with a feeble hand; famine and pestilence combined with war to depopulate his dominions; in the early part of his reign Lewis the eleventh had lent to him the sum of three hundred thousand crowns; and the important counties of Roussillon and Cerdagne were transferred as the security for the money advanced; the value of a country from which France derives a revenue exceeding an hundred thousand pounds sterling, and which contains above one hundred and eighty-eight thousand inhabitants was early discerned by Lewis; he refused to restore the pledge he had been trusted with, and maintained the possession of it by force; the succours that Ferdinand could afford his father were few and precarious; the armies of Lewis were numerous and well disciplined; the war was not marked with any interesting occurrence; but the event of it was decisive; and Roussillon and Cerdagne were annexed to the kingdom of France.

The distress of his subjects and the ill success of his arms might have occasioned some mortification to John; he had already largely exceeded the common term of humanity; and at the advanced age of eighty-two his death might be hourly expected; he expired at Barcelona; the crown of Navarre, which he had obtained by his marriage with Blanch, paffed to the countefs of Foix, his daughter by that princefs; but Arragon acknowledged and fubmitted to the pretenfions of Ferdinand; and the union of that kingdom under the fame monarch as Caftille, revived the name, and eftablifhed the power of modern SPAIN.

Chapter

Chapter the Ninth.

State of the neighbouring powers, when Ferdinand united the crowns of Castille and Arragon.—Of Portugal, Navarre, and Granada.—Of France.— Italy.—Germany.—And England.—Political state of Spain.—Account of the Justiza in Arragon.—Of the Holy Brotherhood.—Address of Ferdinand.— He makes peace with Portugal.—Commences the war with Granada.—Various success.—Exertions of Ferdinand and Isabella.—Dissensions of the Moors.—Ferdinand successively reduces Ronda, Velez, and Malaga.—Domestic history of Abdallah king of Granada.—Granada is invested by the Christians.—Construction of the town of Santa Fé.— Despair of the Moors.—Capitulation of Granada.— Triumphal entry of Ferdinand.—Description of the Alhambra.—Expulsion of the Jews.—Subsequent oppression of the Morescoes.—Progress of navigation. —Discovery of the Fortunate or Canary Islands by the Spaniards.—Extensive discoveries of the Portuguese.—History and character of Christopher Columbus;—his idea of new countries in the West.— His proposals rejected by Genoa and Portugal.—

Are at length accepted by Isabella.—He sails from Palos in Andalusia.

A. D. 1479, 1492. WHEN Ferdinand by marriage and succession united the kingdoms of Castille and Arragon under the name of Spain, that peninsula still contained the independent powers of Portugal, Navarre, and Granada. The former from Cape Vincent stretched along the sea coast to the mouth of the Minho; it nearly occupied the country of the warlike Lusitanians; and the loss it had sustained on the side of the east, was compensated by an accession of territory towards the north. From the Pyrenean mountains Navarre advanced about sixty miles in breadth to the frontiers of Castille, and extended about seventy-five in length, until bounded on the east by the province of Biscay, and on the west by the kingdom of Arragon. The kingdom of Granada for one hundred and seventy miles ranged along the shores of the Mediterranean; but it had gradually receded before the encroaching spirit of Castille; and its breadth might be estimated at about seventy miles; yet narrow as were its limits, and mountainous its appearance, every deficiency was supplied, and every obstacle overcome by industry; the Moors disdained not the toils of

hus-

husbandry; beneath their labours the country assumed the face of a garden; and Ferdinand confessed with a sigh of envy and ambition, that the fairest district of Spain was possessed by the natural enemies of his faith and crown.

It was not within the peninsula of Spain that the views of Ferdinand were confined; the neighbouring states of Europe claimed, and partook of his attention. Recovered from the wounds which she had received in her long and repeated conflicts with England, France displayed the features of a mighty and vigorous monarchy. The bloody policy of Lewis the eleventh, though immediately oppressive, had laid the foundation of the grandeur of his successors. He had broken the strength of the nobility, and established the power of the crown. Nine thousand cavalry, and sixteen thousand infantry in regular pay, restrained within the bounds of obedience the national levity; his address had allured, or his menaces had intimidated the states to render several taxes perpetual which had been formerly imposed only for a short time; and he had delivered the king from a precarious dependence on the will of his people. By fraud or force he had possessed himself of Burgundy, Artois, and Provence; and his recent acquisition of Roussillon and Cerdagne, pointed him out as the more peculiar object of jealousy and suspicion to Spain.

From

From the western coast of Spain, the opposite shores of Italy could not but attract the notice of Ferdinand. The fertile kingdom of Naples obeyed a bastard son of the house of Arragon, who had wrested it from that of Anjou; yet the race of the latter was not extinct, nor had they relinquished their title to the Neapolitan crown. The count of Maine and Provence, the heir of this family, conveyed all his rights and pretensions to Lewis the eleventh and his successors; the king of Naples could not revolve without anxiety their formidable claims, nor had he less to dread from the turbulence of his own nobility, ever prompt in arms to assert their enormous privileges, and confederate against their sovereign.

In Venice the form of government was republican; a people who for safety had fled from the sword of the ferocious Attila to the sequestered isles of the Hadriatic, and whose habitations might be doubtfully assigned to the earth or water, soon became alike familiar with both. Necessity had early compelled them to penetrate into the heart of Italy by the secure though laborious navigation of the rivers and inland canals; they were impelled by avarice when they were no longer urged by want; their vessels were continually increasing in size and number; and they assiduously visited all the harbours of the gulf But the Venetian government, which had originated

nated in a number of families, reduced by misfortune to the fame level of humble poverty, had in the acquifition of wealth declined from its ancient fimplicity; and though its deliberative, legiflative, and executive power, as calculated for the order of nobles alone might be regarded as excellent, yet if confidered as formed for a numerous body of people, it muft have appeared a rigid and partial ariftocracy. The republic however rapidly advanced in rank and affluence; the arts of induftry and commerce were encouraged; all the nations of Europe depended on it not only for the commodities of the eaft, which were imported in Venetian bottoms, but for various manufactures fabricated or finifhed with fuperior dexterity or elegance; and though the military genius of the citizens of Venice was naturally frigid, or was repreffed by the jealoufy of her nobles, yet on the fea, her peculiar element, her armaments were conducted with valour and wifdom, and augmented her glory and extended her dominion.

The advantage of trade in fixteen fucceffive centuries had gradually extended Florence from the rock of Fæfulæ to the banks of the Arno. But though the fource of her profperity was nearly the fame, her conftitution widely differed from that of Venice; it partook as much of democratical turbulence and licencioufnefs, as the other of aristocratical rigour; but about the middle of the fifteenth century Cosmo of Medicis arose; and Florence beheld herself governed by one of her merchants, without arms and without a title. His wealth, his liberality, and his zeal for learning, established his pre-eminence among his fellow citizens. His riches were dedicated to the service of mankind; he corresponded at once with Cairo and London; and a cargo of Indian spices and Greek books was often imported in the same vessel. He gained such an ascendant over the affections as well as the councils of his countrymen, that though the forms of popular government were preserved, and though the various departments of administration were filled by magistrates distinguished by ancient names, and elected in the usual manner, he was in reality the head of the commonwealth; his grandson Lorenzo imitated and surpassed him in generosity and literature, and at least equalled him in authority; and transmitted a considerable degree of his power to his descendants, who ruled in Florence with almost absolute sway.

Genoa had once been the rival of Venice, and disputed with her the sovereignty of the sea. The names and families of her naval commanders, Pisani and Doria, were familiar and illustrious throughout Europe; and their abilities supported her through a contest of one hundred and thirty years; but she was

at

at length compelled to yield to the fuperior fortune or refources of her implacable enemy; her factions had increafed as her ftrength diminifhed; and obliged her to feek for domeftic peace under the protection of a foreign lord; and alternately to court the controul of the duke of Milan or the French king.

Milan had in the beginning of the fourth century of the Chriftian æra, been exalted by the emperor of the weft into the feat of government; about the middle of the fixth century it had been deftroyed by the Burgundians; and three hundred thoufand male inhabitants are reported to have perifhed by the fwords of the barbarians; it had rifen from its afhes, had refifted the authority, and been overthrown by the arms of the emperor Frederick the firft. Yet its depreffure was but tranfient; and it foon again reared its head, though with diminifhed fplendour; it had fcarce fuffered more from the rage of foreign enemies than from domeftic faction; the chief power amidft fucceffive contefts had imperceptibly been attained by the Vifconti family, who in recompenfe for their attachment to the imperial intereft, had been created dukes of Milan; Valentina, a daughter of that houfe, had married Lewis duke of Orleans, brother of Charles the fixth; in their marriage contract, which the pope confirmed, it had been ftipulated, that upon failure of heirs male

male in the family of Visconti, the duchy of Milan should descend to the posterity of Valentina and the duke of Orleans. That event took place; and Charles duke of Orleans urged his right to the crown, founded on the contract of his mother Valentina. It was disputed by Alfonso king of Naples, who claimed under the will of the late duke; and by the emperor, who contended that upon the extinction of male issue in the family of Visconti, the fief returned to the superior lord, and was re-annexed to the empire. Both pretensions were rejected by the citizens of Milan themselves, who, enamoured of freedom, aspired to establish a republic; but the jarring interests of each party were favourable to the ambition of Francis Sforza, the natural son of Jacomuzzo Sforza, whose courage and abilities had raised him to be a distinguished leader of those bands which made war a trade, and hired themselves out to different states. Francis succeeded his father in the command of the martial adventurers who had followed his standard; he had married a natural daughter of the late duke of Milan; and this claim, slight in itself, became formidable from his address and valour. After a long struggle he ascended the ducal throne; the defects of his title were forgotten in the admiration of his abilities and virtues, and he was permitted to bequeath in peace his sceptre to his son.

Rome,

Rome, after having succeffively submitted to the rapacity of the Goths, the Huns, and the Vandals, trembled at the hostile approach of the Lombards. Famine and pestilence conspired with the rage of the Barbarians against the ancient mistress of the world; her streets were deserted; her edifices exposed to ruin and decay; and the mouldering fabrics were easily overthrown by inundations, tempests, and earthquakes; the imperial magistrates had abandoned the scene of desolation; and towards the close of the sixth century, the reins of government dropped into the hands of her bishop. The name of Gregory must ever be dear to the Vatican; during more than thirteen years that his pontificate lasted, the misery of his flock was alleviated by his incessant care; he introduced order and plenty again into the capital; he deserved and obtained the name of The Father of his Country; he directed the operations of the provincial troops; and repelled by his arms, or diverted by his address, the savage Lombards. The bishops of Italy and the adjacent islands acknowledged the Roman pontiff as their special metropolitan; and during several ages the see of Rome received and claimed no other mark of respect; but towards the beginning of the ninth century, their pretensions to infallibility, as the successors to St. Peter, were revealed; and they asserted their power as heads of the church to universal jurisdiction. Their authority was supported by the superstition and credulity of mankind; in all ecclesiastical controversies their decisions were received as oracles of truth; nor was the plenitude of their power confined solely to what was spiritual. They dethroned monarchs; disposed of crowns; absolved subjects from the obedience due to their sovereigns; and laid kingdoms under interdicts. Their success inspired them with insolence; they forgot the sanctity of their situation; and engaged as principals or auxiliaries in every war that was kindled in Europe; the surrounding nations could not remain blind to their inordinate ambition; the veneration for their sacred character began to abate; and towards the close of the fourteenth century was nearly extinguished.

But while their spiritual authority declined, their temporal dominion advanced; and the same turbulent spirit of intrigue that proved fatal to the first was propitious to the last. From the donation of Constantine they pleaded their claim to the greatest part of Italy; but the fictitious deed has been exposed by the pen of Laurentius Valla; and it was from the hasty liberality of Pepin and Charlemagne that we may date their pretensions to a territory beyond the walls of their city; they derived more considerable advantages from the credulity of the Norman adventurers

venturers who conquered Naples, and from the
superstition of the countess Matilda; and the ecclesiastical state was gradually extended over the
Campagna, and embraced several of the adjacent
cities.

One general system prevailed through the Italian powers; and while they engaged in perpetual and endless negociation to adjust the interests
of the different states, their contests in the field,
when they had recourse to arms, were decided in
mock battles, by innocent and bloodless victories.
When the danger became more imminent, instead
of their own subjects, they had recourse to the
Condottieri, or leaders of bands, who readily embraced and fought for the party, which allured
them by the most ample proffer of pay or
plunder.

Of hardier mould, the Germans still retained
the traces of their ancient ferocity and martial
spirit; when the successors of Charlemagne relaxed from the vigour of his administration, every
baron exercised a sovereign jurisdiction within his
own domains; every duke and count aspired to
independence; and towards the middle of the
thirteenth century, the imperial authority had
dwindled into an empty title. Rodolph of Hapf-
burg, the founder of the house of Austria, had
been elected emperor; not that he might re-establish order, but because his territories were too

inconsiderable to excite the jealousy of the German princes: several of his successors were raised to the throne from the same motive; and almost every prerogative was wrested from their feeble hands. The capacity of Frederic of Austria, the third emperor of that name, was far from vigorous; he listened with terror to the progress of the Turks, who had planted the standard of Mahomet on the walls of Constantinople; he trembled for the safety of his capital; and his embarrassments were increased by an unsuccessful war which he had waged in hopes of the crowns of Hungary and Bohemia. Unfortunate abroad, he was despised at home; and, during his reign, the calamities of the German empire rapidly multiplied; the causes of dissension among its numerous members were infinite; and these gave rise to perpetual private wars, which were carried on with all the violence that usually accompanies resentment, when unrestrained by superior authority. Rapine, outrage, and exaction, became universal; the cities united in a league to check the pride and oppression of the nobility; the nobility formed confederacies to maintain tranquillity among their own order; Germany was divided into several circles, in each of which a provincial and partial jurisdiction was established to supply the place of a public tribunal; but the remedy was ineffectual; and the empire was still

involved

involved in darkness and anarchy, when on the death of Frederic, his son Maximilian succeeded to the imperial crown, who had been previously elected king of the Romans, and who by his marriage with the daughter of Charles of Burgundy had acquired Flanders, Franche-Comté, and the Low Countries.

The arms and victories of Henry and Edward in France had diffused throughout Europe the name and renown of the English; their valour had been immediately felt in Spain in the revolution which restored Peter the Cruel; but the minority of Henry the Sixth had been fatal to those conquests which had been obtained by the mature policy and courage of his father; and in France, Calais alone had stemmed the returning torrent which had overwhelmed the fortunes of the English; during more than twenty years England herself had been distracted by the rival pretensions of the houses of York and Lancaster; and though the ascendancy of the former seemed established in the reign of Edward the fourth, the embers of civil war were rather concealed than extinguished.

Such was the situation of the principal powers of Europe, when Ferdinand united the crowns of Castille and Arragon; and though his territories were considerable, and the general disposition of his neighbours pacific, yet his ambitious views were contracted by the limits which were placed to his authority; the privileges of the nobility in Castille; the immunities of several of the cities; and the influence they possessed in the *Cortes*, or Assembly of the States, restrained the will of the sovereign; the military orders of St. James, Calatrava, and Alcantara, rivalled him in power; and although in Arragon the form of government was monarchical, the genius of it was purely republican. The real authority was vested in the parliament, which consisted of four different descriptions. The nobility of the first rank; the equestrian order, or nobility of the second class; the representatives of the cities and towns; and the dignitaries of the church, with the deputies of the inferior clergy. No law could pass in this assembly without the assent of every single member; peace, war, and revenue, depended on their resolutions; and they claimed the privilege of inspecting every department of justice and administration, and of redressing all grievances. According to a regulation introduced at the commencement of the fourteenth century, the *Cortes* was convoked once in two years; after it was assembled, the king had no right to prorogue or dissolve it without its own consent; and the session continued forty days.

Besides her parliament, Arragon possessed another institution peculiar to herself in her justiza,
or

or supreme judge; this officer was chosen by the king from the second class of nobility; but he could be removed only by the voice of the Cortes. He acted as the protector of the people, and the comptroller of the prince; his person was sacred; his power and jurisdiction were almost unlimited; he was the supreme interpreter of the laws; had a title to review all the royal proclamations and patents; by his sole authority could exclude any of the king's ministers from the conduct of affairs; could call them to answer for their maladministration; and he was himself solely accountable to the Cortes for the manner in which he executed his high office. It was through him the Arragonese pronounced their oath of allegiance; and the words of it sufficiently proclaim their jealousy of the throne, and their love of independence: "We," said the justiza to the king, in the name of his high-spirited barons, "who are
" each of us as good as you, and who are altoge-
" ther more powerful than you, promise obedi-
" ence to your government if you maintain our
" rights and liberties; but not otherwise." Nor were these lofty expressions a vain form; but according to their oath, they established it as a fundamental article in their constitution, that if the king should violate their privileges, it was lawful for the people to disclaim him as their sovereign;

sovereign, and to elect another (even a heathen) in his place.

Had Ferdinand presumed publicly to have exalted the power of the crown at the expence of the people, he most likely must have fallen in the unequal contest; but he proceeded silently to undermine that strength which he dared not openly attack; his profound sagacity in concerting his measures, his persevering industry in conducting them, and his uncommon address in carrying them into execution, fitted him admirably for an undertaking which required all these talents. He prevailed on the knights of St. James to place him at the head of that order; and when his reputation was established by the success of the Moorish war, he influenced by threats or promises the fraternities of Calatrava and Alcantara to follow the example of that of St. James; and to elect as their chiefs Isabella and himself. Innocent the eighth, and Alexander the sixth confirmed the choice by the sanction of the papal authority; subsequent pontiffs rendered the masterships perpetual in the crown; and a new accession of power and revenue was imparted to the kings of Spain.

Another engine in the hands of Ferdinand was the *Holy Brotherhood*; that name had been appropriated to an association, which about the middle of the thirteenth century had been formed

by

by the cities of Arragon, and in which they were soon after imitated by those of Castille. The Holy Brotherhood exacted a certain contribution from each of the associated towns; they levied a considerable body of forces in order to protect travellers, and to pursue criminals; they appointed judges who opened their courts in various parts of the kingdom; whoever was guilty of murder, robbery, or of any act that violated the public peace, was seized by their troops, was carried before judges of their nomination who, without paying any regard to the exclusive and sovereign jurisdiction which the lord of the place might claim, tried and condemned the criminal. But this salutary institution which restored, with the prompt and impartial administration of justice, internal order and tranquillity, was regarded with peculiar jealousy by the nobles, whose castles were too often the seats of oppression, and who complained of this new fraternity as an encroachment on one of their most valuable privileges; they remonstrated against it in an high tone; and on some occasions refused to grant any aid to the crown unless it were abolished; Ferdinand was sensible however not only of the good effects of the Holy Brotherhood with respect to the police of his kingdoms, but perceived its tendency to abridge, and at length to annihilate, the territorial jurisdiction of the nobility; whenever

ever attacked, he invariably protected it; and when supported by the whole force of royal authority, the nobles of Spain found themselves incapable of resisting its weight.

Yet whatever advantages Ferdinand might derive from these measures, he could never hope without a numerous and obedient army to establish the dignity of the crown on a broad and solid basis; and he was conscious it was only in a long and successful war that the troops of Spain could be trained to discipline, and accustomed to respect the voice of their sovereign. On his accession to the throne of Arragon he had been desirous of terminating his differences with Portugal by an equal and honourable treaty; that court consented to resign all pretensions on Castille, and to relinquish the hand of the princess Joanna; the articles were finally signed at Alcacovas; and Ferdinand at peace with his Christian neighbours, revolved in the Moorish kingdom of Granada a more popular object of hostilities.

The sceptre of Granada was at that critical moment held by Abul Hoffein, who in his youth had been distinguished by his valour, and in his age was not found deficient in spirit. Though embarrassed by the pretensions of his son Abdalla, who was impatient of sovereignty, he declined not the impending contest; and to the demand of tribute that was urged by Ferdinand, boldly replied,

replied, " That in the same place where they
" coined money at Granada, they forged arms
" also to defend it." The answer sunk deep in the
mind of Ferdinand; and no sooner was he delivered by his treaty with Portugal from all apprehensions on that side of his dominions, than he
encouraged the marquis of Cadiz to invade the
Moorish territories; the inroad of that Castilian
nobleman was regarded by the Moors as the act
of his sovereign; they flew to arms to avenge it;
they surprised the town of Zahara on the confines
of Andalusia; placed a strong garrison in the citadel which arose on a craggy rock, and was
deemed impregnable; and swept away the inhabitants into captivity. The capture of Zahara
was retaliated by that of Alhama, which is situated about twenty-five miles from Granada, and
is still celebrated for the salubrity of its baths. A
Spanish officer had remarked the weakness and
negligence of the garrison; he imparted his observations to the marquis of Cadiz; and a select
detachment marched under his conduct, scaled
the walls of the castle, and massacred the slender
band that had been left to guard it; the citizens,
in the town below still continued to defend themselves; but their tumultuous valour was ineffectual against the ardour and rapacity of the assailants; three thousand who escaped the sword became the slaves of the Christian victors, and expiated

piated by their sufferings the fate of the inhabitants of Zahara.

These desultory enterprises were only the prelude to a more serious conflict for which the Moors and Christians anxiously prepared themselves; the forces of Granada were first in motion; the royal standard was unfurled; and Abul Hossein rushed forwards at the head of three thousand cavalry and forty thousand infantry to recover Alhama. The reputation of Ferdinand was equally concerned to protect it; the zeal of his nobility enabled him to assemble a numerous army; and the garrison of Alhama had scarce felt the calamities of a siege, before they beheld the banners of their sovereign advancing to their relief; Abul Hossein dreaded to encounter his adversary in the open field; yet twice he resumed the enterprise, and as often abandoned it on the approach of Ferdinand; nor were the Christians exempt in their turn from lamenting the vicissitudes of war; and the king of Spain after beholding the bravest of his followers perish in the fruitless attempt, was compelled to retire with disgrace from the walls of Loxa.

The repulse only served to stimulate Ferdinand to more vigorous efforts; his ardour was participated or surpassed by Isabella; the influence of superstition was called to their assistance; and the people readily believed the moment was arrived
which

which had been so long predicted, when the disciples of Mahomet were to be expelled from Spain; every province displayed the busy face of war; every port resounded with naval armaments; formidable armies were levied, and numerous squadrons equipped; and the supplies which were granted with liberality by the states, were managed with economy by Isabella. Yet though their resources were far inferior, and divided by domestic contention, the resistance of the Moors was by no means inglorious. Abdalla the son of Hossein had seized the capital of Granada, and rejected the authority of his father. He was impatient to sanction his unnatural revolt by some signal and splendid achievements. As a strong detachment of the Christians under the marquis of Cadiz climbed the steep mountains of Axarguira, in the neighbourhood of Malaga, they were suddenly assailed by an ambuscade of the Moors, who arose from their craggy lurking-places, and rushed to the attack with dissonant shouts. The ranks of the Spaniards were already disordered by their march over broken ground; the soldiers were confounded by the unexpected charge; an instantaneous panic was communicated to every bosom; and though the marquis of Cadiz by the swiftness of his horse escaped through secret paths, the greater part of his followers perished by the sword of the infidels. The success

of

of his countrymen elated Abdalla; he marched from Granada, and advanced without beholding an enemy to the frontiers of Andalusia. But he was not suffered to retreat with the same impunity; the count of Cabra, with a select band of cavalry, flew to chastise his temerity; a thick mist concealed their approach, which was dispelled by the sun, when the infidels beheld with terror the Christian squadron ready to charge their rear. They were themselves incumbered with spoil; they were ignorant of the number of their adversaries; and the error into which they were betrayed extinguished all confidence in their leader; each man was only solicitous for his personal safety; and, the moment that the trumpets of the enemy sounded, the rout began. Amidst dismay and slaughter Abdalla was not more conspicuous for the splendour of his arms than for his daring valour; two horses were slain under him in fruitless efforts to animate and rally his trembling and broken troops; but the day was irrecoverably lost; the prince himself was gradually surrounded and oppressed; his golden armour adorned with jewels was the prize for which the crowd contended; and Abdalla would probably have fallen a victim to the avarice of the soldiers, had he not been rescued from their hands by the count de Cabra, anxious to preserve the most glorious mark of his victory.

In Cordova, Ferdinand and Isabella received

their

their royal captive; and Abdalla entered in chains that city which had been the seat of his ancestors' power and magnificence. Yet he was not suffered to regret long the loss of freedom; Abul Hossein exulted in the disgrace of his rebellious son, and delivered from the immediate dread of a formidable competitor, prepared to continue the war with increase of vigour. To distract the measures of the Moors it was resolved to release Abdalla; and that prince subscribed to whatever terms were proposed as the price of liberty. He consented to become the vassal of Spain, and to pay an annual tribute of twelve thousand crowns; but the conditions which had been imposed in the hour of subjection were broken on the return of freedom; nor did Abdalla blush at a violation which was sanctioned by the precepts of Mahomet.

Yet the advantages of restoring the Moorish prince to his countrymen were such as Ferdinand and his council had foreseen; while the Christian arms in four campaigns successively recovered Zahara, reduced Ronda, Velez, and Malaga; and displayed their victorious banners on the banks of the Rio Verde, and the shores of the Mediterranean, the strength of the Moors was consumed in a wide and bloody civil war. Abul Hossein resisted the pretensions of his son Abdalla, but he was forced to yield to the superior fortune or address of his brother Mohammed el Zagal,

Zagal, whose ambition was not restrained by the guilt of fratricide. Yet on the throne Mohammed was instructed how ill he could depend on the fidelity of his subjects; the ties of society were dissolved; the regal title had lost its weight; and the Moors were eager for new revolutions. Abdalla with a chosen band surprised or was admitted into Granada; and the reign of Mohammed was confined to the southern corner of Andalusia, which is watered by the Rio Verde. The strong fortress of Baza was besieged by the forces of Spain; in a desperate sally the garrison indulged themselves in an useless carnage of their enemies; but it was the struggle of expiring independence; Mohammed himself was detested among the Moors as a cruel usurper, and dreaded by the Spaniards as an active and enterprising foe; the few partners of his hopes or associates of his crimes were industrious to secure themselves by a timely submission; Guadix and Almeria opened their gates to Ferdinand; after a gallant defence of eight months Baza was obliged to capitulate; and Mohammed stript of his dominions, from the just revenge of his nephew appealed to the generosity of the Christians; an ample estate was granted to him by Ferdinand for the support of his dignity; he was prevailed upon to employ his valour in the field against his countrymen; and the plains of Granada were ravaged by his

fol-

followers; yet the applauses of his new allies, could not drown the reproaches of his mind; he awakened to the infamy of waging war against his Moslem brethren; and he solicited and obtained permission to seek a retreat in Africa with the Moors who preferred their ancient faith to their native habitations.

Whatever might be the exultation of Abdalla at the abdication and retreat of Mohammed, it was alloyed by a review of his own distress and danger. He had been besieged by the Christians within the walls of Loxa; and though in repeated sallies his valour had been displayed, his fortune had not been changed; covered with wounds, the honourable testimonies of his intrepidity, he had been compelled to sign a capitulation which delivered Loxa to the enemies of his faith, and confessed himself once more their vassal; he was permitted to retire to Granada; and it was not long before that last retreat was assailed by his enemies.

The conquest of Granada has been adorned by the romantic fancy of Dryden; the circumstances on which he founded his play have been collected by an ingenious modern traveller; and though perhaps they command not our belief, they admirably illustrate the spirit and manners of the age. The most powerful families in the reign of Abdalla were the Abencerrages and Alabeces, the Zegris and

and Gomeles. High above the rest towered the Abencerrages, unequalled in gallantry, magnificence, and chivalry; of these Albin Hamet stood deservedly the foremost in the favour of his sovereign. His influence excited the envy of the Zegris and Gomeles, and to accomplish his ruin, they descended to the blackest artifice. An insidious villain of the race of Zegri availed himself of his intimacy with the king to insinuate a dark tale of treason and adultery; he affirmed the Abencerrages to be ready to rise in arms; and assured the monarch, that in the gardens of the palace of Alhambra, he had surprized Hamet in wanton dalliance with the queen. The story found ready admission into a jealous bosom; and the house of Abencerrage was doomed to destruction. They were summoned successively to attend the king in the court of Lions; and no sooner was each unhappy victim admitted within the walls, than he was seized by the Zegris and beheaded. Thirty-six of the noblest had already perished, when the bloody perfidy was revealed by a page who had escaped after witnessing his master's execution. The news was rapidly circulated; all Granada flew to arms; and the streets were deluged with the blood of the contending factions. The authority or address of Musa, a bastard brother of the king, prevailed on them to suspend their rage; and to the chiefs

of

of his nation Abdalla explained the source of his conduct; the conspiracy of the Abencerrages, and the adultery of the queen. At the same time he solemnly pronounced the sentence of the latter; and she was to be delivered alive to the flames in thirty days, if she did not produce four knights to vindicate in arms her innocence against four of her accusers. The bravest warriors of Granada were emulous to enter the lists in her defence; but it was to a Christian sword the royal criminal entrusted her cause. She conveyed a letter to Don Juan de Chacon, lord of Carthagena, and invoked him by the generous duties of knighthood to become her champion, and to bring with him three valiant friends. The answer of Chacon assuaged her fears, and assured her that he too highly valued the honour she had conferred on him to be absent at the hour of trial. On the fatal day the populace accused the negligence of their queen, who had not named her defenders; Musa, Azarque, and Almoradi, the judges of the combat, intreated her in vain to accept their services; she reposed with security on the Castilian faith, and descended with a firm step from the Alhambra to the scene of encounter; the lists were prepared; the trumpets of the Zegri sounded; and from eight in the morning till two at noon their defiance was unanswered; but when the anxiety of the multitude was increased to the highest pitch, and even the confidence of the queen was shaken, a shout of transport burst from the crowd; four horsemen, armed after the manner of the Turks, entered the square; one of them requested permission to address the queen; and as he knelt before her, he let drop the letter she had written to Don Juan; she instantly acknowledged her Christian champions, and declared her willingness to rest her innocence on their valour and success. With Don Juan, the duke of Arcos, Don Alonzo de Aguillar, and Don Ferdinand de Cordova shared the glory and danger of the romantic and perilous adventure. On the signal, they furiously spurred their coursers against their adversaries, and three of the Zegri were instantly overthrown and extended lifeless on the plain; the fourth, the traitor himself who had forged the falsehood, maintained a more obstinate struggle; but he sunk at length covered with wounds at the foot of Don Ferdinand; and his last breath confessed his treason, and the innocence of the queen. Amidst the acclamation of the multitude, and the congratulations of the Moorish chiefs, the victorious knights retired without disclosing their nation or quality; but though Abdalla in tears repented his credulity, he could not efface the resentment, or change the settled purpose of the queen; she renounced for ever his society, and sought a retreat in the kingdoms

doms of Fez or Morocco; a fimilar indignation was felt by the Abencerrages; they quitted Spain; and Granada was deprived of her ableft champions at the moment that they were moft neceffary to her defence.

Whatever might be the domeftic griefs of Abdalla, he was allowed but a fhort time to indulge them: he had fcarce received the intelligence of the reduction of Baza, and the fubmiffion of Mohammed, before he was embarraffed by the prefence of the ambaffadors of Ferdinand, who demanded in the name of their mafter the furrender of Granada. In many a bloody encounter Abdalla had experienced his own inferiority; in prolonging the conteft he was probably deftitute of hope; and however rigorous, he would have gladly fubfcribed any conditions which would have preferved the Moors of Granada as a people. But the decent pride of a prince was ftill cherifhed in adverfity; nor could he fign without a ftruggle the final extinction of a kingdom which had flourifhed beneath the government of the Moflems for above feven hundred years. His anfwer revealed his fallen ftate; he acknowledged his obligations and engagements to Ferdinand; but he prudently eluded them under the pretence that he was no longer mafter of his own capital, and that on the firft intimation of the

treaty,

treaty, the indignation of the Moors would be fatal to his life.

Abdalla flattered not himself that any reply could divert the purpose of Ferdinand; he prepared for war; and in her prosperity, the kingdom of Granada would not have been unequal to the contest. Thirty cities, and ninety-seven fortified towns were once included within the limits of her jurisdiction; and a tribute of seven hundred thousand crowns in gold was not only sufficient for the support of a large standing army, but might have allured the rapacious tribes of Africa to have crossed the sea in her defence. But when Abdalla dismissed the ambassadors of Ferdinand, the kingdom of Granada was confined to her walls or to the adjacent plain; and of four hundred thousand inhabitants which in her most flourishing state those walls contained, scarce one hundred thousand remained to share the danger or increase the calamities of a siege. Yet these were inflamed by sullen despair and religious fanaticism; the first taught them to die; the last promised after death, paradise, the sacred reward of the faithful.

For that reward they were not permitted long to sigh in vain; and the ardour of Ferdinand and Isabella to plant the standard of Christ on the last retreat of the Mahometans of Spain, was communicated to their subjects. The Cortes and prin-

principal cities of Caftille and Arragon contributed with alacrity to the glorious enterprife; their liberality was emulated by the clergy, defirous of fignalizing their zeal in a caufe confecrated by religion; an army of feventy thoufand foldiers whofe valour had been already approved, and difcipline confirmed in repeated conflicts with the infidels, marched beneath the conduct of Ferdinand himfelf. They were animated by the prefence of Ifabella; and the chivalry of Spain, who admired her manly fpirit, were impatient to merit her approbation; as they moved along they laid wafte the fertile plains of Granada; and in the ninth year from the commencement of the Moorifh war, they incamped beneath the walls of the devoted city.

On the banks of the Xenil and the Dauro, and at the extremity of a pleafant and fertile vale, the city of Granada occupies a ftrong and commodious ftation; but in a conteft where the forces were fo unequal, neither her natural pofition, nor the enthufiafm of her citizens, could preferve her independence; the defpair of the Moors repeatedly precipitated them againft the lines of the befiegers; but their fallies, the effufions of rage and fanaticifm, were more frequently fatal to themfelves than their adverfaries; the Spaniards carried on their approaches with caution and regularity; and one incident alone ferved tranfiently to revive and finally to found the hopes of the infidels; as Isabella beguiled the hours of the night in reading, her taper, negligently placed, involved in an instant her apartment in flames; she escaped from the fire; but it was rapidly communicated to the camp, which was constructed of huts thatched with reeds or straw. On the first alarm Ferdinand half dressed mounted on horseback, and flew with the cavalry he could hastily assemble to repulse the attempts of the besieged; his firm posture awed the Moors; and they were content with observing the conflagration. But the misfortune served only to stimulate Isabella to a new undertaking; and she determined to provide against a similar accident in future. Two long and broad streets were traced in the form of a cross; the neighbouring quarries supplied plenty of stone, and the work was facilitated by the skill and labour of the pioneers; instead of a camp a city arose; from the piety of its royal foundress it obtained the name of *Santa Fé*, or Holy Faith; and its construction sufficiently revealed the perseverance and resolution of the besiegers.

Many an anxious look was cast by the unhappy citizens of Granada towards the coast of Africa; but the Mahometan kings of Fez and Morocco were too intent on each others destruction to prop the sinking fortunes of their brethren in Spain; and the famine which raged through the city was aggravated by the plenty which flowed into the camp.

camp. Affailed by the fword, and exafperated by hunger, the Moors abandoned themfelves to all the horrors of defpair; they crowded round the tombs of their anceftors, and invoked their affiftance; they filled the mofchs with their cries, and alternately deprecated the wrath, or blafphemed the name of their 'prophet; thence ftarting to arms they iffued tumultuoufly from the gates, and rufhed againft the works of the befiegers; but Ferdinand could rely on the ftrength of his fortifications; he patiently awaited the effects of famine; nor expofed his foldiers to the headftrong fury of the infidels. Difappointed of a glorious, they returned to the terrors of a lingering death; they furrounded the Alhambra, menaced the life of their fovereign, and purfued him with execrations as the author of their miferies.

At length the tempeft feemed to have exhaufted its force; the multitude oppreffed by fatigue funk into a momentary filence; and the tranfient calm was improved by Abdalla to obtain all that he could now hope for, an honourable capitulation. Ferdinand was too defirous to fecure his triumph to hefitate on the terms; the articles were formally ratified by an oath; the Moorifh king confented to furrender his palaces and capital; to do homage, and fwear allegiance to the victor; to fet at liberty all Chriftian flaves without ranfom; and to deliver five hundred of the principal inhabitants as securities for the punctual execution of the treaty. In return, Ferdinand engaged to protect the vanquished in the possession of their arms, their horses, and their estates; to preserve their moschs inviolate, and allow them the free exercise of their religion; to govern them according to their own laws, and to choose from among themselves their magistrates; to abate during the term of three years their taxes, and never to impose heavier than those which they had been subject to under their former kings; and to provide shipping for all who should wish to dispose of their lands, and to retire with their effects to Africa.

If humanity could not influence Ferdinand, policy at least prompted to him alleviate the distress of a people who were so speedily to become his subjects; and no sooner were the hostages delivered than plenty was poured into the famished city; relieved from the immediate terror of a slow and painful death, the concern of the Moors revived for the honour of their nation and the sanctity of their faith. A wild enthusiast rekindled the rage of the multitude; his voice was heard through the streets denouncing the indignation of Mahomet, and menacing with the flames of hell those who impiously treated with the followers of Christ; a motley group of twenty thousand fanatics obeyed his summons, and besieged the

the gates of the Alhambra; Abdalla could no longer command, and the frantic infurgents derided his intreaties; but they trembled at the menace of Ferdinand; the king of Spain threatened to intercept all further fupplies, and to avenge on the hoftages their guilt. They were awakened by the ftern admonition to a fenfe of their forlorn condition; the laft murmur of refiftance expired, and they fubmitted to the will of their conqueror.

It was on the fecond day of January, in the year fourteen hundred and ninety-two, that Ferdinand and Ifabella entered in triumph the proftrate city of Granada; as they advanced towards the Alhambra they were met by Abdalla, accompanied by fifty horfe; the Moorifh prince alighted from his courfer, pronounced with a dejected countenance and tremulous voice the degrading words, " We are your flaves, invincible mo-
" narch; we deliver up this city and kingdom to
" your clemency and moderation;" he would have fallen at the feet of his lord and mafter, but he was prevented by Ferdinand, whofe fpirit was neither moved by adulation, nor capable of generofity; he promifed the royal fuppliant a fafe retreat, and an income adequate to his dignity; but Abdalla could not forget he had once been a king; the prefence of the victor muft have been irkfome to him; he folicited and obtained leave

to

to retire to Africa. As from a neighbouring hill he cast a last look on his palace and capital, a torrent of tears proclaimed the anguish of his soul; his grief was reproved by the indignant reply of his mother the fultaness Ayxa, " Thou doft well to " weep like a woman for that kingdom which " thou kneweft not how to die for like a man."

The inmoft receffes and glories of the Alhambra were thrown open to the eyes of Ferdinand; as in the pride of victory he paffed through the *gates of judgment,* the Chriftian chief might have been inftructed by the humble piety of the Muffulman; and the frequent infcription on the walls, *there is no conqueror but God,* might have checked the infolence of profperity; but the moment of fuccefs is feldom propitious to admonition; and it is not probable that the inftability of his own fortune, and the fallen ftate of Abdalla recurred to the mind of the victor, while he gazed on thofe wonders which have refifted the rage of time, and ftill command the admiration of the traveller.

The exterior of the Alhambra prefents a rough and irregular pile of buildings which forms a ftriking contraft to the order and elegance within. Through a fimple and narrow gate, the fpectator is conducted to a feries of beauties which almoft realize the fabulous Tales of the Genii. The bath, the firft object which ftrikes his fight, confifts of an oblong fquare with a deep bafon of

clear

clear water in the middle; two flights of marble steps leading down to the bottom; on each fide a parterre of flowers, and a row of orange trees. The court is incircled with a periftile paved with marble; the arches bear upon very flight pillars, in proportions and ftyle different from all the regular orders of architecture. The ceilings and walls are incruftated with fret work in ftucco, fo minute and intricate, that the moft patient draughtfman would find it difficult to follow it unlefs he made himfelf mafter of the general plan. The former are gilt or painted; and time has not faded the colours, though they are conftantly expofed to the air; the lower part of the latter is Mofaic, difpofed in fantaftic knots and feftoons; a work new, exquifitely finifhed, and exciting the moft agreeable fenfations.

From the bath a fecond door opens into the court of the lions, an hundred feet in length, and fifty in breadth, environed with a colonade feven feet broad on the fides, and ten at the end; the roof and gallery are fupported by flender columns of virgin marble, fantaftically adorned; and in the centre of the court are the ftatues of twelve lions, which bear upon their backs a large bafon, out of which rifes a leffer. A volume of water thrown up, falls again into the bafon, paffes through the beafts, and iffues out of their mouths into a large refervoir, whence it is communicated to the other apartments.

Thefe

These apartments are decorated with whatever the art of the age could invent or commerce could supply. The floors glitter with marble; the walls and the windows are enriched with mosaic; and through the latter the rays of the sun gleam with a variety of light and tints on the former; the air is perpetually refreshed by fountains; and the double roof equally excludes the extremes of heat and cold; from every opening shady gardens of aromatic trees, beautiful hills, and fertile plains meet the eye; nor is it to be wondered that the Moors still regret the delights of Granada, and still offer up their prayers for the recovery of that city, which they deem a terrestrial paradise.

While Ferdinand gazed with admiration on his new conquests, his bigoted mind revolved a scheme equally injurious to their interests and his own. In almost every age and country the Jews have been the objects of contempt and persecution; yet in oppression that unhappy race have continually multiplied; and their address in pecuniary negociations has not been more advantageous to themselves, than to the government in which they have been tolerated. But the understanding had not yet burst from the shackles of bigotry; and the fifteenth century was still darkened by religious prejudice; no sooner had Ferdinand celebrated his triumph than he commanded ed all the Jews who would not embrace the Christian faith, to quit his dominions within six months. Their attachment to the law of Moses was superior to every other consideration, and the effects they could conceal from the vigilant rapacity of the conqueror, they transported with them into Africa; in Tunis and Algiers they preserved their peculiar rites and unsocial manners; and have gradually increased in number and riches under the most arbitrary and sanguinary government.

If the Jews accused the humanity, the Moors might impeach the faith of Ferdinand and his successors. Every article of the capitulation was in its turn eluded or openly violated; and they were reduced to the alternative of renouncing the koran, or abandoning their native country. About seventy years after the taking of Granada they were driven into revolt by the rigour of administration; as they acted without allies and almost without concert, they were after a bloody struggle of above two years subdued. And at the commencement of the seventeenth century, their doom was finally signed by Philip the third. Every person of Moorish extraction without exception was commanded under the severest penalties to retire out of Spain; the order in appearance was punctually obeyed; yet an edict in the beginning of the eighteenth century

assures

assures us that several preferred their native soil, though with the sword suspended over their heads; about that period a fresh persecution was kindled by the breath of the inquisition; the wretched remnant of the Moorish race was driven into exile, and their effects, which were estimated at twelve millions of crowns, were confiscated.

From the conquest of Granada by Ferdinand and Isabella to the present time, the joint numbers of the Jews and Moors, who have been banished or sacrificed to the bigotry and rigour of the Spanish government, are supposed to have amounted to two millions of persons; the loss of so many industrious hands has been severely felt; and the traveller who beholds the present state of Granada, can scarcely credit her ancient prosperity. Instead of luxuriant plantations and venerable forests, the eye is assailed by black and barren wastes; and it is only in the massy ruins which are scattered over the hills, that her former magnificence can be traced.

But to an inaccurate observer, the detriment which Spain sustained by the expulsion of the Moors, was compensated by an event extraordinary as it was important to Europe. The discovery of the mariner's compass in the dawn of the fourteenth century had encouraged the navigators to abandon their ancient timid and lingering course along the shore, and to launch boldly into the ocean;

ocean; about the middle of that century a more enterprising spirit guided the Spaniards to the Canary or Fortunate Islands, near five hundred miles from their own coast; and above an hundred and fifty from that of Africa. Yet the chief glory of penetrating beyond those limits which nature seemed to have imposed, and of opening a new field to the daring genius of men, must be ascribed to the Portuguese. The situation of their kingdom, bounded on every side by the dominions of a more powerful neighbour, did not afford free scope to their activity by land, and the sea remained the only theatre on which they could distinguish themselves. About the beginning of the fifteenth century their vessels explored the coast of Africa, doubled Cape *Horn*, which had bounded the progress of former navigators, and reached Cape Bojador. Beneath the auspices of prince Henry, who to the martial spirit of the times added all the accomplishments of a more enlightened and polished age, the Portuguese rapidly advanced in the study of geography and the science of navigation; they discovered and planted the islands of Porto Santo, and Madeira; the wines and sugars which were imported from the latter, encouraged them to proceed; they doubled Cape Bojador, advanced within the tropics, and in the space of a few years reached the river Senegal, and became familiar with the

coast

coast from Cape Blanco to Cape de Verd; the countries which they had discovered were confirmed to them by the papal authority; and they were exhorted to proceed in their laudable career by the bull which granted to them an exclusive right over all the regions which they should descry from Cape Horn to the continent of India.

To gain that continent by a shorter route than hitherto had been known, was the darling object of the Portuguese councils; the spirit of nautical adventure received some check from the death of prince Henry, and slumbered during the warlike reign of Alfonso; but it revived under John the second; Bartholemew Diaz, an officer whose sagacity, experience, and fortitude, admirably qualified him for the undertaking, stretched boldly to the south, and after encountering a succession of tempests in unknown seas, beheld his labours and perseverance crowned by the lofty promontory which bounds Africa on that side; to behold it was all that the violence of the winds, the shattered condition of his ships, and the turbulent spirit of his crew allowed him: the appellation of *Cabo Tormentoso*, or the *Stormy Cape*, was expressive of the boisterous elements which forbade his nearer approach; but on his return the name was changed by the discernment of his sovereign; and it received and retained that of the Cape of *Good Hope*, the auspicious omen of future success.

But

But while John revolved the means of improving the discovery of Bartholomew Diaz, a new and more distinguished character arose, whose genius, vast and fertile as the countries he explored, with them, must command the admiration of posterity. Christopher Columbus was a subject of the republic of Genoa; and though neither the time nor place of his birth can be accurately ascertained, was descended of an honourable though impoverished family. The indigence of his ancestors had compelled them to a sea-faring life; and the disposition of Columbus was happily adapted to the profession which necessity had imposed on him. He had acquired some knowledge of the Latin tongue; and had been instructed, and had rapidly perfected himself, in geometry, cosmography, astronomy, and the art of drawing; thus peculiarly qualified he began his career on that element which conducted him to so much glory. For five years his adventurous spirit was confined within the limits of the Mediterranean, or exercised in voyages to the northern seas or coasts of Iceland; he afterwards entered into the service of a famous sea captain of his own name and family; and displayed his courage in frequent cruises against the Mahometans and Venetians; in an obstinate engagement with the latter, off the coast of Portugal, the vessel on board which he served took fire, together with one of the enemies ships; amidst the general horror, his presence of mind did not forsake him; he threw himself into the sea, and with the assistance of an oar reached the land though at the distance of two leagues.

The ardent spirit of Columbus could not be appalled by danger; and no sooner had he recovered his strength than he repaired to Lisbon, and entered into the Portuguese service, the school for nautical adventure. He was soon esteemed for his skill and experience; and his marriage with a Portuguese lady, the daughter of Bartholomew Parestrallo, one of the captains who had discovered and planted the islands of Porto Santo and Madeira, confirmed him in his darling pursuit; he got possession of the journals and charts of that celebrated navigator; and indulged his impatience to visit the countries Parestrallo had described, in frequent voyages to Madeira, the Canaries, and the Portuguese settlements on the coast of Africa.

The reputation of a skilful navigator satisfied not the ambition of Columbus; his mind, naturally vigorous and inquisitive, revolved new schemes of discovery; he reviewed every circumstance suggested by his superior knowledge in the theory and practice of navigation; and after comparing attentively the observations of modern pilots, with the hints and conjectures of ancient

authors,

HISTORY OF SPAIN. 451

authors, he at last concluded, that by sailing directly towards the west, across the Atlantic Ocean, new countries, which probably formed a part of the vast continent of India, must infallibly be discovered.

The spherical figure of the earth was already known, and its magnitude ascertained with some degree of accuracy. From this it was evident that the continents of Europe, Asia, and Africa, formed but a small part of the terraqueous globe. It was suitable to the ideas entertained of the wisdom and benevolence of the Author of Nature, to believe that the vast space, still unexplored, was not covered with an unprofitable ocean; and it appeared probable that the continent on this side the globe was balanced by a proportional quantity of land in the other hemisphere. Canes, and timber, and trees, had been driven by westerly winds on the coasts of the Azores; and the dead bodies of two men, whose singular features resembled neither the inhabitants of Europe, nor of Africa, were cast on shore there.

These observations were combined by Columbus, and convinced him that other countries existed in the western ocean, which were probably connected with the continent of India. With his sanguine and enterprising temper, speculation led directly to action; and he was impatient to bring the truth of his system to the test of experiment.

riment. Long abfence had not extinguifhed the affection which he had imbibed to his native country, and he wifhed that it fhould reap the fruits of his labour and invention; but from his refidence in foreign parts the Genoefe were unacquainted with his abilities and character; they rejected his propofal as the dream of a chimerical projector; and loft for ever the opportunity of reftoring their commonwealth to its ancient fplendour.

The king of Portugal, in whofe dominions he had long been eftablifhed, had the next claim to his fervices. Here his talents were known and efteemed, and the genius of the people accorded with his own. But John unfortunately referred him to a council who had advifed the difcovery of a paffage to India by a different route from that which Columbus recommended. They could not fubmit to condemn their own theory, and acknowledge his fuperior fagacity; while they deferred paffing judgment, they advifed John to difpatch fecretly a veffel to purfue the courfe Columbus had pointed out; but the ungenerous attempt was attended by the difappointment it deferved; contrary winds arofe; no fymptom of approaching land appeared; the courage of the pilot failed; and he returned to Lifbon, execrating the project as equally extravagant and dangerous.

Colum-

Columbus quitted with indignation a court capable of such mean treachery; and while he commissioned his brother Bartholomew to found the inclinations of the king of England, he himself repaired to Spain. He found Ferdinand and Isabella engaged in the war with Granada; the former, wary and suspicious, was not disposed to bold or uncommon designs; the latter, though sanguine and enterprising, was chiefly influenced by her husband; and though the character of Columbus secured him respect, though his grave and courteous deportment, his exemplary attention to all the duties and functions of religion, conciliated the regard of the Spaniards, his proposals were received with coldness; his project was treated as chimerical, and the advantages which he reserved for himself were considered as exorbitant.

Fatigued by incessant objections, Columbus had already quitted Santa Fé to join his brother in England, when his journey was arrested by a messenger from Isabella. Granada had surrendered; the moment of triumph is ever propitious to new enterprises; and while the mind of the queen was elated by prosperity, it was recalled to the plan of Columbus, by Alonso de Quintanilla, comptroller of the finances in Castille, and Lewis de Santangal receiver of the ecclesiastical revenues of Arragon; these ministers had early declared themselves the patrons of Columbus; they
painted

painted in glowing colours the honour that would accrue, after re-eftablifhing the Chriftian faith in thofe provinces of Spain from which it had long been banifhed, from difcovering and communicating it to a new world; they reprefented that if fhe did not decide inftantly, the opportunity would be irretrievably loft; that Columbus was on his way to foreign countries, where fome prince more fortunate or adventurous would clofe with his propofals, and Spain would for ever bewail the fatal timidity which had excluded her from the glory and advantages that fhe had once in her power to have enjoyed.

The doubts and fears of Ifabella were vanquifhed by the arguments of Quintanilla and Santangal; an invitation was difpatched to Columbus to return, and was received with that exultation which an ardent mind muft feel on being permitted to attempt a favourite enterprife. Yet Ferdinand ftill remained unmoved; as king of Arragon he refufed to take any part in the expedition; one eighth part was defrayed by Columbus himfelf; the reft was fupplied by Ifabella as queen of Caftille, who referved for her fubjects an exclufive right to all the benefits which might arife; yet the whole of the expence exceeded not four thoufand pounds; and about eight months after Granada was recovered by the Chriftians, Columbus with three fmall veffels,

and

and lefs than an hundred mariners, failed from the port of Palos in Andalufia, to traverfe the Atlantic Ocean, and explore a new world in the weftern hemifphere.

END OF THE FIRST VOLUME.

www.ingramcontent.com/pod-product-compliance
Lightning Source LLC
Chambersburg PA
CBHW022112300426
44117CB00007B/682